*Labor, Management,
and Social Policy*

John R. Commons
1862–1945

Labor, Management, and Social Policy

ESSAYS IN THE JOHN R. COMMONS TRADITION

EDITED BY GERALD G. SOMERS

THE UNIVERSITY OF WISCONSIN PRESS · MADISON, 1963

Published by The University of Wisconsin Press
430 Sterling Court, Madison 6, Wisconsin

Copyright © 1963 by the Regents of
The University of Wisconsin

Printed in the United States of America
by Vail-Ballou Press, Inc., Binghamton, New York

Library of Congress Catalog Card Number 63-10533

CONTRIBUTORS

ARTHUR J. ALTMEYER was chairman of the Technical Board which assisted a Cabinet committee set up by President Franklin D. Roosevelt to prepare the recommendations incorporated in the 1935 Social Security Act. He served as a member and chairman of the Social Security Board 1935–46 and as commissioner for Social Security 1946–53. Recently he has been adviser to various governments and organizations in the development of national social welfare programs. He is also chairman of the Board of Trustees of the Retirement Fund of the Coat and Suit Industry in New York and an occasional lecturer in the Department of Economics, University of Wisconsin.

JACK BARBASH is professor of economics and labor education at the University of Wisconsin. He served as economist with several government agencies including the U. S. Department of Labor, the National Labor Relations Board, and the U. S. Senate Committee on Labor and Public Welfare. He has also been a staff member of several labor unions: the AFL-CIO Industrial Union Department, the Amalgamated Clothing Workers, and the Amalgamated Meat Cutters and Butcher Workmen of North America. His published works include *The Practice of Unionism* (1956), *Labor's Grass Roots* (1961) and *The Changing Order in Union-Management Relations* (1963).

ELIZABETH BRANDEIS is professor of economics at the University of Wisconsin. She has taught in the Department of Economics since 1924, her major field of teaching and research being labor legislation and social security. She is author of Part 2 in Volume 3 of the *History of Labor in the United States,* by Lescohier and Brandeis (1935); the chapter on "Social Security" in *Problems of the Postwar World,* edited by T. C. McCormick (1945); and the chapter on "Organized Labor and Protective Labor Legislation" in *Labor and the New Deal,* edited by Derber and Young (1957). She is currently chairman of the Wisconsin Governor's Committee on Migratory Labor.

ABNER BRODIE, professor of law at the University of Wisconsin, is a member of the bars of New Jersey, Michigan (inactive), Wisconsin, and the United States Supreme Court. He engaged in the private practice of law in Newark, New Jersey, 1931–40 and 1947–48; and in Detroit, Michigan, in 1948. He was employed in the U. S. Department of Labor 1940–42 and the U. S. Department of Justice 1946–47. He is coeditor of *Labor Relations and the Law* (2d ed. 1960) and *The Employment Relation and the Law* (1957). He has been a member of the University of Wisconsin Law School since 1949.

NATHAN P. FEINSINGER is professor of law at the University of Wisconsin. He was a public member of the National War Labor Board 1942–46 and chairman of the National Wage Stabilization Board 1951–52. He was appointed chairman of the President's Commission on the Airlines Controversy in 1961. He is author of *Cases and Materials on Labor Law* and of articles in various periodicals on labor law, collective bargaining, mediation, and arbitration.

DAVID B. JOHNSON is associate professor of economics and associate chairman, Department of Economics, University of Wisconsin. He was formerly chief, Labor Relations Branch, Division of Organization and Personnel, U. S. Atomic Energy Commission. On the subject of wage law he has also published "Prevailing Wage Legislation in the States," *Monthly Labor Review* (August 1961).

ROBERT OZANNE is director of the School for Workers and professor of economics at the University of Wisconsin. He was formerly an organizer for the Retail Clerks International Association. His fields of interest are wage theory, labor history, collective bargaining, and union administration. His publications include articles on unionism and wages in the *Quarterly Journal of Economics* (May 1959) and the *Industrial and Labor Relations Review* (April 1962), and on occupational differentials in the *Review of Economics and Statistics* (August 1962).

KENNETH H. PARSONS is professor of agricultural economics at the University of Wisconsin. His special fields of interest are the general economics of agriculture, agricultural policy, economic development, and institutional economics. He is editor of the posthumous publication, *Economics of Collective Action*, by John R. Commons (1950).

GERALD G. SOMERS is professor of economics at the University of Wisconsin and editor of the Industrial Relations Research Association. He was formerly the director of the industrial relations centers at West Virginia University and the University of Wisconsin. His publications in the labor market field include *Labor Supply and Mobility in a Newly Industrialized Area* (1960) and *Adjusting to Technological Change* (1963).

L. REED TRIPP is professor of economics and director of the Industrial Relations Research Center, University of Wisconsin. He was chief economist to the Wage Stabilization Board 1951–52 and field chairman of the University of Wisconsin's Economic Project at Gadjah Mada University, Jogjakarta, Indonesia, 1957–59. He served earlier as research economist in industry and government posts, and has continued to be active in labor arbitration and as government consultant. Among his publications are *Labor Problems and Processes* (1961) and *The Role of Labor in the United States* (1963), a publication of the U. S. Information Service for distribution overseas.

PREFACE

John R. Commons has been acclaimed as the founder and principal exponent of "institutional economics" in the United States. Although one may find widespread agreement with this statement, there will be considerably less agreement on selection of a central theme of his work. He has been known as a pragmatist, theorist, and historian, as well as an institutionalist. His multidisciplinary interests have focused on economics and law, but they have also included political science, sociology, and psychology. His work as a scholar and, frequently, as an activist has included concentration on taxation, banking institutions, political processes, and administrative commissions, in addition to his study of labor and general economic analyses. There is little wonder, then, that Commons' contributions may appear to be diffused and that some question the dimensions of his role in the development of economic thought.

Two aspects of Commons' work which stand out clearly, however, prompt this volume of essays, written to mark the centennial of his birth in 1862. None can deny the profound impact of Commons and his associates on the study of unionism, collective bargaining, and labor-social legislation; and there are few scholars whose activities were so closely associated with the establishment of public policy in these fields. The essays in this volume reflect these two dominant strands in Commons' writings and activities.

It is this linkage of scholarly inquiry to public policy formation that provides a distinctive characteristic of Commons' approach. It is significant that the subtitle provided for his *Institutional Economics* was "Its Place in Political Economy." His very definition of an institution is instructive in this regard: "Collective action in control, liberation and expansion of individual action." Even though Commons' analyses of economic phenomena departed from the classical and neoclassical economic doctrines that continued to dominate the discipline during his time, he cannot be considered antitheoretical. He made continuous efforts to generalize from his pragmatic investigation of institutions, to trace cause and effect, to develop a coherent statement of economic principles. If his theorizing was rooted more deeply in empiricism and institutional behavior, this was expressly because of his preoccupation with public policy. Analyses of social problems are likely to be influenced by pragmatism when their author becomes involved in drafting concrete legislation to meet those problems. This was frequently Commons' role.

In the field of labor and social legislation, the happy wedding of empirical investigation and policy-oriented analysis has continued since Commons. Not content with the application of long-established economic doctrine to the labor field, scholars in recent years, following the lead of the Webbs in Britain and Ely and Commons in the United States, have turned to direct investigation of the organization and functioning of unions and collective bargaining, labor market behavior, and socioeconomic conditions of older workers. Many of these same scholars —still in the Commons mold—have been called upon to serve as arbitrators, government officials, and legislative consultants, participating actively in the formulation and implementation of policy on questions they have studied.

Only a few of the essays in this volume are directly concerned with Commons and his writings, but they are all in the Commons tradition. They deal with current and, frequently, controversial questions in the labor field. In keeping with Commons' approach, a major goal of the writers here is intelligent social policy, to be reached through analytical constructs reflecting careful examination of historical developments, current institutions, and behavioral characteristics.

Three major areas of public policy in the labor field converge in these essays: union-management relations, social security, and the labor market. In each area a long history of legislative concern continues unabated into the present. Although labor relations legislation in the United States predates the Wagner Act and unionism's upsurge of the 1930's, it has been an increasingly important focus of national attention since that time. Social security has been consistently in the public eye since the Social Security Act came into being in 1935; each proposed legislative extension has been, and continues to be, hotly contested. Problems of wages and employment have long played a central role in American protective legislation, but no session of Congress has witnessed greater interest in these subjects than that concluded in the fall of 1962.

The essays are appropriately begun with a general discussion of John R. Commons' approach to public policy. Kenneth Parsons describes the process by which Commons transformed European ideas of social reform, stemming from the German historical school, into an American "progressive" approach to economic reconstruction.

In the second section, devoted to unionism and labor-management relations, Robert Ozanne discusses the theory and history of the labor movement, developed in the writings of Commons and his associates, in the light of recent criticism and research findings. Reed Tripp develops an "institutional theory" of collective bargaining growing out of the Commons-Perlman approach; and Jack Barbash presents an analysis of the organizational structure and governing institutions of the central house of labor—the AFL-CIO. With these theoretical and empirical discussions serving as a useful background, Nathan Feinsinger traces the growth of public policy in the labor relations field, indicating the increasingly important role concepts of the public interest play in collective bargaining negotiations.

Arthur Altmeyer introduces the final section, on the labor market and social legislation, with an assessment of Commons' influence on the growth of social security in the United States and an analysis of current developments and proposed changes in the legislation. Abner Brodie suggests measures to correct deficiencies noted in workmen's compensation programs. Migrant labor problems in Wisconsin are discussed by Elizabeth Brandeis, who proposes additional protective legislation. Asking "Are prevailing wage laws outmoded?" David Johnson analyzes the strengths and weaknesses of this aspect of government regulation. The essays conclude with a discussion by Gerald Somers of current and proposed measures to improve the functioning of the labor market.

In his writings and practical affairs, John R. Commons viewed Wisconsin as a laboratory for socioeconomic and legislative experiment. It is appropriate on this occasion that members of the faculties of economics and law at the university in which he studied and taught provide a group of essays rooted in the Commons tradition.

G. G. S.

October 1, 1962

CONTENTS

I JOHN R. COMMONS' POINT OF VIEW

1

KENNETH H. PARSONS

The Basis of Commons' Progressive Approach to Public Policy

John R. Commons was a progressive devoted to the gradual improvement of the economic system of his times. He was concerned with issues of public policy in the development, stabilization, and humanization of an economic system which honored and depended upon the self-directed activities of businessmen, laborers, and farmers both as participants in the economy and as citizens. Much of his life was devoted to understanding the predicament of laborers in the burgeoning American industrialization. From this concern came not only significant contributions to the study of the history of industrial society, trade unionism, and labor legislation but also social inventions in public administration, especially those relevant to programs for industrial relations, accident prevention and insurance and unemployment compensation. Although he worked creatively on public utilities, monetary policy, economic stabilization, and taxation, his most persistent interests were in the labor field, and his major works in economic theory all carry the imprint of this interest. As he commented in the opening chapter of *Institutional Economics*, "The problem now is not to create a different kind of economics—'institutional' economics—divorced from preceding schools, but how to give to collective action, in all its varieties, its due place throughout economic theory." [1]

I

In considering the intellectual and moral commitments which gave direction to Commons' point of view, it is well to remember that he was born in 1862, during the Civil War. He was to witness as a student and young man the far-reaching political and social convulsions that followed this war. The era was characterized not only by reconstruction, panics, and depression but also by completion of the railway system, the end of the frontier of free land, the granger movement, antimonopoly campaigns, the rise of industrialism, and the emergence of a stable unionism in the American Federation of Labor. Commons responded to the issues of his time by his concern with poverty and with what came later to be known as business cycles, as well as with problems of monopoly power.

His first major publications treated the problem of monopoly. An essay on "Protection and Natural Monopolies" appeared in 1892 in the *Quarterly Journal of Economics,*[2] and in 1893 his first book, *The Distribution of Wealth,* was published.[3] Although Commons' analysis of monopoly was along lines which were to be followed up by economists of later decades, the review criticism of the book centered almost wholly upon his radicalism,* which was epitomized in his proposal that "the right to employment" should have the status of a property right,[4] with compensation for unemployment and loss of jobs.

In 1899 Commons had a fairly long essay in the *Arena* entitled "The Right to Work." Here he restated his basic thesis, this time supported by the doctrine of natural rights. He noted that "lack of employment" was attributable to one of three circumstances: "arbitrary discharge ... loss of employment through improved machinery and trusts ... or loss of employment through depression of trade."

Free industry is the right to leave the ranks of wage-earners, without let or hinderance from one's employer, or lord, and to enter the ranks of capitalists and employers, *if one is able.* Monopoly now has antiquated this right, since the small capitalist, to say nothing of the *quondam* laborer, cannot compete with the large and established industry. Instead of starting anew

---

* For a recent comment on this point see L. G. Harter, Jr., *John R. Commons— His Assault on Laissez-faire* (Corvallis, Oregon State Univ. Press, 1962), pp. 35–37.

as a capitalist, the laborer can only hope to get promotion or to invest his savings within the industrial organization where he finds himself.... The successor and substitute for the rights to free industry and free employment, must, under new conditions, be the right to a definite and *right* standing, within the existing industrial enterprises. This is the Right to Work.[5]

Commons never abandoned his thesis that the worker deserved and should somehow be given *rightful* status as a worker. The Wisconsin Compensation Act of 1932 was the culmination of his long persistence in this cause.

Commons' outlook and approach seem to have been deeply influenced by a few major events in his career. First there was what he called "my Five Big Years" between his dismissal at Syracuse University in 1899 and his appointment at the University of Wisconsin in 1904. During these years he became acquainted with American industry, business, and government; he constructed the first index of wholesale prices (for the Democratic party campaign of 1900, and was summarily dismissed when the index rose); he made a study of immigration for the U. S. Industrial Commission; he worked as a labor conciliator for the National Civic Federation with Ralph Easley and learned the art from a master; and he made the study of the Restriction and Regulation of Output by Capital and Labor. But he was "born again," as he said, when he "entered Wisconsin, after five years of incubation." [6]

The renascence in Commons came from a combination of circumstances most fortunate for him. The State of Wisconsin was then a great laboratory for experiments in the progressive reconstruction of the economy, and the University provided him with an opportunity to do fundamental research. He became an adviser to officials and administrators in devising new procedures for economic, social, and political adjustment. In this experience we sense three or four crucial episodes. He found in the writings of Charles Peirce, especially, a philosophical formulation which put his thinking on a more solid footing; his study of the American shoemakers enabled him to work out the foundations of a non-Marxian, and even anti-Marxian, theory of industrial evolution; and his sharing in the design and administration of the Wisconsin Accident Compensation Act of 1911 confirmed his thesis that conflicts of interests in industry could be resolved constructively and used as a tool of economic progress. All of these experiences were influenced by and in turn enriched his program of fundamental research. In his great research treatises, *Legal Foundations of Capitalism* (1924) and

Institutional Economics (1934), he reconsidered as an investigator many of the issues with which he had been concerned as a young man; but the context was different. He now had a mastery of economic and legal history which enabled him to understand how property, markets, trade unionism, industrialism, and capitalism itself had evolved in the experience of Western man.

II

In order to understand what Commons did, we need to see what he was trying to do. He was first of all concerned with social and public issues, with the ways in which private purposes are made consistent with public purposes. He assumed that private persons and concerns pursue self-interest, and held that the private and individual have their significance within going concerns which restrain, liberate, and expand individual action through working rules, enforced by various sanctions.

As regards the value problem, Commons was concerned primarily with what he called public value; one of his major courses in the last years of his teaching was so entitled. In his consideration of public value, the major point may well have been that he was really at peace with the fundamentals of the inherited system. Although he was a great innovator, and was considered a radical and reformer by some people throughout his life, the key to his constructive contributions in public affairs, it now seems, is that as he came to understand deeply the development of the Anglo-American political and economic system he was able to accept the system and the fundamental precepts and principles upon which it is based. As an analyst he worked within the basic premises of the main tradition of Western economics, except that he attempted to broaden the analysis sufficiently to embrace conflicts of interest, collective action, and the remarkable structure of property relations which has developed in Western capitalism. But the principal point to be emphasized here is that Commons accepted as worthy public purposes the emphasis upon liberty, equality of opportunity, and the dignity and self-direction of the individual to which the democratic system was intentionally dedicated—to be assured and experienced through order, security of expectations, and reconciliation of conflicts. Willing participation was for him the leading principle of social organization.

No one has summarized the issues of public value more succinctly than G. H. Mead in his essay on "Scientific Method and the Individual Thinker": "This modern conception" of freedom of action, observes Mead, "the cult of increasing knowledge and of continually reconstructing the world ... proceeds from the standpoint not of formulating values, but giving society at the moment the largest possible number of alternatives of conduct, i.e. undertaking to fix from moment to moment the widest possible field of conduct. The purposes of conduct are to be determined in the presence of alternative possibilities of action." [7] Working within this interpretation, Commons concentrated his attention upon the range of alternatives open to participants within the social organization, of which the economic system is a major part. Commons' position on public value is closely related to his faith in experience as the source of the elements of working rules; the derivation of the common law out of customs is a conspicuous example.

Since an evaluation of Commons' philosophical views is not possible here, we shall limit this aspect of our comment to noting a few relevant remarks by Commons in his *Institutional Economics*. In reviewing the influence of John Locke upon economic thought, he remarked:

Locke's mechanistic idea of the mind was that of a passive receptacle of ideas. . . . This too, was characteristic of the physical economists, culminating in Karl Marx, who reduced the individual consciousness to a mere copy of the production and acquisition of wealth. In order to unite, in the idea of an expected repetition of transactions, Locke's corpuscular sensations, reflections, and volitions, it required a still further notion of the mind as the whole body in action, . . . with this whole body as a *creative* agency looking towards the future and manipulating the external world and other people in view of expected consequences. This remained for the most recent psychology and economics to accomplish.

He added in a footnote: "Pragmatism, Gestalt psychology, institutional economics." [8] *

Among the significant premises of Commons' formulation we should also note his determination to work out a volitional economics, a formulation of economics which would recognize that human beings were persons with wills of their own. Closely related is his thesis that "economics deals with the individual as a citizen endowed with rights,

* Professor Commons referred frequently in class to his intellectual debt to Peirce's essay on "How to Make Our Ideas Clear" (*Popular Science Monthly*, Jan. 1878). Also he once remarked privately how grateful he was when he found that Peirce had in this essay "worked out many of the problems I had been thinking about."

duties, liberties, and exposures, in varying degrees imposed by various concerns. . . . Peirce's pragmatism, applied to institutional economics, is the scientific investigation of these economic relations of citizens to citizens." [9]

Commons' acceptance of the instrumentalist viewpoint in philosophy provided him with a theory of mind, as a creative interaction in events, consistent with his formulation of willing participation as the leading principle of social organization. He resolved early in life to formulate a volitional economics.[10]

III

Commons' early years at Wisconsin were devoted to study of the history of labor and industrial society, in which he and his associates first collected and then interpreted basic documents in the industrial evolution of America.[11] In this extensive effort, his article on the "American Shoemakers, 1648–1895" [12] was a strategic achievement, both in terms of his own ideas and for the interpretation of the labor movement.[13]

The selection of the shoe industry for the intensive study of industrial evolution was not a random choice. Enough of the records of the "Company of Shoomakers" of Boston, founded in 1648, were preserved to enable Commons to analyze the functioning of a guild and all successive industrial stages in this new country. As he says in the opening sentence of "American Shoemakers": "The boot and shoe makers, either as shoemakers or 'cordwainers,' have been the earliest and the most strenuous of American industrialists in their economic struggles." Furthermore, there were advantages in studying industrial evolution in America: "certain considerations in European history . . . have obliterated or confused the pure economic facts. Industrial evolution, considered as a mere economic process, had to work its way up through superimposed racial, military, tribal, feudal, ecclesiastical, and gild regulations and restrictions. . . . It is this bald simplicity of American individualism, without much covering of races, armies, gilds, or prelates, that permits us to trace out all of the economic sutures in their evolution from infancy to manhood." [14]

Here then was a historical record which could serve as a laboratory for the investigation of the economic facts of industrialization. Out of his study of the evolution of shoemaking from custom, or "bespoke," work through the retail and wholesale order stage, he concluded: "It was the widening out of these markets with their lower levels of competition and quality, but without any changes in the instruments of production, that destroyed the primitive identity of master and journeyman cordwainers and split their community of interest into the modern alignment of employers' association and trade union. The struggle occurred, not as a result of changes in tools or methods of production, but directly as a result of changes in markets." The conflict of labor and capital resulted from the changing economic functions integral to the widening of the market. These he termed "revolutionizing facts"—because, one infers, they provided the clues to a theory of the labor movement altogther different from that propounded by Marx.[15]

Karl Marx [he noted] was the first to challenge the world with a keen analysis of economic evolution, but his standpoint is that of the mode of production and not the extension of the market. His two assumptions of a given "use value" and a given "average social labor" serve to obliterate, the one the part played by the price-bargain, the other the part played by the wage-bargain. With these assumptions out of the way he is able to concern himself with the production of "surplus value" by his theory of the working day and the cost of living. But these are secondary factors, results not causes. The primary factors are on the side of the market, where competition is carried on at different levels. Instead of "exploitation," growing out of the nature of production, our industrial evolution shows certain evils of competition imposed by an "unfair" menace. Instead, therefore, of an idealistic remedy sought for in common ownership, the practical remedy always actually sought out has been the elimination of the competitive menace through a protective organization or protective legislation.[16]

The insights from the shoemaker investigation served as a foundation for Commons' later work on labor theory, labor history, and industrial government. In the introduction to the *History of Labour in the United States* Commons adds to his thesis regarding the significance of market structure for industrial conflict, recognition of the crucial importance for unionism of citizenship in the face of economic instability. In all of this he was investigating the "rightful" place of labor in the American economy.

Commons' idea of "protective organizations" matured in policy as fair competition buttressed by equality of bargaining power. The conception of "protective legislation" expanded in public policy from hour and wage legislation to unemployment compensation and eventually into the social security system. The general principle was that of a stabilized and humanized capitalism.

Participation in the "agitation, enactment, and, for the first two years, in the administration of the accident compensation and safety laws" [17] adopted in Wisconsin in 1911 rounded out and probably confirmed in a definite way his progressive approach to public policy. Only two or three issues can be noted here. Commons' approach to accident insurance and prevention had the effect of changing the whole "possible field of conduct" (to use Mead's phrase), especially that of employers, regarding industrial accidents. In place of reliance upon the common law rule of negligence, the Wisconsin law of 1911 was based upon the triple idea of (a) making industrial accidents an economic liability of industry, which was (b) to be covered by insurance, with the expectation (c) that the costs of accident insurance could be covered by "efficiency in accident prevention," to be achieved by a new interest in safety; each establishment would have a separate liability rating for insurance purposes according to its own accident record.

The administrative procedures adopted under the law provided that (a) safety standards were to be drafted by committees consisting of the representatives of the employers and employees directly concerned, with a deputy of the Industrial Commission acting as secretary; and (b) these formulated rules and regulations were given the force of law by being issued as orders by the Industrial Commission. By these means the safety regulations adopted were assured of being reasonable. This procedure brought the orders "within the legal doctrine of reasonableness, and avoided the constitutional prohibition against taking the property of employers without due process of law; that is, in this case, without their consent." [18] Also adoption of safety practices with the greatest promise of practical effectiveness made reasonableness in effect the "upper practical limit of idealism," [19] under the circumstances.

Among the principal inferences which Commons seems to have drawn from this experience with accident prevention and insurance, two deserve special note. First, the interpretations of reasonableness were gradually elaborated into his theory of reasonable value, especially on public issues, which underlay much of his faith that capitalism could become a reasonable capitalism. Secondly, his insights from experience with the responsible participation of representative but immediately conflicting interests became generalized in his view as the possibility of achieving order and mutuality of interest out of conflicts, through negotiation, conciliation, and compromise.

IV

Professor Commons was invited by the governor of Wisconsin to draft a public utility law that would regulate rates and yet meet the judicial tests of due process. Out of this experience came, after seventeen years of study and writing, Commons' greatest research achievement, *Legal Foundations of Capitalism*. In searching legal and economic history for principles of valuation, he "found eventually that what we were really working upon was not merely a theory of Reasonable Value but the Legal Foundations of Capitalism itself." [20]

Although this book of Commons reports comprehensive investigation, we can note only a few issues central to a progressive approach to public policy suggested by the terms development, power, property, and custom. These issues are of major concern today, particularly in considering the possibilities of a gradual or progressive approach to development policy in the less developed areas of the world.

Legal Foundations is a study of the way the form, or structure, of an economy changes as development moves from feudalism and the guilds to a modern market, opportunity-oriented economy. This transformation centered, in the Anglo-American experience, upon the changing nature of property rights and relations. Understanding the development of the system of property relations provides in turn a key to understanding both how political power is controlled and how private economic power came to emerge. A brief review of a few points in Commons' analysis may indicate how he formulated the central issues.

The rule of the British monarchs in the centuries following the Norman invasion was as absolute as that of a modern dictator. The British people gradually achieved both individual liberty and secure zones of economic opportunity through reduction of the unlimited prerogatives of the king to the sovereign powers of a constitutional monarch. The landlords were the first class to have their liberty implemented with property.

Among the strategic points of the development of property and liberty were the commutations of feudal dues to fixed money liabilities, which eventually became taxes upon the land levied by parliamentary procedures. Through rules restricting the zones of arbitrary acts by the monarch, the exercise of power by the monarch and his agents was eventually reduced to predictable and controlled limits; a "compromise set of working rules" [21] established the rudiments of representative government and the independent judiciary, with public officials subject to trial by the same laws and courts of the realm as private persons. The essence of the achievement, from the perspective of economic development, was that the curbing of the powers of unlimited prerogative created a zone of freedom and discretionary action—what Commons called the "indefinite residuum," an "orbit where the will is free." [22]

The "indefinite residuum" beyond the power of the monarch is the basis of what we now call opportunity; secure occupation and exploitation of opportunities became the rights of property. In a parallel manner, the liberty of persons assured by this same curbing of the arbitrary powers of rulers is the basis of personal liberties; these liberties became citizenship when made secure by the "compromise set of working rules."

Thus Commons' analysis shows not only the integral and reciprocal relationship among limited sovereignty, opportunity, and individual liberty, but also how these assured working rules permitted rightful opportunity to develop into property and rightful liberty into citizenship.

The common law method of developing law is essentially that of choosing customs deemed beneficial and making these customs into generalized working rules sanctioned by the power of sovereignty. In this way the customs of landlords and tenants became the basis of the common law of landlord and tenant; similarly the customary trade practices of the guilds were selectively generalized into the common law of business.

In an age of subsistence agriculture, handicrafts, and limited commerce, the first definite property rights developed by this method were essentially the exclusive right to use a physical thing.[23] This led to a common-sense notion of property as physical objects held for personal use. Although this idea of property persisted for centuries, and persists even today, the development of a market economy gradually enlarged the idea of property to the rightful withholding from others, and the value of property to the capitalized expected market earnings from the use of the object. This Commons calls intangible property, which follows the law of opportunity; and an economy characterized by intangible property is what Commons means by capitalism.[24]

Through this analysis of the nature and evolution of property and property rights, Commons was able to reconsider the nature of property rights in the job, the issue which had brought such calumny upon him thirty years before. Through his analysis of the development of property rights in land and the law of business and credit, he was able to trace out the ways in which the customs of landlords and tenants, businessmen, and borrowers and lenders had gradually developed into the common law (as well as the ways in which the common law was supplemented by equity law and statute law). However, the customs of organized labor as late as 1924 had not been accepted in the United States as a similarly reasonable basis for a common law of industrial relations. This lack of acceptability by the courts, Commons argued, was based upon such considerations as the doctrine that, "for the purposes of the Fourteenth Amendment, a corporation is deemed to be a person and not an association of persons," "whereas the union appears as a conspiracy of individuals...." The ideals and customs of laborers "are quite peculiar and differ in important respects from those of business. Primarily they spring from ... insecurity of jobs and positions...." [25] Subsequently, the law of collective bargaining in this country did accept many of the customs of laborers and developed very much along the evolutionary lines envisaged by Commons.

This meager sketch may suggest something of the way in which Commons formulated basic issues in the evolution of the structure of a modern exchange economy. Out of experience came customs in the struggle to survive and get ahead; and out of customs came ways of resolving disputes which could be strengthened and generalized into law. The achieved security of expectations together with limited government fostered the development of property. But private economic power was also a consequence, as liberty became implemented by property in an age of capitalism.

As Commons formulated the problem of power he distinguished political power from economic power and both from moral power or persuasion. Political power rests upon the legal use of physical violence to enforce sanctions; economic power upon the ability to withhold, sanctioned by collective action and property. Both are irreducible entities in an industrial economy which honors liberty and opportunity. But the method of arriving at "reasonableness" in the use of power is different in the two kinds of power. The power of governments is kept in check basically by the procedures of representative government, the independent judiciary, and the trying of public officials in the same courts as private persons. Private economic power can be destroyed by government, by Communist revolutions for example, but the stabilization and humanization of an economy characterized by economic power are a matter of bargaining, of balancing power with power—which Galbraith has called countervailing power. Thus Commons would permit private economic power—within wide limits—and keep such power reasonable through collective bargaining and the long-honored doctrine of reasonable restraints of trade.

V

Commons accepted as desirable a stabilized and humanized capitalism. In an essay published in 1925 [26] he compared his views of a reasonable, stabilized capitalism with Marxism and socialism.

We need to remember, he noted, that Marx published the Manifesto in 1847,

following ten years of the lowest degradation reached by the working people of England and Europe since the time of the Napoleonic Wars. . . . There is much reason to conclude, had capitalism continued in the same direction after 1847 as it did during the 30 years after 1817 when Ricardo wrote his *Political Economy*, that Marx's revision of Ricardo would have proven to be correct, for Marx described, in fact, what had actually been happening. . . . But there occurred after 1850, and increasingly since that time, what may be named, in part the Self-Recovery of Capitalism and in part its Forced Recovery, until today what may be named the Stabilization of Capitalism is apparently strengthening the system more than ever before.[27]

The self-recovery of capitalism began, in Commons' interpretation, with the general incorporation laws of the 1850's, in both America and Europe. Prior to this time charters were granted by special acts of legislatures, which led to political corruption. But the universal right of incorporation counteracted Marx's prediction regarding the concentration of capital by permitting concentration of capital along with decentralization of ownership. Also, this self-recovery was aided by legislation.

It is by legislation, such as public utility laws, blue sky laws, watered-stock laws and similar measures, that well-meaning capitalists can be protected in the greatest of all safeguards of capitalism, the confidence of millions of investors. . . . The outcry of many capitalists against legislation on the ground that it interferes with business is quite one-sided. It is this very legislation which has helped to save capitalism in our western civilization, and it is the lack of this legislation that has left it, in Russia, unprotected against communism and agrarianism.

. . . .

The culminating oversight of Marx in his theory of socialism, and the one which comprehends all others, [was] the failure to see the importance of Custom, and what, in Anglo-American jurisprudence, is called the Common Law.[28]

Commons then goes on to explain why the changing fact of custom and common law has "set up the principle of stabilization." What are later recognized as the "rights, duties, liberties and liabilities of private property" are in fact in existence as customs before being given the sanction of law. Common law arises out of customs as needed, when "disputes arise which must be decided promptly in order to keep the association, or community, or nation in a peaceable frame of cooperation." [29]

Marx was not alone in failing to see the interconnections between custom and the common law, and between customary behavior and private property; neither did Ricardo nor Adam Smith. "For them there was no intervening principle of human behavior, between the compulsory edicts and the laws of sovereignty, on the one hand, and the individual bargains of private property on the other hand. Private property, for them, was actually created by the sovereign and it logically followed that the sovereign could abolish private property. For them there was nothing between the Individual and the State. Ricardo and the capitalistic economists would eliminate the state from business; Marx and the socialists would make the state supreme." [30]

The stabilization of capitalism in Commons' interpretation is a complex of several major parts, as may be noted in a brief summary. One aspect of this was the stabilization of the price level and of the value of money. "The greatest and most fundamental stabilization [of modern capitalism] has been that of credit and prices through the cooperation of the banks organized in the Federal Reserve System." [31] A second was the stabilization of the structure of the economy through gradual modification of the nature of property rights, of which the most comprehensive is the "historic process of stabilization through custom and law." A third aspect was stabilization through legislation such as that defining procedures for the issuance of stocks or the regulation of public utilities. A fourth method of stabilization was by placing effective limits upon the exercise of economic power, through judicial support of fair competition, the value of good will, and the support of reasonable, but not unreasonable, "restraints of trade."

All of these aspects of stabilization are interrelated in public policy. For example, stabilization through placing reasonable limits upon the exercise of private power is an extension of the principle of stabilization through attention to customs. "This process of stabilization of capitalism through custom, has been passing through two stages, the first of which is the stage of conspiracy and anti-monopoly; the second, the stage of legalization and regulation. The conspiracy stage reached its climax in the Sherman anti-trust law of 1890, and the regulation stage can hardly be said to have had a beginning prior to the Twentieth Century." [32]

The possibilities of this stabilization of capitalism occurred to neither Adam Smith nor Karl Marx because neither of them accepted the possibility of progress through the reconciliation of conflicts of interest. Smith, as Commons said, accepted the "principle of harmony of interests" and believed that people were injured by "such institutions as slavery, government monopoly, tariffs, bounties, navigation laws," etc., but that a "perfect freedom of action on all sides, in the pursuit of private property, could not injure anybody," "since in an age of Abundance the opportunities would be unlimited." Karl Marx held the view not only that history was ruled "by an impelling force that worked out its evolution regardless of the will of man," but also that the inevitable struggle between the owners and nonowners of property would be ended by a worldwide revolution, followed by a temporary dictatorship of the proletariat and "then a final harmony of interests . . . after everybody has accepted the principles of communism. . . . But this entire harmony of interests, whether under capitalism or under socialism, falls to the ground if once we recognize that social conflict has always been and always will be a fundamental fact in the progress of mankind." [33]

Thus the idea of the stabilization of capitalism, in Commons' view, must rest fundamentally upon ways of resolving and reconciling conflicts of interest. This conflict is not merely a class struggle, it is a struggle of persons in many classifications, for "this conflict is as many sided as there are classifications of people according to their economic interests." [34] Thus not only is stabilization coming to be recognized, and should in Commons' view be recognized, as a major public purpose and a dominant issue of public policy, but the very nature of the "public" grows out of the resolution of conflicts of interest.

Commons develops his ideas of public and private purpose most fully in *Legal Foundations of Capitalism*. The public is not, he observed, something antithetical to the private. "The question always is, not, *What* is a private purpose over against a public purpose? but, Is the private purpose *also* a public purpose, or *merely* a private purpose?" [35] This position in turn rests upon the thesis that the public perspective is achieved through the resolution of disputes. Thus the public viewpoint is rooted in the judicial function and is found in all societies. "This judge, however, necessarily takes a public point of view, since his decisions must conform to what other judges have decided in similar disputes and to what the customs or laws of the community authorize and support. In applying the common rule he is conforming to public purpose. Hence the public point of view is inherent in every transaction, and just as much so in primitive society as in a credit economy." [36]

VI

The work and thought of John R. Commons are now a part of our history; a full generation has passed since his last major writings. If one were to evaluate his gradual or progressive approach to public policy, therefore, one would need to look back over the history of this country and assess the influence of his ideas in those fields where he was particularly active; this is done in several essays in this book. But Commons strove also for generality, especially in the later decades of his career. In conclusion, therefore, we choose to consider the relevance of his thought to a few issues in the public policies of nations emerging from colonialism. It is here that Western thought faces the direct competition of revolutionary Marxism. Consequently, it is this arena which presents the greatest challenge to a gradualistic and progressive approach to policy. In translating Commons' ideas into concepts relevant to the analysis of issues of public policy in underdeveloped areas, one encounters major problems in semantics—particularly in the term capitalism. This word meant something quite different to Commons than to Marx, and the difference goes to the very core of their viewpoints. Marx studied the performance of capitalism in the early stages of industrialization, partly at least from parliamentary inquiries concerned with the poverty and misery of the working classes in the early decades of the nineteenth century. He elaborated his insights within an Hegelian system of ideas which emphasized property as exploitation and predicted the ultimate collapse of the system.

The major documents that Commons studied in his interpretation of the development of the Anglo-American economic system were also available to Marx as he wrote, had he chosen to study them. But Commons studied economic history constructively, one might say, as a participant-citizen trying to understand how the economic system had been transformed from a traditional feudal, guild, and handicraft economy into a modern market, opportunity-oriented system. In his analysis, he traced out the changes in the nature of property and the meaning of property rights, as rightful access to opportunities and negotiability of contracts matured into the intangible property of market freedom, and as the negotiability of debts grew into the incorporeal property of bonds and impersonal liability for debts. Whereas Marxian doctrine leads to revolution and the subordination of economic affairs to the control of the state, Commons' analysis leads to what he called a reasonable and stabilized capitalism in which political and economic powers are kept within reasonable limits and in some sort of equilibrium with each other. The relevance of Commons' progressive approach to policy in the underdeveloped world may be explored somewhat more precisely by concentrating on two issues, those of power and of the common law approach to deriving law from customs.

The American system of economy and politics was deeply influenced by the revolutions of the seventeenth and eighteenth centuries. These revolutions were turned against the restrictive practices of governments at a time when the productive powers of a market-industrial economy were beginning to be enjoyed. We inherit the doctrines of classical liberalism from this era; as Guido de Ruggiero writes in the *Encyclopaedia of the Social Sciences:* "At an early stage of its development therefore the forces of liberalism concentrated on the crucial problem of limiting the interference of the state and of transforming state policy into a vehicle for promoting the liberties of individuals and groups." [37] Liberalism in economic policies, of which laissez faire is a logical expression, was a part of this liberal philosophy. These liberal ideas were deeply influential in Western Europe and America through the middle of the nineteenth century. In terms of the power issue, the problem of power was essentially that of holding the power of the state to a minimum. In this view it is not economic but political power which is to be guarded against.

As the deficiencies and social consequences of a laissez-faire policy in industrial organization became evident, a major reaction was toward socialism, with reliance upon the state in the operation of the economy. Marxism is only the most powerful of the various versions of socialism.

We are again living through an age of revolution; this time, worldwide. The economic circumstances are vastly different from those of the revolutionary era of the seventeenth and eighteenth centuries. During the intervening centuries the market-oriented industrial system has penetrated the farthest reaches of the globe by trade, by colonial policies, and by the economies of empires. Marxian doctrines offer superficially plausible interpretations of the poverty and backwardness of the underdeveloped areas as economic "exploitation" by the imperial and propertied interests. Consequently, we are now witnessing a revolutionary era which "idealizes" the power of the state and considers private economic power the scourge to be avoided.

The major issue in development policy of the underdeveloped world is to find a middle ground between these two extreme views, one reacting against the participation of the state in the economy and the other against all forms of private economic power. Commons considered it essential to avoid unlimited power of any kind. However, the methods by which political power is kept within reasonable limits are different from those which so contain private economic power.

The exercise of arbitrary political power by the state is to be avoided or kept within bounds by representative government, the independent judiciary, and related institutions, as discussed above. Historically, the freedom assured to persons in the Anglo-American tradition by the reduction of royal prerogative to the constitutional exercise of power opened the way for the rise of economic power based upon the ownership of property and collective action. The problem of keeping economic power within bounds is partly a matter of government policies of taxation, inheritance, etc., but the day-to-day problem of economic power in the functioning of the economy is met in Commons' view mostly by balancing power with power. To this end he favored a policy of equalization of bargaining power between employers and employees, as well as the use of the sovereign powers of government to supplement the weak economic power position of farmers.[38]

Thus Commons' analysis faces both ways on the power problem.

Both economic and political power must be recognized and kept within bounds.

> Once it is realized that there is no such thing as an automatic harmony of economic interests, either under capitalism or future socialism, and that economic conflicts are not merely conflicts between individuals, which can be decided in court after the damage is done or is imminent but are conflicts between classifications and even classes of individuals, which might be adjusted before a break occurs, then some progress can be made toward approaching not an ultimate ideal of harmony, but merely that series of next steps which will keep the concern improving from day to day—the Reasonable Stabilization of Capitalism.[39]

Commons' genetic approach to the development of the economy as a social organization rests upon his views regarding the constructive function of customs. The neglect of custom he termed "the culminating oversight of Karl Marx ... the failure to see the importance of Custom, and what, in Anglo-American jurisprudence, is named the Common Law." [40] In this constructive interpretation of customs, Commons may well have the major key to gradualism in economic development, due to the primacy of order in making both freedom and efficiency possible.[41] The use of customs can be a way of developing tough controlling and stabilizing institutions out of the experience of a people. But the selection of customs to be generalized and strengthened is a process of deliberate selection, not natural selection in the Darwinian sense— and the selection in Commons' view is a judicial function. Every society worthy of the name has a vast complex of customs by which members of the group come to have security of expectations regarding the behavior of the other members of the group. In this way the customary laws of land use and occupancy, inheritance, marriage and contracts, among other laws, come into operation. The constructive selection and development of customs into law is a part of the process of self-government.

This explains in part why colonialism had such a disorganizing effect upon traditional societies; where government is by prerogative, the working rules are likely to be imposed from above. Where the superimposed laws and edicts conflict with customs the latter must give way, being discredited in the process. Now, with the emergence of independent states in Africa and Asia, the way would seem to be opened for an unprecedented use of customary patterns of activity as the source of public laws or working rules sanctioned by the people. Starting from the customs and experience of the people, there is, of course, a major problem of systematization of rules. The genius of the common law method is that it provides both for a system and for gradual change in the rules before conflict reaches revolutionary proportions.

Notes

1   New York, Macmillan, 1934; Madison, Wisc., Univ. of Wisconsin Press, 1959, p. 5.
2   *Quart. Jour. Econ.*, 6 (July 1892): 479–84.
3   Macmillan.
4   *Distribution of Wealth*, pp. 79–85.
5   *Arena*, 21 (Feb. 1899): 131–42. Pp. 139–41, 138 cited.
6   *Myself* (Macmillan, 1934), pp. 65, 63–94, 95.
7   A chapter in *Creative Intelligence—Essays in the Pragmatic Attitude*, a symposium edited by John Dewey, New York, Holt, 1917. See pp. 222–24.
8   *Institutional Economics*, 1: 16–17. See also pp. 152–53.
9   Ibid., p. 157.
10   See *The Economics of Collective Action* (New York, Macmillan, 1950). Intro. by K. H. Parsons, p. 13.
11   Their work culminated in the eleven-volume *Documentary History of American Industrial Society* (1910–11) and the *History of Labour in the United States* (1918; eventually four volumes, 1926–35).
12   First published in *Quart. Jour. Econ.*, 24 (Nov. 1909): 39–84. Republished in *A Documentary History of American Industrial Society* and in *Labor and Administration* (1913).
13   See Commons' Introduction to *History of Labour in the United States*, Vol. 1; and Selig Perlman, *History of Trade Unionism in the United States* (Macmillan, 1922), espec. chap. 12, "An Economic Interpretation."
14   *Quart. Jour. Econ.*, 24: 39, 77, 78.
15   Ibid., pp. 50, 59.
16   Ibid., p. 76.
17   In *Institutional Economics*, p. 854, Professor Commons has written extensively on this experience; no attempt will be made here to review it in detail. See ibid., Accidents and Unemployment—Insurance and Prevention, pp. 840 ff.; and *The Economics of Collective Action*, chap. 16, "Capital-Labor Administration."
18   *Institutional Economics*, p. 857.
19   Ibid., p. 860.
20   *Legal Foundations of Capitalism* (New York, Macmillan, 1924; Madison, Wisc., Univ. of Wisconsin Press, 1957), pp. vii–viii.
21   Ibid., pp. 104–5.
22   Ibid., chap. 6, "The Rent Bargain—Feudalism and Use-Value," at p. 221. This brief comment can only suggest the kind of distinction made.
23   Ibid., chap. 2, "Property, Liberty and Value."
24   Ibid., chap. 7, "The Price Bargain—Capitalism and Exchange-Value."

25 Ibid., chap. 8, "The Wage Bargain—Industrialism." Citations at pp. 291, 296, 304–5.
26 "Capitalism and Socialism," *Proceedings of the Wisconsin State Bar Association*, Vol. 15 (Madison, 1925), Reports of the State Bar Association of Wisconsin. A somewhat abbreviated version of this essay was also published in the *Atlantic Monthly* (Nov. 1925) under the title "Marx Today: Capitalism and Socialism." All citations here are to the essay as published by the Bar Association.
27 "Capitalism and Socialism," p. 63.
28 Ibid., pp. 65, 71.
29 Ibid., pp. 73, 72.
30 Ibid., p. 71.
31 Ibid., p. 76.
32 Ibid., p. 74.
33 Ibid., pp. 79, 77, 80.
34 Ibid., p. 81.
35 *Legal Foundations*, pp. 326–27.
36 Ibid., p. 242.
37 "Liberalism," *Encyclopaedia of the Social Sciences* (1933), 9: 435.
38 See his analysis of the U. S. Supreme Court decision on the 1933 Agricultural Adjustment Act (U.S. vs. Butler, 297 U.S. 1.56 St. Ct. 312, 1936), in the *Economics of Collective Action*, chap. 14.
39 "Capitalism and Socialism," p. 82.
40 Ibid., p. 71.
41 See Frank Knight, "Economic Objectives in a Changing World," in *Economics and Public Policy*, Brookings Lectures, 1954 (Brookings Institution, 1955), at pp. 50–54.

II UNIONS AND COLLECTIVE BARGAINING

2

ROBERT OZANNE

The Labor History and Labor Theory of John R. Commons: An Evaluation in the Light of Recent Trends and Criticism

Introduction

John R. Commons' major contributions to the study of labor history were the compilation of the ten-volume *Documentary History*,[1] the writing with his students and associates of two volumes in the *History of Labour*,[2] and the formulation of his "extension of markets" theory on the origin and evolution of trade unionism and the origin of class conflict.[3] In addition, few teachers in any field have attracted as able and productive a group of graduate students as those who assembled in Madison, Wisconsin, to work on the many investigations which Commons initiated.

The impact of the documentary volumes and the *History of Labour* has been enormous. These works have provided the major factual basis for most of the subsequent general labor histories, even including those which reject the theoretical conclusions of Commons and his one-time student Selig Perlman.

The Challenge to Commons' Theory on the Origin of Unions

While several facets of Commons' interpretations (and particularly Perlman's) on the evolution and nature of trade unionism are still subject to criticism, the brilliant insight combined with painstaking documentation of Commons' "extension of markets" theory resulted in its general acceptance. In recent years there appears to be only one frontal criticism of this "origin" theory, that of Lloyd Ulman in *The Rise of the National Trade Union*.[4] To understand and evaluate Ulman's disagreement we must at least summarize Commons' origin theory.

In contrast to Marx, who had seen the origin of class conflict in the changing methods of production and the changed ownership of tools attendant upon the growth of power machinery, Commons attributed the earliest class division to the extension of markets brought about by improved transportation. Commons' theory evolved from documentary studies which clearly revealed the existence of unions and strikes in the American pre-factory period, 1790–1820.

After delineating five distinct stages of production—those of (a) the itinerant craftsman, (b) the retail shop, (c) the wholesale order, (d) the merchant-capitalist, and (e) the factory—Commons placed the origin of unionism in (c), the wholesale order stage. Here serious employer-employee conflict first arose because improved transportation put the merchants of one town in competition with merchants of other towns, thus giving rise to strong downward wage pressures. While Marx saw the origin of conflict in the factory stage, (e), Ulman points to the retail shop stage, (b), as the probable origin of unions, because this was the stage "in which distinct classes of employers and employees first arose."[5] If Ulman is correct, the significance which Commons saw in improved transportation and extension of markets disappears. Commons rejected the retail shop stage because so long as the shop was producing on order for retail customers the master could keep prices high enough to pay satisfactory wages. During this stage of production, Commons found, workmen and masters belonged to associations similar to the European guilds of earlier times and, as in the days of the guild, made common cause as producers.

Ulman denies that any guildlike harmony of interests existed during the retail shop stage and points to the presence of full-scale strikes at this stage in the building trades:

> But the most serious objection to Commons' attempt to classify local market unions as "guilds" is suggested by the fact that these unions—especially those in the building trades—frequently engaged in strikes to reduce hours, to raise wages, or to prevent reductions in wages. If these local unions really

did resemble the medieval guild, it is difficult to explain why they should have engaged in strikes against the employers in question. The strike record in the 1820's and 1830's hardly suggests the existence of a community of interest between union member and employers similar to that which characterized the guild organization. On the contrary, it suggests that the mere existence of monopoly in the local product market (where it in fact occurred) was not a sufficient condition for the payment of wages above equilibrium levels, but that it merely made the payment of such wages more feasible—if unions were on hand to demand them. Commons does not attribute great importance to this development, it will be recalled, because the merchant-master's local monopoly allegedly made it possible for him to grant wage demands by raising prices.[6]

Ulman is, of course, correct that strikes in local market industries such as the building trades could not have been affected by the extension of the market which came with improved transportation.

How does Commons explain the rise of unionism in the building trades and certain other local market industries such as the newspaper branch of the printing industry? Since it was he who carefully documented the earliest building trades strikes, he could hardly have been unaware of the challenge to his extension-of-markets theory posed by strikes and unions in such local industries. In fact he devotes six pages to "fitting" this apparent building industry discrepancy into his general theory.[7]

In this explanation Commons saw the building industry as being in the merchant-capitalist stage of production as early as 1791. He explains the separation of worker and master builder as due not to extension of markets resulting from improved transportation but to the practice of "small contractors bidding against each other and making their profit out of the labourers' wages, their position was that which in manufacturing industries came to be known as the 'sweating system,' characteristic of the succeeding merchant-capitalist system." [8] Thus in the building industry the menace was not the competition of workmen in neighboring cities felt because of improved transportation but the competition of fellow townsmen who through a bidding procedure cut prices and thus put downward pressure on wages. Commons made the unionism in the building trades a special case in his theory, in which conflict between labor and capital arose from extreme competition caused by changed financial practices and not from improved transportation. The building trades employer by 1791 had lost control of the industry to the capitalist landlords and bankers, who in turn reduced the employer to a mere labor contractor. It is unfortunate that in his criticism of Commons Ulman takes no cognizance of Commons' detailed explanation of the origin of building industry unionism.

Ulman's attack on Commons' extension-of-markets theory does serve to point up the fact that early unions in local-market industries originated from causes other than extension of markets; Commons however not only had said as much but had documented and interpreted the phenomenon.

The Formation of National Unions

Ulman's second criticism of Commons encompasses the causes of the rise of national (nationwide) trade unions. Commons' extension-of-markets explanation, he feels, is too narrow and limited: "This explanation of the institution [nationwide unions] with reference to only one artificially isolated phenomenon cannot be expected to explain the whole truth." [9] For a broader explanation, Ulman offers the following factors, some of which inhibit and some advance the formation of nationwide unions: (a) geographic mobility of workers, (b) extension of markets, (c) the multiplant firm, (d) the big firm, (e) technological innovations, and (f) the state of business.

The following explanation by Commons of the rise of nationwide unions during the 1860's appears to be as broad as Ulman's:

> The first and most far-reaching cause, as illustrated by the stove moulders, was the competition of the products of different localities side by side in the same market. . . . In other trades, where the competitive area of the product was still restricted to the locality, the paramount nationalising influence was the competition for employment between migratory out-of-town journeymen and the locally organised mechanics. This describes the situation in the printing trade. . . . The third cause of concerted national action in a trade was the organisation of employers. . . .
>
> The fourth cause was the application of machinery and the introduction of division of labour, which split up the old established trades and laid industry open to invasion by "green hands." [10]

Point two above is a direct answer to Ulman's next criticism, that "Commons' theory also fails to account for the presence of national unions in industries which did not have national markets." Ulman further feels that Commons' theory fails to catch the significance of the role of the multiplant or big firm in the development of the national union.

Specifically, it [Commons' theory] fails to account for the absence of national unions in some industries which had national markets. In such cases, local unionism was also nonexistent—or at least sporadic and ineffectual. It follows that where there could be no locals there could be no nationals. The outstanding examples were those industries in which big firms predominated and in which conditions were peculiarly unconducive to unionism with respect to organizability, bargaining power, and even industrial skill. Commons and his associates emphasize the intensifying effects of competition in discussing the widening of market areas, but they say little about the growing size of the business unit and the multiple-plant firm or "combination." Yet it is obvious that industries characterized by the latter phenomena were just as well qualified as more competitive industries, composed of smaller business units, if extension of markets is taken as the prime criterion of national unionism.[11]

Since big firms arose well after the rise of national unions and since their primary effect was on the very existence of unionism within them, not on whether the union structure would be local or national, Commons quite appropriately discussed these effects in their most significant context: "As soon as the trust became the sole employer of labour in an industry, the relations between labour and capital were thrown almost invariably into the state of affairs which had preceded any organization of labour whatsoever. By abolishing competition among employers for labour and by giving the employer unlimited power to hold out against a strike, 'trustification' destroyed every bargaining advantage which labour ever enjoyed." [12]

To sum up, Commons' *History* volumes disclose a broad list of causes for the growth of nationwide unions, each carefully weighed as to importance. Ulman's charge that he explains it only through "one artificially isolated phenomenon" is not borne out by examination of Commons' text.

The Attack on *"Manualist Psychology"*

With Commons' origin theory as a taking-off point, Selig Perlman went on to put forward his own theory on the nature of a mature trade union movement.[13] One of the additions he made to the historical work of the Commons group was the role of what he labeled the "manualist psychology" of the workingman. Not only Ulman but two of his University of California colleagues, Charles A. Gulick and Melvin K. Bers,[14] have concentrated much of their criticism on this part of Perlman's theory. Because the theory drew much from Commons, both attacks on Perlman's manualist psychology are briefly discussed here.

Ulman does not quarrel with Perlman's main thesis, that the goals of trade unionists are job-centered. But when Perlman derives these goals from the psychological nature of the workingman and from the scarcity of job opportunities, Ulman parts company with him. Where Perlman labels the workers' psychological outlook "pessimistic," Ulman sees only "optimism." How does each arrive at his viewpoint?

Perlman used the term "pessimistic" in two ways. First, he said, the worker is pessimistic about his own innate inability to compete for jobs and economic rewards in a competitive world. Hence he readily accepts union controls which ration scarce jobs and assure each his fair share. Second, on the basis of experience the worker is pessimistic about the number of available jobs relative to the job seekers. Hence workers fashion a union which tries to assert maximum control over job territory, limits apprenticeships, restricts overtime, occasionally insists on "make-work," develops seniority and other regulations to preserve scarce job opportunities for the "in" group.

Ulman looks at the same facts and reads their meaning differently. Unemployment and job rationing are not evidences of pessimism, since "the scarcity of which the worker was conscious might have been induced by the wage policies of the union . . . [forcing wages above competitive levels]. Under such circumstances could consciousness of scarcity have implied 'economic pessimism'? . . . job rationing might well have appeared as the essential means to a desirable end. . . ." If labor believed that the demand for its services was "inelastic," continues Ulman in the vocabulary of the price theorist, "the prospect of a ride uphill—a rise in price unpenalized by a shrinkage in opportunity —should inspire optimism even among the innately cautious. . . . Can achievement of security by forcing the employer off his demand curve be regarded as evidence of pessimistic resignation to one's economic fate . . . ?" [15]

These differences are disagreements in semantics rather than in substance. Each is correct in the light of the usage of words which he has selected. In the common meaning of the term "pessimism," which Perlman has selected, unions that insist on seniority, restriction of apprenticeships, and make-work are correctly described as "pessimistic" about the availability of jobs. Ulman has chosen to discuss these restrictive union practices from the viewpoint of the price theorist. From this esoteric approach, he correctly describes the same unions as "optimistic" when they anticipate a rise in wages unpenalized by a shrinkage in opportunity. Perlman has accurately described the workers' motives. Ulman, on the other hand, has given us the price theorist's evaluation of the probable secondary results of the unions' restrictive practices. Up to this point Ulman has apparently by-passed rather than refuted Perlman's view of labor as pessimistic.

Additional evidence of labor's optimism is seen by Ulman in that "the nineteenth-century union sought wherever possible to maximize gains as well as to cut losses." [16] He quotes Gompers: " 'I would not want any man to believe that our movement is satisfied. There is not anything satisfying in what we have accomplished. It is gratifying but simply whets our appetite for better and better and still better things.' " Then he contrasts Gompers' and Perlman's views: "Although both Perlman and Gompers stand together in their advocacy of 'pure and simple' unionism, there is a difference between the defensive, pessimistic brand described by the former and the aggressive, optimistic variety for which Gompers testified." [17] Here Ulman improperly put Perlman in the position of claiming that labor was generally pessimistic about everything. Perlman was well aware that labor had no pessimism regarding its long-run chances for economic betterment; that unions were frequently optimistic in the sense that they took long chances, risking their very existence in strikes for economic gains, and in such struggles were frequently very aggressive.

If we apply the label "pessimistic" in the narrow and limited sense in which Perlman used it, it seems as appropriate today as in the nineteenth century. Today a large share of union energy is devoted to problems of job scarcity. Demands for shorter hours, for supplementary unemployment benefits, and for rigid seniority, as well as the persistence of jurisdictional strife, all stem from labor's pessimistic view of the number of job seekers relative to the available jobs. There is no conflict between the limited area of pessimism attributed to unions by Perlman and the aggressive optimism which Ulman sees in other aspects of union activity.

Gulick and Bers disagree with Perlman's psychological explanation in a more fundamental way, as the following excerpts illustrate:

As noted above, an adequate theory of the American labor movement must explain why it is that broad schemes of social reorganization have been rejected in favor of a narrowly oriented job-conscious unionism. Perlman's explanation runs largely in terms of the alleged "psychology of the laboring man."

.   .   .   .

The emergence of a "job-conscious" labor movement in the United States was a phenomenon almost unique in labor history. Yet without resorting to an analysis the essence of which is to divide Western humanity into spurious psychological categories it is possible to find an explanation of it.[18]

There is nothing "spurious" or mysterious about manualist psychology as seen by Perlman. In fact it is an important link in understanding why workers have rejected "broad schemes of social reorganization . . . in favor of a narrowly oriented job-conscious unionism." Manualist psychology is merely a common tendency, stronger in manual workers than in others, to grasp at simple, close-at-hand solutions to their job problems. Manualists do not readily grasp abstract solutions. In Perlman's words: "To the workingman, the freedom that matters supremely is the freedom on the job, freedom from unjust discrimination, which enables him to face his boss 'man to man.' Compared with this tangible sort of freedom, the 'higher' freedom, the freedom to elect the managers of industry who are to supplant the present day private boss, or the freedom which the intellectual talks about, appears too remote to enter into actual calculations." [19]

Thus manualist psychology helps explain why American workers will militantly support strike action to make wage gains or to preserve their jobs but will only half-heartedly support the more abstract and less job-centered political solutions, even when the latter are more fundamental and far-reaching.

Writing in 1953, Gulick and Bers saw a likelihood that American labor might abandon job-conscious unionism: "It would be folly to predict an indefinite extension of job-conscious unionism as 'the' labor movement in this country. Yet such a prophecy appears to flow directly from Perlman's theory of the 'psychology' of the laboring man." [20] Within two years of this prediction the CIO, which held the only hope for a less job-conscious labor movement, merged with the AFL, an admission that the younger, industrially organized unions were made in the same basic job-conscious mold as the older organizations.

It is interesting to observe the American labor movement's struggle with the unemployment problem in 1962. For several years before that the AFL-CIO executive council had supported various Keynesian fiscal proposals, including increased government spending and increased income tax exemptions, designed to step up the rate of economic activity. But the rank and file failed to understand these abstract and complicated solutions. Their cure for unemployment was the simple, age-old remedy of cutting the hours of work. In 1962 the AFL-CIO executive council succumbed to rank-and-file pressure, and perhaps to its own latent manualist psychology, and came out for the thirty-five-hour week. Despite five years of excessive unemployment no voice within the labor movement has been raised in support of what Gulick and Bers would call basic reforms of the social and economic system.

Why do labor movements in other countries, in addition to having job consciousness, support labor political parties and socialist political programs whereas the American labor movement has refused to support a labor party and rejected socialist political leadership?

Where union movements have accepted socialist programs, as in Germany, Britain, and Russia, Perlman attributed it to the work of intellectuals who sometimes gained positions of leadership in unions. The timing of the granting of suffrage, the role of the state, the closeness of the feudal heritage, and other national and cultural differences explain why intellectuals had more influence in some countries than in others.

Manualist psychology, while a limiting factor in union behavior, is not completely static. Thus the American labor movement, post-Jones-Laughlin and Taft-Hartley, seems to be moving slowly, haltingly, and with much prodding by its leadership, toward more use of the political weapon, all the time retaining as a first priority its job-conscious outlook. Conversely, labor movements in Western Europe, while retaining their highly developed use of political party, are faltering in their enthusiasm for their long-cherished goal of nationalization of industry, perhaps because of the more compelling lure of concrete job-conscious achievements immediately available through collective bargaining.

The Impact of the Frontier

Both Commons and Perlman were criticized for subscribing to Turner's questionable theory of the impact of the frontier.[21] They used it to help explain why the early American labor movement vacillated between trade union action and efforts to escape from the wage system through producer cooperation, greenbackism, free land, and other middle class panaceas.

One need only read the writings of William Sylvis, president of the Molders and the National Labor Union, and of Terence Powderly, grand master of the Knights of Labor, to observe how their belief in producers' cooperatives retarded the development of stable trade unionism. The existence of cheap land undoubtedly drained off some fraction of labor discontent. The early labor leaders Thomas Skidmore and George Henry Evans actually made free land one of labor's chief goals. It is difficult to document the number of workmen who went from factory to farm, but the fact that immigrant workers saved enough money to remit millions of dollars annually to their mother countries is evidence that wages were high enough to permit saving and presumably the purchase of land. Commons and Perlman further used Turner's thesis of the disappearance of free land about 1890 as a partial explanation for labor's turning away from middle class panaceas toward stable trade unionism.

Did the frontier "close" about 1890 or did the economic frontier broaden while the physical frontier receded? Despite considerable research the historians are in disagreement on this question.

Since conflicting forces are continually at work in the social scene, I see nothing contradictory in the Commons-Perlman notion that the decline of free land, the simultaneous growth of manufacturing in the second half of the nineteenth century, and heavy immigration helped to turn the workers' outlook toward the city instead of the country, thus stimulating interest in unionism rather than in land ownership or producer cooperation. This does not mean that opportunity suddenly ceased. Perlman found that widening economic opportunity in the 'twenties retarded scarcity consciousness and hence unionism. From Perlman's viewpoint the decline of cheap land was only one factor in turning away labor from middle class ideologies. The other significant factor was the emergence in top labor leadership posts of foreign-born class-conscious leaders such as Samuel Gompers. Having shed his doctrinaire socialism and adapted his program to the job consciousness of the American worker, Gompers still retained his socialist acceptance of the inevitable growth of big industry and a permanent working class.

An Alternative Hypothesis

Ulman labels his own views on the origin of unions, their evolution from local to nationwide organizations, and their basic goals an "alternative hypothesis" to the Commons-Perlman theories. So far as an "origin" theory is concerned Ulman is vague. He implies that unions originated in the retail shop stage, one step prior to Commons' placement of them in the wholesale order stage. The cause of unionism in both the building trades and the cordwainers he thinks is "wage cutting." [22] But this term explains little compared to Commons' detailed description of the source and nature of the competitive forces which brought on wage cutting and separated worker from employer.

Ulman then offers an "alternative" to Commons' and Perlman's explanation of why labor in America relied on collective bargaining rather than political action. Commons' explanation was that the American political structure, with separation of powers and court checks, made the political method difficult and unsure. An additional roadblock was the fact that the American worker's political allegiance had been formulated before the rise of trade unionism. Long experience with this situation taught labor the folly of diverting much energy from collective bargaining to the uncertainties and diversions of politics. Ulman merely looks at the other side of the coin. He attributes labor's concentration on collective bargaining to its success. The two views are complementary.

Gulick and Bers do not offer an alternative hypothesis. For the most part they restrict themselves to criticism of Perlman's theory. However they do reveal some of the forces which they declare would have changed the nature of the American labor movement. As a case in point, "the presence of a dozen Debs would have altered considerably the tone of the American labor movement." [23] This unsupported espousal of an accident-of-leadership theory is in striking contrast to Commons' and Perlman's careful analyses of such factors as the stage of production and marketing, the nature of industrial organization, the influence of immigration, the nature of the American political system, and the widespread distribution of property, especially land.

Similarly, Gulick and Bers declare that the Commons-Perlman emphasis on the strength of private property as an influential determinant of the course of the American movement is an "overestimate," since "popular sentiment for mortgage moratoria during the Great Depression indicated that certain elements of sanctity [of private property] are dispensable when economic conditions depart *too far from usual experience* [italics mine]." [24] The preponderance of evidence both before and since 1933–34 confirms Commons' and Perlman's estimate of the entrenched position of private property in the United States.

In commenting on Commons' and Perlman's analysis of how the division of political power between state and federal government and among executive, legislative, and judicial branches had rendered the political instrument relatively ineffective, Gulick and Bers pose an unlikely proposition: "it may be useful to reflect upon what a 'labor' Congress and a handful of new Supreme Court justices could do to revamp traditional American institutions if sufficient popular sentiment were being generated over, say a ten-year period." [25] This recurrent notion that the American labor movement would have followed a different course under more politically minded leadership indicates a lack of understanding of the historical forces which shaped the movement. There were, of course, plenty of politically minded leaders of every variety in the movement, yet their preachments fell upon infertile soil; in the end they either were rejected or, like Gompers, revised their programs in the light of their experience.

Current Labor Theory

The criticisms of Commons' and Perlman's theories made by Richard A. Lester in *As Unions Mature* and by Clark Kerr and others in *Industrialism and Industrial Man* [26] are less pointed and less detailed. Lester's emphasis is on the changes which unions have recently undergone as they have expanded, matured, and gained public acceptance. He refers to his analysis as "developmental," in contrast to Perlman's "static" theory, which "rests on a normative psychology of 'job-consciousness' in manual workers, which seemingly is universal in its application and unchanging over time." [27] Lester's interpretation is generally consistent with Perlman's analysis of job consciousness, but he adds a wealth of detail on changing union structure, leadership, and management relations. His main conclusions:

1. As the rate of union expansion slows down, a psychological ageing tends to spread throughout the organization, especially if it already covers most of its jurisdiction.
2. With the passage of time and the accumulation of experience, central control at union headquarters tends to expand and democratic checks at the local level weaken.
3. As a union stabilizes and ages, the top leadership becomes more administrative in character and the differences between union executives and management executives diminish.
4. The more successes unions achieve, the more they tend to reduce their

areas of potential expansion and innovation and, consequently, some of their dynamic qualities.

5. With increased bargaining experience and rising living standards, the differences between manual and white-collar workers tend to narrow and the areas of conflict and worker protest tend to be reduced.

6. As unions gain employer acceptance and their objectives broaden, the differences between unions and other community organizations tend to decrease.

7. Increasing security for the union and for the present leadership serves as a moderating influence; less rivalry and fewer challenges reduce the pressures and incentives for militant exploitation of a union's bargaining power.

It is predicted that these long-run tendencies and trends will continue in effectiveness over the forthcoming decades, tending to level out in some cases but not being completely offset or reversed.[28]

This description of the maturation process of unions is a real contribution to labor theory, despite the fact that Lester is frequently dealing with details, rather than with the fundamental goals and nature of unions as Perlman does.

In seeing a progressive lessening of labor-management tensions, I believe Lester has underestimated the inherent dynamism in trade union activity. It is generally not true that labor has drawn away from a militant exploitation of its bargaining power. The annual gains of unions in wages and fringe benefits in recent years are more economically important than the gains of any earlier period. Moreover, these gains are engaging unions and management in an increasingly significant struggle over the distribution of corporate income. That collective bargaining generally results in elaborate legalistic contracts instead of strikes, and that the typical strike is disciplined and without violence, should not be interpreted as softness or collaboration with management. The current collective bargaining struggles of the well-established unions may take a different form from the sit-down strikes of the 'thirties, but their economic importance should not be underestimated. The bitter six-month steel strike of 1959 warns us to be wary of predictions that the strike is "withering" away. In broad areas of trade and manufacturing management has not even submitted to dealing with unions.

There is more political ferment within unions than Lester recognized. Internal union political struggles are not a thing of the past, though they have obviously subsided from the instability of the formative years, as witnessed in the first years of CIO.

Lester's labeling of Perlman's job-conscious theory as "static" is substantially correct. While Lester offers this as a criticism, Perlman's recognition of the roots of job-conscious unionism in the relatively stable psychology of the manual laborer has been one of the merits of his theory. Perlman's understanding of the psychology of the manualist enabled him to predict correctly the nature of today's unionism after observing it primarily in its craft stage and before the advent of mass production unionism.

The labor problems of 1962 indicate that today's unions are as much or more concerned with job security and extending job ownership than their predecessors a century ago. This does not prevent some changed responses to different stimuli. For example, the manual worker's job consciousness has not kept labor leadership from putting increased emphasis on political activity either from 1906 to 1914, when the courts blocked labor's normal organizing and bargaining activities, or after the Jones and Laughlin decision of 1937, when the legal obstacles to job security via government had been removed.

Like Lester, Clark Kerr and his associates break new ground in *Industrialism and Industrial Man.* They offer a theory of industrial relations which is not limited to explaining industrial relations; it is put in a setting of global economic development.

The essence of the theory is the overwhelming power of industrialism to force all countries into a similar mold regardless of the cultural, political, and economic institutions and almost regardless of their different historical starting points. Thus middle class America, revolutionary Russia and China, nationalistic India and Ghana, and what is left of colonial empires will under the relentless impact of industrialism move toward very similar societies described as "pluralistic industrialism." In this new society the state will not wither away but will play a central role as a sort of mediator among pluralistic factions, not classes. In place of the traditional economic and social classes the society will have bureaucratic managers, technicians, scientists, occupational and professional associations. The class loyalty of Marx and the plant community of Mayo will both be forgotten. Conflict will be limited to "bureaucratic memos" rather than strikes. "These threads of conflict will continue when class war, and the contest over private versus public initiative, and the battle between monistic and atomistic ideologies have been left far behind in the sedimentary layers of history." [29]

This global framework contrasts with the theory Commons built of union development of a single country. Kerr points up the contrast as follows: "One of the principal deficiencies, even in the classic studies of relations between workers and managers, such as those of the Webbs and Commons, is that they have lacked the perspective of a long-run deductive model of the industrialization process." [30] It is true that neither Commons nor Perlman achieved a worldwide model of the industrializing process. By years of research Commons managed to construct a deductive model for union development of one country, the United States. Even so, it was difficult for him to square all the facts with the model. Perlman, with considerable attention to the industrializing process in America and Western Europe, went forward to construct a broader model covering union movements in four countries: the United States, England, Germany, and Russia. His model over the years has fitted the United States remarkably well and is turning out to be increasingly accurate in its predictions of the other three countries—though there is considerable controversy on this point.

The comprehensive framework of Kerr's group is a new and imaginative way of approaching industrial relations. It may also be over-ambitious. There is certainly overemphasis on the similarities which technology may produce in diverse human beings under varying human institutions and with varying amounts of available physical resources.

For example, may not industrialization have a vastly different pattern in areas with a high ratio of resources to population, such as the United States, Western Europe, and Russia, from that in countries with a low ratio, like India and Egypt? May not industrialization show dissimilar forms of worker protest in countries which have been able to increase productivity more rapidly than population, i.e. the United States, Western Europe, Japan, than in countries where standards of living do not rise because population increase keeps pace with productivity?

Kerr and his associates believe on the basis of their observations that worker protest is no longer a critical factor during a nation's industrializing process; it has been superseded by that wave of the future, the managerial elite, which regularly by subtlety or force sublimates worker goals to the national interest.

But can we cross off the Communist threat so easily? Kerr has observed that to date worker protest "peaks early," thus "turning Marx on his head." This was true in the United States and Western Europe, where productivity exceeded population growth. Will it be true in such countries as Brazil, Argentina, India, Indonesia, where quite different productivity and population trends may develop? The Kerr theory does have room for considerable diversities, but it has underemphasized the very great differences in the role of worker organizations that may arise and persist because of these diversities. Nevertheless illustrative examples in *Industrialism and Industrial Man,* and its generalizations on the similarity in long-run impact of technology despite differing cultural and political regimes, do add a new and useful dimension to thinking on industrial relations.

The CIO Threat to the Commons-Perlman Analysis

Commons' famous article on the shoemakers, which first elaborated his extension-of-markets doctrine, appeared in 1909; the documentary volumes in 1910–11, and two volumes of the *History of Labour* in 1918. Perlman's *Theory of the Labor Movement* came out in 1928. Both continuation volumes in the *History* appeared in 1935. Thus the writings of the "Wisconsin School" were completed while the labor movement was small, craft-dominated, and in a rather precarious position, well before the great upsurge of the 1930's which brought the new millions of semiskilled and unskilled into the movement. Just how well did the analysis of job consciousness stand up in the light of the mass unionism of the CIO?

Perlman failed completely to anticipate the mass unionism on an industrial basis of the mid-1930's. As a matter of fact, as late as 1935 he was more than half expecting an employer counteroffensive similar to the open shop movement of the early 'twenties.

The early days of the CIO with its sit-down strikes and its new, young, turbulent left-wing leadership gave rise to serious doubts as to the accuracy of Perlman's emphasis on job consciousness. However, it shortly became evident that the sit-down strikes of the semiskilled and unskilled were in no sense an effort to dispossess the employers of their property but merely a desperate attempt to establish the same type of job ownership which skilled labor had traditionally sought. The new industrial unions rapidly proceeded to stake out seniority claims and seek arbitration of grievances and stable contractual relations much as their job-conscious forebears did. The left-wing leadership in CIO unions was totally unsuccessful in arousing rank-and-file interest in anything but traditional union objectives, and generally held office only by concealing its left-wing philosophy and any ties with the Communist party.

To note that the CIO unions turned out to be as job conscious as the AFL predecessors is not to overlook certain important contributions made by the generally younger and often more alert CIO leadership. This new leadership was quicker to recognize the importance of political activity. After the liberal reverses of the 1942 Congressional election, the CIO put political action on a year-round basis. This was five years before the passage of the Taft-Hartley Act moved the AFL to take similar action.

But even here the real motivating force in the increased political activity of both CIO and AFL was primarily protection of their collective bargaining rights, which were threatened by antilabor majorities in Congress. This is not to deny that labor's political goals by the 1940's had broadened in terms of peripheral interests considerably over the narrow AFL attitudes of the 'twenties. But even the broadened interest in world affairs, civil rights, and New Deal reforms did not go beyond job-conscious unionism in the field of labor-management relations. These questions have always been of subsidiary concern to the rank-and-file membership, who stubbornly persist in centering their union interest on grievance handling and collective bargaining, as did their predecessors seventy-five years ago.

The deaths of Philip Murray and William Green in 1952 removed the personality factors which had made merger difficult. The CIO had already expelled the Communist-dominated unions, and the AFL had expelled a union for racketeering. By this time no one presumed to see much ideological difference between the two federations. Jurisdiction, that persistent manifestation of job consciousness, was the major stumbling block that separated the labor movement. The 1955 merger by-passed the jurisdiction question, but it refuses to disappear and is today the AFL-CIO's biggest internal problem.

In the 1961 convention President Meany tried to minimize the importance of the troublesome jurisdiction question by placing it in proper perspective with a quotation from Samuel Gompers almost sixty years earlier: "Beyond a doubt, the gravest problem—the danger which, above all others, most threatens not only the success but the very existence of the American Federation of Labor—is the question of jurisdiction." [31] Yet it took an all-night executive council meeting to put together a resolution on jurisdiction which would save the federation from increased internal warfare and possibly new splits.

The current course of the labor movement is a testimonial to the soundness of the Commons-Perlman analysis, formulated long before the labor movement achieved its current size and influence.

The Future Impact of Extension of Markets

Does Commons' extension-of-markets theory, which helped explain the origin and nationalization of the union, have any relevance for charting labor union developments of the future? With the current rapid rate of industrialization in the rest of the world, the process of extension of markets may again influence trade union structure in the United States. A substantial increase in world trade might introduce a new era of intensive, worldwide competition for the product market. This would exert downward wage pressures in high-wage areas such as the United States. Since the road to protection for the American worker in this case would appear to be the tariff, this new extension of markets, unlike that of the nineteenth century, might bring heightened interest in political action rather than in collective bargaining. Unions and employers in affected industries would have common interests in such political action; thus the markets' extension might bring American capital and labor together for mutual survival, while at the same time tending to heighten class antagonisms as management holds a tight rein on wages in the face of foreign competition.

I am aware that today the AFL-CIO strongly supports the principle of tariff reduction. The primary motive for this is not narrow job protectionism but a recognition of the role of increased world trade for American foreign policy. The lower tariff resolution at the AFL-CIO convention of 1961 was hedged with many job-protecting reservations. Should tariff reduction, increased competition in the product market, and some increase in unemployment actually occur in the next few years, an agonizing reappraisal would be forced upon the federation.

Simultaneously with this increased worldwide competition there would be increased emphasis on worldwide unionism. Because of nationalism the structure of this internationalization of unions would follow patterns different from the usual union structural changes within countries, but the goal would be the same: to create a structure which could equalize wage competition. In the past, within national boundaries, such growth of nationwide unions contributed to the unionizing of workers. In the international field the structural adjustment would generally be among already existing nationwide unions and might be expected to increase the role of the international secretariats and confederations.

These trends, both political and economic, would not be totally new developments but rather major extensions of already existing activities, brought on by the increased level of international competition in the product market. While the extension-of-markets doctrine was originated by Commons to help explain both the origin of unionism and the dominance of nationwide unions based on collective bargaining, it may have new and quite different significance for the trade unionism of the future.

Labor History Since Commons

Scholarly interest in labor history seemed to wane along with the declining fortunes of the labor movement during the 'twenties and early 'thirties. The publication in 1935 of Perlman's and Taft's volume of the *History of Labor* marked the end of an era. This encyclopedic volume brought labor history up to date. A few differing interpretations appeared, but significant works awaited the opening up of new sources and the making of new history.

The rapid growth of the labor movement in the late 'thirties heightened interest in labor relations but not in labor history. Accounts of the CIO's success began to appear, along with hastily improvised biographies of the new labor leaders. These works were often turned out by persons close to the labor movement. Inevitably they lacked perspective and sometimes objectivity. The war again delayed serious historical work by cutting off manpower. Wartime government agencies served to acquaint hundreds of academicians with labor-management problems. This experience together with the growth of unions served to bring on what might be referred to as the postwar explosion of universities into labor-management studies. While most of the war-created labor relations experts turned to the fields of industrial relations, collective bargaining, and arbitration, renewed interest and effort were devoted to labor history.

The enlarged labor movement has provided new subjects and a wealth of new sources. In contrast to Commons' general history of the labor movement, the rapid growth of new unions has resulted in many histories of specific unions. Several general histories of the post-1932 labor movement and of the CIO are either under way or appearing.

An interesting development is the new sources which are being uncovered. One such source which was not available to Commons' group is business records. As the early labor battles fade into the past, some corporations have been willing to open their files on these once controversial events. These reveal fascinating details on the events cursorily covered by Commons and other early historians. Some of the records go back to the 1830's; some are as recent as the 1930's. Business historians have been the first to get access to these corporate files. Their publications, however, generally indicate a lack of interest in the labor policies of the company, or perhaps they were not always given unrestricted access to controversial materials.

Unions too are opening their files. While Commons was restricted to published convention proceedings and journals, several historians have been allowed recently to use minutes of union executive boards. In the belief that much union history will never be revealed by documents, some universities are engaged in oral history projects, taping testimonials of current labor leaders. It remains to be seen whether the future historian will be more enlightened or misled by such sources.

Commons' chief sources were court records, daily newspapers, and union publications. These sources are still available and yielding excellent results for those scholars willing to take the necessary time and travel. They are particularly valuable in filling out regional developments.

Commons and his associates were generally economists rather than historians. Current labor historians appear to be about equally divided between the two. Economists such as Commons and Ely originally went into labor history because the traditional historians had long failed to recognize its significance. This is not the case today, when both disciplines are making different and valuable contributions. The historian is especially skillful in putting the labor story in its proper relationship with other social currents. The economist tends to concentrate on the labor story and either consciously or unconsciously ignores the total setting. His merit is that his knowledge of industrial relations and economic theory gives him a unique perspective from which to view and analyze the history of trade unionism and labor-management behavior.

Notes

1 John R. Commons et al., *Documentary History of American Industrial Society*, 10 vols. Cleveland, Arthur H. Clark Co., 1910–11.
2 John R. Commons and associates, *History of Labour in the United States*, Vols. 1 and 2, New York, Macmillan, 1918. In his preface Commons lists 33 persons besides himself as responsible for the cooperative research which went into these two volumes. Commons planned and supervised the research for them, and most of it was done in his seminars over a 12-year period; it is appropriate to refer to the contents as the viewpoint of Commons even when written by one of his associates.

By contrast Commons' influence on Volumes 3 and 4 of the *History of Labor* (Macmillan, 1935) was indirect: the authors Brandeis and Lescohier (Vol. 3) and Perlman and Taft (Vol. 4) had at one time been his pupils. The content of these later volumes is not discussed in this article.
3 This theory was first expressed in "American Shoemakers, 1648–1895," *Quart. Jour. Econ.*, Vol. 24, Nov. 1909.
4 Lloyd Ulman, *The Rise of the National Trade Union*, Cambridge, Harvard Univ. Press, 1955.
5 Ibid., p. 576.
6 Ibid., pp. 576–77.
7 Commons, *History of Labour*, 1: 66–71.
8 Ibid., p. 71.
9 Ulman, pp. 44–45.
10 *History of Labour*, 2: 44.
11 Ulman, p. 45.
12 *History of Labour*, 2: 526.
13 Selig Perlman, *A Theory of the Labor Movement*, New York, Macmillan, 1928; New York, Augustus Kelley, 1949.
14 Charles A. Gulick and Melvin K. Bers, "Insight and Illusion in Perlman's Theory of the Labor Movement," *Industrial and Labor Relations Review*, 6, No. 4 (July 1953): 510–31.
15 Ulman, pp. 581, 583.
16 Ibid., p. 584.
17 Ibid., p. 588.
18 Gulick and Bers, pp. 521, 528.
19 Perlman p. 290.
20 Gulick and Bers, p. 530.
21 Ulman, pp. 572, 591–92.
22 Ibid., p. 599.
23 Gulick and Bers, p. 529.
24 Ibid.
25 Ibid.
26 Richard A. Lester, *As Unions Mature*, Princeton Univ. Press, 1958;

Clark Kerr, J. T. Dunlop, F. H. Harbison, and C. A. Myers, *Industrialism and Industrial Man*, Cambridge, Harvard Univ. Press, 1960.

27 Lester, p. 5.
28 Ibid., pp. 111–12.
29 Kerr et al., p. 296.
30 Ibid., p. 23.
31 Samuel Gompers, Report to 1902 Convention of the AFL, as quoted by George Meany, Transcript of AFL-CIO Convention, *Proceedings* (Dec. 7, 1961), p. 20.

3

L. REED TRIPP

Collective Bargaining Theory

In the intellectual climate since World War II the lack of a theory of collective bargaining has been a frequently voiced complaint. The burden of these criticisms has generally been twofold: (1) that collective bargaining has been a pragmatic or applied field which was foreign to if not in actual contradiction of the laws of economics, and (2) that where scholarship was being devoted to collective bargaining the efforts produced largely scattered spot materials, case studies, unrelated observations or speculations, with little or no systematic framework of interrelated propositions or operational hypotheses.*

* Commenting on the need for such a framework, Joseph Shister attributes the first attempt at an explicit and systematic characterization of the process of collective bargaining to Leiserson in 1922: "Nothing substantial was done between then and 1951 when Chamberlain developed his threefold categorization of collective bargaining" (the marketing theory, the governmental theory, and the managerial theory). Joseph Shister, "Collective Bargaining," in *A Decade of Industrial Relations Research 1946–56,* N. W. Chamberlain, F. Pierson, and T. Wolfson, eds., Industrial Relations Research Association, Pub. No. 19, Harper, 1958.

The Industrial Relations Research Association had a soul-searching session in 1960 in which both a survey report and various speakers revealed the frequency of the complaint that no theory of industrial relations exists. To conceptualize industrial relations would require considerations of the psychology of work for the individual, the small group, and other societal units generally underlying or extending beyond union and management, the two entities whose interplay is the focus of

Old writers apparently did not feel a poverty of theory; indeed many considered that they were contributing to the development of systematic consideration of the collective bargaining process. Noteworthy of course were the Webbs' "higgling in the market," their standard rate as one phase of the common rule, and even their concept of industrial democracy.[1] Pointing out the differences between the customs and working rules * of labor and the "theory of the law-merchant," John R. Commons sought principles of an evolution of "industrial government" from the "wage-bargain." [2] As examples of the assurance of earlier bargaining theorists, one recalls titles like John Davidson's *The Bargain Theory of Wages* (1898) or W. H. Hutt's *Theory of Collective Bargaining* (1930).

It is appropriate to question whether we are really as bereft of theoretical formulation in this field as contemporary criticism suggests. More important, if we find some relevance to current affairs in theoretical formulations of earlier scholarship, is to consider the possibilities for building a modern statement of collective bargaining upon such a historical base to make theory even more useful in explaining current events. This paper will proceed upon the hypothesis that intellectual progress is more likely to emerge from building upon past scholarship than from scrapping or ignoring the lessons of history and starting de novo.

"Theory" as we shall use it here means a system of thought intended to help explain and predict human behavior. Its purpose to the writer is to identify lasting forces at work in human affairs, having survival value in Darwinian terms, and being operational in the moving context of human activities. Its obligation, unpopular as it may be at times, is to distinguish persistent underlying currents from the vagaries of the moment, whimsical or transitory behavior, and even intellectual fads.

We shall view collective bargaining as related to the workplace, usually industrial, but not limited to a particular type of production. To this extent it has an economic core, but it cannot always be confined within economic concepts in a formal sense. For this reason it is useful to consider collective bargaining system formulation and the economic

collective bargaining. While the analysis in this paper will not extend so far, there appears to be no conceptual barrier to the development of a theory of industrial relations of which the theory of collective bargaining would be an integral part.

* The concept of work rules similar to that used by Commons continues to be popular both in the field and in literature of industrial relations. See for example n. 3.

theoretical systems as intersecting sets rather than view one as a sub-system of the other.[3] The main reason for this caveat however arises from the constraints which economists have often imposed upon themselves in formulating their propositions in such a way as to abstract out the "noneconomic" aspects of human behavior. Students of collective bargaining have consistently found sociological concepts and sometimes analogies to political behavior highly useful in explaining this field of human activity. Recourse to related social science material needed to explain other economic phenomena, e.g. economic development, might also be easier to apply if the older and broader scope of "political economy" or Commons' theoretical economics were in vogue today. In such a case, collective bargaining theory could easily be subsumed as a subset under a social-political economic system.

The Market Base

With the foregoing qualifications in mind, it is still highly useful to place the theoretical formulation of collective bargaining upon an economic base. The economic requirements for combining factors of production are reliably basic to any consideration of organization of work from place to place or country to country, though the organizational arrangements themselves, distributive systems, and particularly relationships to government may be highly varied.

The rich variety of possible organizational arrangements and distributive systems is demonstrated in the different countries of the world today, all facing the basic economic problem of combining factors of production to yield their respective national outputs. Man-land ratios, or more accurately, the relative factor endowments among natural resources, capital equipment with various stages of technology, and labor or manpower are basic to any consideration of potential welfare limits of a country's economy, and generate the underlying economic forces which affect the operation of a labor market, if it exists, and other market determinants of distributive income shares.

In a free market system, however, it has long been recognized that the competitive model needs many qualifications in labor market analysis to approach the realities of the wage determination process. Critical to collective bargaining theory is the hypothesis that a free or non-union labor market operates very imperfectly and yields ranges of indeterminacy in wage setting of greater or less width. The scope of this indeterminacy, particularly when one considers a dynamic economy with limits continually changing, has not been quantified and may not be in the foreseeable future. The evidence from empirical studies of behavioral deviations in the local labor market from requirements of a competitive model, both by employer and employee, supports the hypothesis that market actions should not be expected to be reflected fully in wage costs or earnings. Even in Smithian terms this statement would leave considerable margin for monetary wage variations.* To the extent that we recognize human behavior as departing from the rationality assumption, the margins or ranges of indeterminacy become larger.

Lloyd Reynolds has clearly drawn the implications of his empirical labor market data for wage theory.[4] Other empirical studies of labor markets generally support his conclusions. Although studies of certain white collar groups seem to show more rational employee behavior than is found characteristic of production workers, these studies show employer wage-setting behavior to deviate as much or more from the competitive model. In any case, there is no extensive evidence so far that perfectly operating competitive models of money wage setting exist in labor markets.

This conception of a moving range of indeterminacy in free or nonunion market wage setting is by no means intended to abrogate all effects of economic forces on wages. The concept can also recognize disemployment effects of nonmarket wage raising by law, organization, or administrative decision. Instances can be found of very tight labor markets with active bidding upward of wages (even pirating), as in the tool and die industry in 1941 or in particular local shortages of clerical workers. In such instances, otherwise quiescent market forces can be seen, as it were, to "raise their ugly heads." Obversely any great slackness or reserve of unemployed (a phrase recently reappearing in the literature) is usually thought to exercise real pressure or drag on wage movements.

On the second point, it often appears to bargainers that disemployment does not have a direct connection to the wage level within a relevant variation of likely wage decisions at a moment of time. Arthur

---

* Revealed preference utilities or disutilities or even Adam Smith's concept of net advantage are thus consistent with this statement, though it may be argued that they demonstrate a kind of abstract, truistic equilibrium mainly irrelevant to the range of money wage indeterminacy.

Ross made the classic statement of this notion: "The employment effect of a wage adjustment is unpredictable before the fact and undecipherable after the fact"; [5] and so it may appear at the bargaining table. Yet this is surely a matter of degree. Stating the extreme case, one can certainly imagine a wage level so high in a particular industry or in an economy that it would not be profitable to employ many workers. Moving from "the extreme case" to the "relevant range" merely reveals the difficulty of identifying any specific disemployment level, related as such a level is to demand elasticity in product markets, among other things. Yet that such an effect could emerge over time is beyond doubt. It is further likely that disemployment does result from labor costs at times, and along with other factors may account for the closing of the noncompetitive firm or plant. Graphic instances must surely be within the contemplation of union bargainers.

Collective bargaining theory merely asserts that the parties to the bargain can establish realistic and acceptable wages and employment terms more reliably than can labor courts or other alternative devices for setting wages and work rules. It furthermore provides representational machinery for administered decisions, where we hypothesize a likely range for administration. It is this characteristic that has prompted labor economists from Sidney Webb to Sumner Slichter to note the economic basis for collective action by groups of employees as an offset for weaknesses of individual bargaining.

Within such an understanding of the economic environment, earlier writers drew mainly from historical materials certain statements of central tendencies of union behavior. Our first task is to note some of these authorities, ask whether they are related to each other, and finally appraise their relevance to current events. In the world of free markets and private decision making, the trade union was seen by the Webbs as attempting to establish a standard rate and common rule. Commons added to this concept, as he saw the widening of product markets in the United States through increase of transportation and trade become a critical impetus to expansion of unionism. Selig Perlman considered "competitive menaces to the job" the reason that employees sought to organize trade unions even beyond local labor markets, with national unions and a lasting federation emerging in the United States in the second half of the nineteenth century.[*] The interrelationships and

[*] Because of Perlman's historical and philosophical treatment the fact is often glossed over that Perlmanism has a very strong economic or market base. The job

relevance of these concepts will be discussed below. A thread readily at hand upon which a weaving together of these postulates may be posited is job-centered unionism.

The Job-Centered Theory of Unionism

As revisionist work proceeds today on labor theory, one might note initially some dimensions of the concept "job interest." Selig Perlman identified what he considered to be a distinctive manualist psychology defined as a "consciousness of job scarcity." [6] While some aura of magnetic appeal was suggested around the job, the concept was built upon what has been known more commonly as concern for job security. A plenty of jobs, or conversely the fear of unemployment, concerns workers at least as much if not more today than was indicated in the historical materials from which the concept emerged. Recent documentation of this concern by employees themselves is available from collective bargaining developments and surveys of employee attitudes. Restriction of output under incentive compensation by informal pegging of pace among unorganized workers has been related at least in part to "fear of working themselves out of jobs." It would appear that this psychological trait is still a highly reliable element by which to anticipate or predict employee behavior.

For trade union theory, however, the threat of job loss takes on special meaning when related to the earlier concept of the standard rate. The fear of individual employees' competitively undercutting a standard wage is the basic underlying explanation for collective bargaining as against individual bargaining. This concern underlies the "closed shop" issue in some industries (not all) where union members fear that the nonunion employee will undermine union standards. The same anxiety relates to appropriate unit determination under the Labor-Management Relations Act, where majority preference against unionization in a small segment of an industry constitutes a threat to union standards and therefore to union members' jobs in the organized segment, as production may move to lower labor cost centers of a competitive product market.

In considering the modern relevance of concern for job standards, it is evident that the occupation or craft is not a sufficiently wide area.

territory with which he concerned himself referred basically to a product market; this is discussed later.

Although craft unions arose first, the coal mine workers and needle trades operatives were already organized in unions on a largely industrial basis at the time that Perlman was writing. It is superficial in the extreme to assume that his work is relevant only to the craft. The critical feature of Perlman's "threat to jobs" is found in the product or service market more importantly than in the labor market. In the basic steel industry, for example, we see a national and international market for steel. The gradual elimination since World War II of the "Southern differential" in steel wage structures reflects the attempt to make sure that Pittsburgh and Gary jobs would not be lost to a cheaper labor cost steel-producing center such as that in Birmingham, Alabama. Within each major automobile corporation the same development has occurred since the war. It has been evident in other industries, but in some this type of drive was not so successfully completed because of many obstacles, including state legislation that inhibited organization growth, multiunionism, and multiproduct companies which make industry markets highly difficult to identify today. Recognition of the obstacles to the achievement of such drives does not invalidate a basic motivational concept behind union expansion. In fact the identification of positive and negative forces, together with appraisal of their relative strength, begins to give us the tools for prediction of human behavior which we seek in collective bargaining theory.

Some revisionist attempts in labor theory see the elements of social cohesion today much more within the firm than across firms to an industry dimension or product market. Yet there is an obvious difference in orientation between employees in the expectedly continuous employment of a large corporation and workers in the short-term employment of building contractors, small needle trades firms, shipping companies, trucking firms, etc. For the latter the union often provides more stable employee ties than does the employer. Even for employees of the corporate employer, however, the union represents an employee interest in and concern for the wage rate and employment standards of other employers competing in the same product market or markets, if job standards are to be maintained against competitively lower wage levels. Moore's company orientation here for purposes of labor theory [7] is contradicted by Bakke's finding that unions are inherently interested in the employees of other employers whereas management would prefer to confine its consideration to its own employees.[8] If sociological theory finds cohesion solely in the firm, it will miss not only wide segments of organized labor where prime bonds are to a union but also the interesting phenomenon of dual loyalty in large-scale industrial employment, which needs much more investigation.

Finally, we have heard a number of times in recent years that unions do not strive for a standard wage but have developed new bargaining criteria such as sharing productivity gains and following wage patterns. Superficial evidence supports this revision, which undoubtedly accounts for much of the de-emphasis on the concept of job standards as basic to unionism. It may be useful, however, to probe this behavior pattern more deeply.

In the first place, the notion of establishing job standards that need protection has always implied attempts to improve or advance the status quo. Gompers' concept of the union objective as more, more, and more was not as sophisticated as modern measurements of productivity gains but probably came to about the same thing: seeking to obtain as large a share as was bargainable of what a growing economy could yield. The laws of distributive economics in an economy of growth would theoretically be expected to yield constantly growing real wages (though absolute growth proportions might change through time). If labor markets operate imperfectly, collective bargaining by the union would put upward pressure on the distribution system in the attempt to advance job standards. To avoid misunderstanding on this point, however, the statement of the job interest motif should probably be revised to declare more positively the union's aim to "protect and advance job standards" rather than simply to protect jobs in a narrow sense. The familiar bargaining tactics of striking the easiest target first, of asking more from one firm than another on the basis of ability to pay, as well as much pattern following, whipsawing, and similar strategies, would all be consistent with such statement.

One type of pattern following however fits uneasily even under this concept. Occasionally a package demand, emanating from national union power center bargaining, may be imposed on a firm faced by quite different product market competition. In such a case the plant may "run away," enticed by wide geographic areas or industry segments that are unorganized or organized by other unions. The failure of organization drives (influenced at least partly by post-World War II legislation), still unresolved union jurisdictional problems, and the modern complications of identifying products with multiproduct firms and shifting product competition have all made the maintenance of job standards and associated costs difficult. Yet the complete disregard of job standards and associated competitive labor costs can be shown occasionally to be suicidal for the union involved. Frequent plant closure in recent years, when attributable to a noncompetitive labor cost element, bears witness to such suicide. In spite of the complexities of modern industrial life, therefore, the basic underlying union drive must be recognized if we are to understand, explain, or predict the behavior of unions and to know what unions will survive.

It is recognized that the concept of job interest is itself a multidimensional concept, involving many noneconomic as well as economic elements. For illustration, one might mention Veblen's motivational insights on "the instinct of workmanship" and the influence of habitual and routine industrial behavior; [9] or, more currently, Dubin's emphasis upon the interdependence of work with role, status, and other value drives that motivate some part of job interest.[10] K. U. Smith in particular stresses the significance of work as a central life role, in his biosocial theory of the evolution of man at work.[11] Any attempt at a complete theory of industrial and human relations would seek to identify and if possible quantify both the noneconomic and economic dimensions of job interest.

Without waiting for the development of such a social-psychological theory of industrial man, it is useful to recognize the job interest through which focus both of the foregoing categories of motivations, economic and noneconomic, while realizing the complicated internal structure of the job theme. The economist can recognize the strong product market dimension of the drive to protect and advance the job interest complex as the moving force of unionism. We suggest that this set of forces is as necessary and relevant to the understanding or even prediction of survival-oriented union behavior today as when first anticipated by Commons' analysis of the impact of widening markets and later formulated by Perlman's union theory, discussed above. In this sense the Perlman theory, while considered to be psychological and philosophical, also had a strong economic or product market base.

Is Job Interest a Sufficient Explanation of the Union's Current Role in Collective Bargaining?

Even if it be conceded that the attempt to protect and advance job standards continues to represent a basic objective of union organizations, many critics consider job-centered labor theory highly inadequate as a characterization of union behavior in collective bargaining.

The first form of this criticism designates job-centered unions as "bread and butter unionism" and argues that they disregard intangible, human values beyond a narrow economic interest. Although the debate between pragmatist and idealist has centered more around the role of political activity beyond the collective bargaining arena (see section 5 below), such terms as "slot machine" bargaining stress the narrow economic role of unionism in the shop exclusive of any more idealized objectives. Can one identify noneconomic human values in Perlman's manualist ideology?

Actually some of Perlman's students would probably be surprised, shocked, and hurt at the emphasis on market economics in the foregoing section. Perlman was considered as pre-eminently a philosopher, a historian, sometimes as a humanist, and thought by some even to have disregarded hard data and scientific methodology. What then are the intangible elements or value systems that can be detected objectively in his theoretical work?

A basic concept is the dignity of the individual worker, theoretically protected against arbitrary discrimination, which is inherently difficult to eliminate from human affairs. In contrast to the self-employed, a wage or salary worker is dependent on levels of higher authority for work instructions and also for fairness and treatment with respect. He may hope that personnel policies will be enlightened and beneficent but he has no independent assurance of it. The individual worker under unionism has an actual or potential independent recourse which provides him with assurances beyond the nonunion employment relationship. With his fellow employees' support, he can be represented by a leader selected and paid by them. This support and representation can give him the self-confidence that he seeks in the industrial relationship and in meeting any problems that arise. This independent recourse provided by the "outside" union is the irreplaceable element inherently absent from the most enlightened attempts by management to devise a nonunion grievance procedure.

Furthermore the intangible right to a "say" through chosen representatives may be as important psychologically as the actual economic terms reached. In George W. Taylor's concept collective bargaining is "agreed-upon" terms, which are more satisfying psychologically than imposed terms, even if possibly less equitable by given absolute standards. It has been suggested that this "meeting of minds" represents a basic source of willing participation in productive effort and an essential characteristic of the American industrial system of growth and progress.[12]

Thus human values of individual worth, including representation through bargaining and grievance procedures on the job, freedom from the frustrating reality or possibility of unilateral dictation under economic necessity, secure avenues for expression and communication, and democratic participation are all aspects of job-centered unionism at its best. It is both pragmatic and characterized by "religious fervor." Like other religious movements, it is sometimes intolerant; freedom of individual choice may at times be sacrificed to achieve the gains of group action. This combination of intangible human values with pragmatism can be considered without distortion to be what Perlman called the manualist trade union ideology, as an alternative to and rival of Marxism and other ideological blueprints.

We see job-centered unionism then as considerably more than "bread and butterism." But other critics ask, "Where does it stop, as it extends its sway over a given job territory?" (Note again the product market dimension of this job territory, discussed in sections 1 and 2 above, rather than the narrower dimensions assumed by many critics.)

In this connection Perlman's phrases "sovereignty over a job territory" and "communism of job opportunity" need revision in the modern context. In the first place, "sovereignty" connotes political or governmental authority, which today's commentators will insist cannot be conceded to any private or semiprivate group. The connotation was useful in delineating inherent jurisdictional problems as they appeared historically between rival unions. Similarly communism of job opportunity has interest in viewing comparative ideologies, but it also suggested the equalitarian sharing of job rights found in certain unions historically. Wider experience however has shown great diversity in the manner of ordering job opportunities, sometimes following quite different methods of reconciling internal group interests, which depart considerably from equal sharing. In any case the notion of a communism of job opportunity, when combined with the idea of union sovereignty over a job territory, violates widely held social and economic values in implying unilateral union control of jobs. In only relatively narrow circumstances are managements and public indifferent to the way employees or their organizations wish to operate and divide up a given job territory. Thus the concept of bilateralism is essential to collective bargaining.

Bilateral Collective Bargaining Theory

Collective bargaining theory rests upon bilateral determination of terms and conditions of employment. The nonunion case is employer unilateralism, subject only to the very imperfect operation of the labor market mentioned on pages 49–50. The sovereignty concept implies union unilateralism, which is equally inapplicable to collective bargaining on terms and conditions, regardless of the relevance of such sovereignty to internal union affairs. Management and labor undoubtedly would each prefer its own unilateral freedom of decision, and each often considers the participation of the other as a nuisance. Though one may recognize such attitudes, the logic of the American labor-management relationship forces the conclusion that bilateralism as a kind of "necessary evil" is the distinguishing characteristic of modern collective bargaining in this country. Chamberlain has pointed out [13] the evolutionary process running historically from the union unilateralist efforts of early trade unions to the negotiational process we now think of as collective bargaining. Taylor saw the process of private decision making through collective bargaining as often distasteful to both sides but valued in a democratic society as perhaps the only realistic alternative to governmental determination of specific terms of employment.[14]

Related to the nature and degree of control over a job territory is the complex of problems around property rights in jobs. Proprietary rights in jobs constituted a subject of early interest in labor literature, in the period when complete freedom of contract and freedom to dispose of and operate private property were challenged by social regulation and legislation like the Fair Labor Standards Act. Labor relations legislation furthermore established the right of employees to designate a union as their exclusive bargaining agent in the negotiation of wages, hours, and working conditions in an appropriate unit (which might be quite different from the job territory outlined above). Finally even more recent legislation has emphasized the individual employee's right to work, as against union membership requirements. It is evident, even without mentioning seniority rules and legal claims under these, that property rights in jobs involve a complex of many factors. This area of the current scene may well be a highly rewarding one for extensive research.

The nature and degree of control over job territories which unions seek to establish are not easily pinpointed. As suggested above, one can reject "sovereignty" by reason of the bilateral nature of collective bargaining. One can accept, further, the representational rights by reason of established public policy since 1935, the period in which large segments of present unionism became established. There are still unanswered questions as to the extent of proprietary interests in jobs, if any, by individual employees, union organizations, or management.

Nonetheless at least two further criticisms of basing collective bargaining theory on job-centered unionism can be explored in this connection. First, if unions make extensive attempts at job control or exhibit a "proprietary" interest in jobs, are they not interfering in all phases of management? Secondly, the union objective is considered by some critics far broader than the mere job motive: its goal is said to be participation in the management of industry. Can these two tendencies be considered consistent with bilateral collective bargaining? These are two different versions of the union's invasion of management, expressed sometimes by students of labor impatient with traditional unionism or by managements fearful of loss of sole control, as well as by numerous commentators observing the transition from nonunion to collective bargaining relationships. They are behind many portrayals of industrial relations as a power struggle, although generally in a non-Marxian context. They still relate to power in the workplace, but have implications also for the managerial directing function in an economy of growth largely based on private enterprise.

In regard to the first criticism, even a cursory study of seniority rules reveals instances of rigidities which interfere with efficiency. These interferences with efficiency may be justified on human relations grounds or may merely reflect a lack of realistic accommodation between both parties' needs. Whether job rules are consistent with or impede efficiency or technological advance undoubtedly depends upon the way the parties to collective bargaining write and apply these job standards. Under job-centered labor theory, however, the possible limitation upon management which may occur is incidental to the concern with and protection of job conditions. Technical collective bargaining operations are concerned with procedures of accommodation between the necessary role of management to innovate and provide leadership in other respects for a dynamic economy and the basic job interest of unions.

As for the question whether this really represents a power drive of unions to take over or even participate in the role of management, job-centered labor theory asserts that unions lose their identity as advocates of employee interests if they become part of management. The behavioral studies made since World War II which show again that unions have a political type of internal structure support this view. Elected union officials who direct the rank and file in a managerial sense risk the loss of their "image" as aggressive employee advocates. The allegation is made that unions are engaged in a power struggle to take over management. This allegation must be based on the assumption that unions are bent on institutional suicide. If unions are not trying to commit suicide, then the theory that they are bent on taking over management has little merit and is refuted.

Illustrations come easily to mind of union demands for participation in discipline, piece rate setting, or other decisions affecting employees or their work. Yet an experienced labor leader knows that such participation may prevent abuse in some cases but leads him inevitably to the cases where he too agrees to discharge or to the fairness of a time standard. In executing these commands, the union official finds himself in the contradictory position of giving orders to the constituent who elected him. It is much easier in the conflict situations of industrial life to protest a decision made by managerial authority than to be a part of such authority, when the union leader's responsibility is basically to the rank and file.

The prediction of institutional suicide if union leaders identify themselves with management does not require universal belief in or understanding of this eventuality on the part of all members or even all union leaders. Union requests for participation in management decisions sporadically come across the bargaining table. But if a union pursues this type of program intensively and widely in many areas of decision making, the union becomes entrapped in contradictory goals. When the chips are down, a union can be relied upon to cherish its own survival and not risk a suicidal effort to change its nature.

A final criticism of a job-centered collective bargaining theory today comes from what may be designated "the integration school," which probably stems from the human relations writings of Elton Mayo and his followers but has independent currency among prominent sociologists today. Moore's emphasis on cohesion in the firm and his warning against "dichotomization" between management and labor are illustrative.

Page 53 has already cited the misunderstanding of identifying job-centered labor theory solely with an occupation or craft. The job territory typically involved today represents a product or service market, within which labor cost competition propels job shifts, supporting or nullifying job standards. Such a job territory orientation points more toward an industrywide cohesion or horizontal unionism than to the firm, though it may be narrower than a firm if critical product or service groups of workers cut across company lines. The product or service market axis is consistent also with a trend toward a different occupational mix to permit control efforts as technology renders narrower jobs obsolete.* The resulting combination of structures emerging is likely to be as pragmatically shaped as in the past.

In this connection a supporting bit of evidence comes from the tendency toward centralization of union structure on a national basis, which has been emphasized in recent literature. In fact any standard historical treatment of the emergence of the American Federation of Labor in 1886 from earlier attempts at a labor movement, and of the Federation's subsequent long life, points to national centralized authority for individual participant unions as one of the major planks on which unionism could survive in this country.[15] Neither local union autonomy nor federation control in collective bargaining would be successful, according to statements of the job-oriented leaders who were forming the Federation; and history has confirmed their judgment. That younger unions have reached the same conclusion is consistent not only with historical experience but also with the institutional need to protect and advance job interest over a horizontal but industrywide job territory.

Thus union structural studies both on 1886 data and in 1958 support [16] the view that employees' cohesion in forming unions extends over a competitive product market, and this attraction frequently domi-

---

* Cf. Clark Kerr, J. T. Dunlop, F. H. Harbison, and C. A. Myers, *Industrialism and Industrial Man* (Cambridge, Harvard Univ. Press, 1960), where the authors see a pattern of structured professional association emerging even more conspicuously in the future.

nates though by no means eliminates employees' cohesion or even loyalties within the firm. It is entirely true that such "solidarity" does not eliminate factionalism. The forging of some unified program out of conflicting local interests is at times a difficult process. Normally agreement is reached on some major job standards, while considerable flexibility on local conditions is left to the local parties. The existence of the unified standards often reflects a conscious sacrifice of some local flexibility to achieve what are considered to be overweighing advantages of common action.

Moore's major attack, and that of other critics, is on the "received doctrine of dichotomization," which they assert to be Marxian because it recognizes divergent interest and conflict. Moore finds that "early industrialization repeatedly exhibits radical differences between managers and men, but later developments obscure and complicate the division rather than sharpening it." He cites particularly the corporate divorce of management from ownership and the merging or fuzziness of formerly sharp distinctions of authority and career status in the modern social organization of industry.[17]

Job-centered labor theory however cites a functional-motivational dichotomy which remains critical to modern social-economic problems after the foregoing points are made. The discussion above of the alleged union invasion into areas of management control suggested the institutional suicide that would accompany union identification with management functions. We may ask whether this prediction is rendered invalid by the characteristics of later industrialization cited above.

An adequately reliable generalization with respect to managerial goals or psychology to help explain common behavior patterns is just as essential an ingredient of job-centered and bilateral collective bargaining theory as is the "manualist mentality" basic to union theory. A fair image of modern management in the American political economy stresses its role in initiating and directing quick decision making as required, and in stimulating investment and innovation. This role can also be identified as an essential function in a dynamic economy of growth where there are wide areas of private decision making.

No convincing reason has been advanced to explain why this functional-motivational dichotomy between the "spark plug," directing concept of management and the job protection and job advance motivation of unionized workers is less important in mature industrialization than in early stages.* In the effort to eliminate conflict no one is currently suggesting in the United States that management merge with the union organization, after the pattern of, say, producers' cooperatives which has been tried in the past. The converse prescription of the non-union social economy was discussed above as subject to the vagaries of imperfect labor markets and employer unilateralism, which we have noted as alternative to the American collective bargaining institutions.†

Our task then is to identify the functional roles of employer (corporate or otherwise) and employee organization in an operating social-political economy. In the United States, with its wide areas of private decision making, a society of growth has highly production-oriented institutions. Under certain rules of public policy, wide freedom is left to each individual and group, corporate or collective, to seek compensation for his or their role in production. To say that a union policy of more and more has revolutionary overtones is to say that the profit incentive is antisocial. One may have moral qualms about self-interest if he wishes, but the theorist of labor in industrialization is attempting to identify critical operational elements in the industrial segment of a freely dynamic sociopolitical economy. Successful prediction rests upon appraisal of the probable effectiveness of each organization tested against its function, but also upon a judgment of their mutual abilities for successful institutional accommodation in conflict resolution.

With respect to the narrower question of the sufficiency of job-centered theory to assist an understanding of collective bargaining behavior, we have suggested some revisions, and much more research would be in order. The basic framework, however, of product and service market dimensions of job interest, and the functional-motivational dichotomy remain as elements essential to group behavior in this field. The nonunion case or nonunion stage would appear to have similar ingredients, though inactive for a wide variety of reasons, e.g.

---

* Although other authors have seen an apparent decline of protest, these same observers found everywhere in the world "managers and the managed" and defined the labor problem as structuring these relationships, thus in a sense rejecting the "integration" thesis. Kerr, Dunlop, Harbison, and Myers, pp. 12 ff.

† Thus the resolution of conflicting interests is essential to collective bargaining processes. This does not preclude union-management cooperation, profit-sharing formulas, and even stock ownership programs, as "partners in production" evolve devices and procedures for accommodation and resolution of conflict.

refusal by professional employees to sacrifice the freedom of individual bargaining to a group, legal restrictions, lack of development of employer-employee relationship in an agricultural economy, lack of market expansions which increase job threats, etc. Other factors and forms of employee organization are related to political factors cited in the following section.

The Implications of Bilateral Collective Bargaining Theory for Political Action

The trade union ideology so far implied in our discussion of collective bargaining theory represents a focus of effort directed toward improvement of wages and working conditions, including intangible representational values as well as economic gains, but stops short by necessity of trying to manage or take over the control of industry. Though this role of unions is by no means fully attained in the United States, the self-limitations it seems to impose arouse both impatience among labor's friends and fear among its critics. It is furthermore said to be unique, and unrealistic compared to other labor movements around the world, which tend to be much more heavily involved with programs to socialize industry or achieve political control of government.

It may be noted first that while the statement of trade union ideology above implies an emphasis on economic bargaining it by no means precludes participation in the political activities of a democracy. Historically, organized labor in the United States has almost always had some political concern, from advocacy of public education in the early 1800's to our latest political campaigns, though the extent and nature of its political participation has varied widely over different periods. Political reformism was so dominant a theme in early labor history as to complicate—some say frustrate—the efforts of unions even to survive in economic bargaining. One major area where direct political action has been continued consistently by union leaders throughout history has been in attempts to get release from legislation restricting union activities. An illustration is Samuel Gompers' efforts, with other AFL leaders, to get exemption in the Clayton Act of 1914 from the application of the Sherman Antitrust law of 1890 to labor unions. Today the "right to work" laws in several states have evoked effective political action by labor against threats to the existence of unionism. And workers have turned to political action when thwarted on the economic front at various times in American history.

The AFL, however, withdrew substantially from political welfare programs before the depression of the 1930's, somewhat disillusioned with such efforts after vainly endorsing the La Follette Progressive movement of 1924. The reasons traditionally advanced for this withdrawal included 1) the belief that concentration upon political goals, beyond the necessary attempts to get release from restrictive legislation that threatened the existence or hindered the organizing effectiveness of unions, seemed in the past to have detracted from economic effectiveness; 2) the realization that the divisive effects which often resulted from political action increased the already formidable obstacles to union cohesion during the formative period; and 3) the fact that repressive measures were taken by governments seemingly to offset the possible threat of labor's seizing political power. The New Deal undoubtedly stimulated a reappraisal of these views as government-sponsored unionism established itself and new welfare programs were launched by a popular government.

In the United States since World War II the interplay of these forces suggests that a new balance may be becoming established of what might be called evolving industrial citizenship. Whereas before the depression the labor movement was reluctant to speak out on issues of social welfare for fear of divisive effects within the organization and retaliatory restrictions by a majority of the public, labor's political voice has been heard since then much more frequently, loudly, and on many issues not formerly considered of trade union concern. It may be still too soon to appraise the results of this activity or to tot up the balance sheet of legislation passed during the period—some of it restrictive to unionism, some of it progressive social measures. A few observations can be made, however, on elements of change observable in this role of industrial citizenship and its relationship to collective bargaining.

As a job territory for a particular union extends widely, for example in a nationwide basic steel industry, the maintenance of fundamental job interests almost necessarily encompasses a concern for public policies directed toward full employment. Since durable and capital goods industries have traditionally been highly cyclical, job-oriented unionism in steel is driven by its own logic to advocate high-level employment policies and economic stabilization. By the same token the job threat of the future may prove to be lower wage standards in foreign competition for world markets, a factor long recognized as relevant to their jobs and wage levels by labor movements in Great Britain and Scandinavia.

Similarly, public policies for improvement in the operation of the labor market and in facilities for relocation and training that may be required to meet the impact of technological change and to ameliorate the transitional human hardships incident to displacements and shifts in the process of economic growth necessarily go beyond the potential limits of what individual companies, unions, or their collective bargaining arrangements can achieve by themselves.[18] The extension of wage payments to include fringe benefits has also involved intricate inter-relationships and combinations of public programs and private collective bargaining terms. All of these policies, from full employment to social security, affect businessmen, farmers, and other groups as well as labor, but they generally have had their greatest impact upon the jobs and compensation of wage earners.

There is no doubt of employees' concern and labor leadership's interest in such issues of public policy in mid-century America. A major function performed at the federation level has of course traditionally been to serve as a voice whenever labor wanted to speak out on legislation and governmental policy issues, and to lobby as appropriate. The next step from lobbying is to try to influence the selection of public representatives at the ballot box.

But delivering a solid vote in election of candidates is a difficult task in the United States, in which unions show a greatly variegated record of success and failure. The policy objectives noted above may not be highly controversial in the entire community, but the means for their achievement are. Elements in voting behavior are a complex of many loyalties and attitudes, of which union affiliation can generally explain only a part.

A democratic political system invites all groups and individuals to turn to government, and consequently ultimately to political action and the ballot box, to decide over-all policy matters. The key question under consideration here, however, is whether labor in the United States will find the public route and political power more appealing than collective bargaining as the method of settling terms of employment and work rules, which have generally been the province of private decision making in the American economy. In part the nature of the issues gives a clue to the answer. A complicated and interrelated industrial economy undoubtedly requires a broad framework of public policies and probably positive public actions to facilitate and assist the process of private decision making in the market economy. Thus promotive monetary and fiscal policies in a Keynesian sense represent the modern version of a long line of promotive public policies in United States history, from protection of infant industries to canal and railway development and support of subsidized agricultural research. Historically these public efforts have more often taken the form of promoting free enterprise than of substituting governmental for private decision making. In fact newly developing or even preindustrialized societies use direct governmental controls more often than has the United States, with its complex industrial economy; wartime has been the chief exception to this.

Within this frame of reference, then, labor's political route extends from job-conscious unionism to invoking the machinery and processes of politics when the breadth of an issue involved, by a pragmatic test, requires public or governmental measures, and the goals are shared by other segments of the public. The voting behavior is still more likely to be identifiable as an urban or rural vote, Southern vote, "up state" vote, occasionally as a religious or a women's vote, than as a polarized "labor vote"; but the labor vote can be identified in local issues of job concern, state issues involving organizational threats, and less reliably in broader issues of social welfare. Union members may be active workers in a political party and assist it to victory at the polls. The union organization's activities, like those of other community groups, have an interplay with political organizations to varied extents, including fund raising. As a group institution in a democracy the union organization has in recent years come more conspicuously to include in its activities political education and political action. These have been added to the core of bargaining behavior toward evolving a balanced program of industrial citizenship in a complex world. It is still too early however to know where this balance will rest. The political aspects have not so far tended to dominate. They have rather been supplementary or complementary to job-centered collective bargaining.

The question remains whether these evolving structures, activity patterns, and the foreseeable extension of these tendencies are moving toward the substitution of governmental for private sector decisions in the future. It would seem superficially that pragmatically determined behavior might easily lead to the substitution of governmentally set terms or work rules in favor of any group obtaining governmental control. We have seen both management and labor seek government support of their positions at the bargaining table as opportunity or apparent need arose. Is it not likely that investment controls, as in Britain or Sweden, or governmental wage determination in favor of either labor or management, or profit limitations or floors would seem the most practical solution to particular sets of problems that might arise? We have certainly approached wartime emergency problems with such tools: collective bargaining processes have been extended into government to provide participation of labor and management through tripartitism in formulating and administering policies recognized by all groups as essential to the effective prosecution of the war. If such participation worked in wartime, why not in peacetime? One may note that the extension of collective bargaining processes in government units to meet pragmatic problems is consistent with Commons' approach to establishing safety standards and workmen's compensation laws in an earlier period. President Kennedy's Labor-Management Committee, considering problems of automation and wage-price policy in 1961 and 1962, suggested an approach of this sort to matters of general public interest.

The historical evidence with respect to political processes in the United States suggests, however, that it would be difficult for any polarized group to establish a dominant position. There have been many "blocs"—as farm, silver, Southern, etc.—with strategic bargaining position in national governmental affairs. When labor, traditionally among the less solid political groups, has favored particular welfare policies, progress toward the objective has generally depended on the program's appealing to other groups as well. Labor advocacy attracts some votes, repels others, and chiefly serves to put issues before the public rather than to deliver votes.

Pragmatically the governmental route may be adopted for particular programs where there is general support. One might argue for example that a governmental old-age security program is more conducive to labor mobility and therefore more compatible with a market economy than the existing mixture of social and collectively bargained pensions. But a pervasive preference for private decision making is widespread in labor itself as well as in other segments of the public from which natural political alliances might proceed. This prevailing value system, which may of course change through time, provides along with our intricate political processes the most likely deterrent to the establishment of a labor welfare state, if the term be taken to imply the substitution of governmental for specific private decision making within public facilitating policies such as those outlined above. In essence then collective bargaining on economic and noneconomic terms remains central to American trade unionism within the discernible broader framework of industrial citizenship in a democracy.

Implications of Collective Bargaining Theory for Comparative Systems and Development

Possibly even more critical for labor theory than the political realities in the United States which we have discussed, and even more likely to give one pause in considering the intertwining of collective bargaining and politics, is the strain that develops inherently within a labor movement which has achieved a labor government, because of the unions' double function to protest or advocate vis à vis the employer and to act as the governing group or the public employer, particularly in nationalized industries. This situation parallels that of unions participating in management. In the model of a planned state under a labor government the union or group of unions can lose the former function if they take on the latter one. The blueprints as applied in most planned states, whether led by labor or other groups, rarely permit as much freedom of union action as those of less highly planned societies. This might be ideal if the millennium had arrived, but skepticism persists as to its imminent arrival. On this point we see a continuum of intellectual commentary from the pragmatist to the idealist, with a kind of "pragmatic socialist" of Scandinavia somewhere in between.

Two aspects of this question are of considerable interest today. One is the predictability of a given sociopolitical economic model from a number of behavioral and institutional variables, with prominence given among these variables to management type and experience and to trade union action patterns. Thus Marx predicted that communism would come about through old and decadent capitalism, which contained the seeds of its own destruction; after gulfs had widened between rich and poor, "capitalists" and workers, unions with the aid of the Communist party would be the vehicle of violent overthrow of the capitalist state. Perlman's formulation was a refutation of this Marxian prediction: communism had come in Russia, and could be predicted to come readily to other countries in a precapitalistic or preindustrial state, in the absence both of strong employers and of old and mature unions. Perlman's prediction, and thus his refutation of Marx in this connection, was born out some thirty years later by events in China and further Communist penetration into preindustrial areas of Southeast Asia and elsewhere.

The major variables in Perlman's schema are of interest in further possible prediction. Abstracting from a wealth of social, political, and economic behavioral evidence drawn from history, he stressed three main independent variables: the age, experience, and aggressiveness of employers ("capitalists" in his terminology); the age, experience, and maturity of trade unions; and the role of the intellectual, which historically has been associated with idealistic social reform of a sweeping nature. Looking at the Russian case, Perlman found (1) weak employers, (2) "immature" (one might say young or even embryonic) trade unions, and (3) a strong, positive role of "intellectuals." At the other extreme the United States model revealed (1) very strong employers, (2) strong trade unions, (3) a much less prominent role of intellectuals. The same three variables in the British model showed (1) a slightly less aggressive employer type after 1920 than in the United States, (2) a strong and mature trade union movement, (3) much greater value attributed to the intellectuals, particularly the Fabians. Currently the Scandinavian models and those for Australia, West Germany, and Japan are instructive when viewed in terms of these variables. So is the case of China, mentioned above, where the Communist party came to power with peasant acquiescence or support, in the preindustrialized setting.

Perlman's analysis, like other hypotheses of social trends, identifies critical institutional probabilities. If it is read in the light of quasi-Marxian determinism, the influence of human will, which Commons stressed along with modifying or humanizing capitalism, is ruled out. Such determination would omit specifically the possible roles of men like Gompers and Walter Reuther in United States labor and of influential centers of human effort and leadership in other countries of the world, as well as wide varieties of intellectualism itself between pragmatism and abstraction. If the analysis however is understood as helping us identify the likely institutional tendencies, it can assist the scholar in understanding what is happening around him and assist the policy maker in choosing devices for development toward desired institutional ends.*

Thus separately from the historical understanding of comparative economic systems and the broad predictability implied, we see the second aspect of collective bargaining theory in its relation to government as having a relevance to newly developing countries seeking economic growth. The models of economic growth that such countries see before them run a gamut from a wide range of private decision making, democratic and relatively free market institutions, and customs with legal support of economic opportunity in the United States, to the compulsory Communist growth model of Russia and China. In between are various democratically planned or autocratically ruled states, some with trade unions, some without, some socialist democracies, some cartelized economies, etc. Perhaps the "social welfare" state has the greatest emotional appeal for a newly independent country. But such a model, based on Scandinavia, or Britain in some periods, may be difficult for a new nation to operate at a satisfactory growth rate, since it appears to strain even the best educated and most experienced administrative civil services. The two models usually considered to have placed the heaviest stress on production orientation and growth are probably the United States, during most of its history, and Communist Russia and China, with possibly Japan and Bismarckian Germany constituting variations of forced growth.

The literature of economic development suggests that to move a society from stagnation to growth is a highly complicated affair. It would seem, however, that an effective orientation toward capital formation and production rather than toward consumption is a necessary minimal ingredient. Initially such production-mindedness and production-oriented policies may have to arise among agricultural producers and those industrial management units, either public or private, that exist or can be created in the preindustrialized stage. Thus the strong-employer role cited above may be essential even if adapted in part to public sectors. The form of labor organization consistent with economic growth and free institutions will be increasingly relevant to the success

* The survey of varieties of industrialism made by Kerr and his associates unfortunately falls short of providing a predictive basis for distinguishing trends toward the Communist, welfare, or capitalist models.

of any industrialization process, provided it is not nipped in the pre-industrial stage by a Communist revolution or other form of dictatorship.

When Commons wrote *Legal Foundations of Capitalism* in the early 1920's he could trace the evolution of the rent bargain, with Anglo-American common law built upon customary relationships of landlord and tenant, and discern tolerably well the evolution of the price bargain. In the latter case, the U. S. Supreme Court had affirmed earlier developments and necessary changes from the *lex mercatoria* to assure property, opportunity, and effective (more recently called workable) competition out of granted privileges and governmental monopolies of earlier periods. Commons found, however, that the wage bargain defied similar treatment of its evolution, since the Supreme Court of the 'twenties seemed oblivious to the very different customs and work rules affecting job rights, in contrast to rights in tangible and intangible business property. Using the same approach he had found useful in other spheres, and studying the emergence of operating principles and work rules of labor relations from common customs, as well as the customary resolution of conflicting interests, Commons saw instances of what he called industrial government; but he had to project this development largely to the future because of its embryonic stage, and particularly because of the seeming absence of governmental recognition of this process.[19]

In fact the growth of common law in collective bargaining has continued far beyond the period in which Commons wrote. It is still developing, and intertwines currently with the use of arbitration as a medium for conflict resolution. In this sense the Supreme Court's support of the arbitration process for resolution of grievance conflicts in the now famous "Steelworker Cases" of 1960 [20] constitutes a significant step along the route of this evolutionary process.

The distinguishing aspect of American growth has been and continues to be a wide range of private decision making within a framework of positive public measures to promote economic well-being. A basic aspect of the private decision-making sphere has been the core focus of the American labor movement on collective bargaining with large segments of American employers. It is in this sense that collective bargaining has been called a way of life. Within even the broader framework of mid-twentieth-century industrial citizenship in a democracy, the emphasis on collective bargaining remains the distinguishing feature of the American industrial relations system and an important avenue for representation in the democratic social-political economy as a whole.

The question of relevance of this model abroad can be better analyzed in the specific if its basic tenets, including its subtler aspects, can be articulated in Commons' tradition of approaching policy goals in the light of human experience. For example, as production growth is stimulated in newly developing countries, can unions act in economic bargaining to protect employees from unnecessary abuses (some might say "exploitation") in the process of growth? Can they hope to assure some "equitable" division of the gains from production growth, or will their efforts inhibit the growth itself? Operating through political activity, as unions are generally doing today, can they establish representational planning with management in a plant or for the planned economy, in order to drive toward production targets? What strains develop in this process? What have been specific experiences of different countries with wide varieties of institutional history? Can these be adapted to culturally unique, indigenous efforts for growth around the world? Can they help to overcome the obstacles which have so far frustrated the economic development of underdeveloped countries? What role, if any, can labor relations legislation play, and are present labor laws in most such countries consistent with such a role?

These are questions requiring much further research, directed toward public policies as well as prediction. For revisionist work in labor theory, they point to the need for a recognition of the American collective bargaining system within its broader context of mid-twentieth-century industrial citizenship, and for an integration thereafter of more recent materials, particularly in the field of economic and social development and related public policy issues, with the earlier scholarship referred to above as assisting an understanding of industrial evolution, comparative systems, and labor movements.

Notes

1   Sidney and Beatrice Webb, *Industrial Democracy,* New York, Longmans, Green, 1920.
2   John R. Commons, *Legal Foundations of Capitalism* (Macmillan, 1924; Madison, Univ. of Wisconsin Press, 1957), chap. 8, pp. 303 ff.
3   Cf. John Dunlop, *Industrial Relations System* (New York, Henry Holt, 1958), p. 5.

4 Lloyd G. Reynolds, *The Structure of Labor Markets,* New York, Harper, 1951.

5 Arthur M. Ross, *Trade Union Wage Policy* (Berkeley, Univ. of California Press, 1956), p. 19.

6 Selig Perlman, *A Theory of the Labor Movement* (copyright, 1928; New York, Augustus M. Kelley, 1949), p. 8.

7 Wilbert E. Moore, "Notes for a General Theory of Labor Organization," *Industrial and Labor Relations Review,* 13, No. 3 (April 1960): 387–97.

8 E. Wright Bakke, *Mutual Survival, the Goal of Unions and Management* (New Haven, Yale Labor and Management Center, 1946), pp. 3–10.

9 Thorstein Veblen, *The Instinct of Workmanship,* New York, 1922.

10 Robert Dubin, "Industrial Research and the Discipline of Sociology," *Proceedings of the Eleventh Annual Meeting,* Industrial Relations Research Association (Madison, Wisc., 1958), Pub. No. 22, pp. 152–72.

11 K. U. Smith, *Behavior Organization and Work,* Madison, College Printing and Typing Co., Inc., 1962.

12 George W. Taylor, *Labor-Management Relations in the Days Ahead,* address, Industrial Relations Center, University of Wisconsin, Madison, 1948, p. 7.

13 Neil Chamberlain, *Collective Bargaining* (New York, McGraw-Hill, 1951), pp. 32–35.

14 George W. Taylor, *Government Regulation of Industrial Relations,* New York, Prentice-Hall, 1948.

15 W. A. Millis and R. E. Montgomery, *The Economics of Labor,* Vol. 3 in *Organized Labor* (New York, McGraw-Hill, 1945), p. 78.

16 R. A. Lester, *As Unions Mature,* Princeton Univ. Press, 1958.

17 Moore, pp. 388–89.

18 Cf. Jack Barbash, "The Union Response to Technological Change," in *Changing Patterns in Industrial Relations,* 1961. Annual Conference Proceedings, Industrial Relations Center, McGill University, Montreal.

19 Commons, chap. 8, espec. pp. 304–5.

20 United Steelworkers of America v. American Manufacturing Co., CCH, U.S. 40 Labor Cases 66, 628; United Steelworkers v. Warrior and Gulf Navigation Co., CCH, U.S. 40 Labor Cases 66, 629; United Steelworkers v. Enterprise Wheel and Car Corp., CCH, U.S. 40 Labor Cases 66, 630.

4   JACK BARBASH

The Government and Politics of the AFL-CIO

I

This is an examination of the American Federation of Labor and Congress of Industrial Organizations (AFL-CIO) in terms of the government and politics of a federation. I will concentrate on the governmental means which have been fashioned to shape the relationship between the federation and the internationals, and on the roles of individual leaders and of rival blocs.

The main line of labor movement government in the United States functions on four tiers. From the bottom up these tiers are (1) the local union, (2) the intermediate body, (3) the international union—for the most part a national union but called "international" in common usage, and (4) the federation—that is the AFL-CIO—and the subject of this paper.

The local union is the nuclear unit in union organization. Frequently though sublocal units—that is shop committees, departments, sections—may provide a more direct union-member relationship. The sovereign entity in the American labor movement is the international union. But the organization chart of a typical international union will not normally show an uninterrupted line from the international to the local. More characteristic is for the line to be broken by one or more levels of government, intermediate between the international and the local, in the nature of district councils, regions, state bodies, joint boards, joint councils, or conferences. The common property of these intermediate bodies is that they are multilocal and usually but not exclusively function within the boundaries of one international.

The federation is, most importantly, an association of sovereign international unions (131). Secondarily, the AFL-CIO is composed of central bodies (820 local and 51 state, including Washington, D.C.), trade and industrial departments (7), and directly affiliated local unions (360 with 71,000 members). Administratively the federation is 15 headquarters departments and 23 regional offices capped by an elected president and secretary-treasurer.

The central bodies and the trade departments constitute two types of subfederations, as it were. Central bodies in the cities and states are composed of the locals of federation-affiliated internationals in their respective states and localities. The departments of the AFL-CIO —railway employees, metal trades, building and construction trades, maritime trades, industrial union, union label and service trades, and most recently food and beverage—bring together internationals affiliated to the federation with a common interest in the trade or industry suggested by the name of the department. The departments include subordinate local councils. The local councils of the Railway Employees' Department are called "system federations." The local councils of the departments are made up of locals of the internationals affiliated to the national department.

The directly affiliated local unions are locals which have no attachment to an existing international union; hence the federation functions for them in place of an international union. This is regarded as a transitional stage until the directly affiliated local union is brought into an established or newly formed international. The directly affiliated local union may also be a member of a "council," which is a loose league of these locals in a given industry grouping, with no constitutional authority of its own except what is imparted to it by the federation.

In a very real sense, then, the federation is not a union in the conventional meaning of the word, in that it does not engage in collective bargaining nor does it have individual members, always excepting the federation's relationship to the directly affiliated locals where, as has been said, it partakes of the functions of an international. The federation is rather an association of unions and primarily an association of international unions.

The concept of an association of unions goes back to the founding of the National Trades Union in 1834. From the National Trades Union to the Knights of Labor and the intervening union associations the decisive constituencies were local central bodies of one sort or another. The formation of the American Federation of Labor (1886) marked a decisive shift to the international union as the major constituent in the national association of unions. The ultimate triumph of the national over the central body as the strategic organizational vehicle is of a piece with the ascendancy of collective bargaining over politics as the priority item on the agenda of the American labor movement.

In general the trade and industrial departments have pursued three categories of objectives: (a) protection of the department's corporate jurisdictional interests in relation to government and within the federation; (b) coordination of activities of affiliated unions in organizing, collective bargaining, legislation, and information; and (c) for two departments (building trades and industrial union) mechanisms for moderating rivalry among affiliates. The central body is primarily concerned with political and legislative functions and to some degree provides limited aid to local affiliates in collective bargaining. A well-established city central may also be influential in ironing out jurisdictional difficulties.

II

The supreme body of the federation is the biennial convention, composed primarily but not exclusively of delegates from the affiliated internationals; their voting weight is determined by their per capita payments to the federation. The per capita payment is seven cents a month supplemented from time to time by temporary assessments—usually of one cent. The per capita payments from the internationals constitute about three-fourths of the total income of the federation. The second largest source of income is per capita and other payments from the directly affiliated local unions.

Between conventions the operating executive authority is exercised by an executive council composed of 27 vice-presidents, in addition to the two executive officers, the president and the secretary-treasurer. An executive committee within the executive council functions as a kind of agenda or steering committee. The president, secretary-treasurer, and executive council are elected by the convention at large. On political but not constitutional grounds council members are likely to be chosen to represent (1) the very largest unions; (2) an important industry grouping, i.e. building trades, public employees; (3) the established balance between former AFL and former CIO unions; and most recently (4) spokesmen from the Negro trade union community.

A general board is established consisting of the principal officer of each international union affiliate. The only clue which the constitution provides as to the functions of the board is that it "shall decide all policy questions referred to it by the Executive Officers or by the Executive Council." [1] The constitution is otherwise silent as to the position of the general board in relation to the executive council. In practice the general board is a forum for gaining wider acceptance of important policies of the federation, i.e. a major-policy-approving body but not a policy-formulating body.

The constitution provides for specified committees and staff departments. The committees are designated as Legislation, Civil Rights, Political Education, Ethical Practices, International Affairs, Education, Social Security, Economic Policy, Community Services, Housing, Research, Public Relations, Safety and Occupational Health, Veterans' Affairs, and Organization. The headquarters staff departments are Auditing, Civil Rights, Community Service Activities, Education, International Affairs, Investment, Legislation, Organization, Political Education, Public Relations, Publications, Research, Social Security, General Council, and Library. Appointment to the staff of the departments and the membership of the committees is the prerogative of the president. In practice the staff is appointed by departments' heads in consultation with the president. The committee is, in general, a policy advisory group, and the staff department is a headquarters administrative unit. The exception is the Committee on Political Education (COPE), which is primarily an operating unit with both a headquarters and a field staff. The Organizing Department has a permanent field staff of 153 (as of 1961) assigned to 23 regions, each under a director.

The locus of effective power in the present federation is in the executive council, which is a barometer of the major pressures and counter-pressures. Mr. Meany as AFL-CIO president carries great weight in the council but on issues involving diverse interests he has to fight for his position. Debate is frequently intense and occasionally bitter. The men who make up the council are accustomed to power in their own organizations and do not lend themselves as rubber stamps, even to a man as determined as Mr. Meany.

The federation convention partakes of the functions of a national spotlight, a meeting ground for the labor movement's top leadership, a plebiscitary body, and a debaters' forum. Alignments on controversial issues are pretty well determined off the convention floor. The convention registers the votes and the supporting debate. On occasion the convention provides a pressure of urgency in resolving a particular issue. The 1961 convention provided the coercive effect against which Mr. Meany inched through an internal disputes program between the building trades and the industrial unions. It also provided the staging ground for an easing of strained relations on the civil rights issue.

III

In addition to internal housekeeping administration there are two large classes of federation functions: (1) the federation's functions as a department of external affairs for the labor movement; that is, its role as spokesman to the national community; (2) the functions involved in relationships between the federation and the national unions, and on occasion between the federation and the subfederations.

The federation meets a need for cohesiveness and solidarity on the part of its constituent elements. Even without a prevailing socialist ideology, solidarity is an article of working class faith, nurtured by a national labor center. It was this that the president of an important national union must have had in mind when he said, "We derive our moral and spiritual sustenance from being an integral part of the entire labor movement." [2] This solidarity is reinforced by a feeling which union leaders have of being outside of the main status channels of the society. Robert Hoxie captured this attitude more than a half century ago: "So far as workers are concerned, there is no society as a whole and no long run but immediate need and rival social groups." [3] Even in these days of "big unionism" the unionist's place in the outside society derives—as I think they see it—from power, not from prestige.

But there are more than morale sentiments involved here. Affiliation to the federation confers legitimacy in the national and local labor movements. Thus Mr. Hoffa can boast of his successes as an independent at the same time that he and his colleagues maintain a drum-fire campaign for readmission into the federation. Indeed, much of the history of the labor movement can be and is written in terms of a search for a viable formula for federation. There are, to be sure, unions that boast of their freedom from labor movement encumbrances on ideological and economic grounds, but these are exceptions.[4]

Measured in man-hours of work the federation's representative function is, by all odds, the most important. By representative function I mean the federation's role as the symbol of and spokesman for all the unions on questions of public policy. This role is supported by a large headquarters staff in Washington, in the nature of a technical secretariat for each class of function. In few areas have federation attitudes changed so drastically as they have toward legislative and political action. To be sure, federations have always been involved in legislation and politics, but until 1933 the main emphasis was on defensive legislation. The burden of effort was directed against specific obstructions and injustices like the labor injunction and the "yellow dog" contract. Even immediately after the New Deal the AFL gave only general support to social security, labor standards, and labor relations legislation. The CIO brought a new spirit to legislation and politics but much of this spirit lacked organizational support in the local community. Until recently, except for a few unions, the serious labor movement efforts were aimed at such issues as repeal of the Taft-Hartley and "right to work" laws.

The profound change that has been taking place in the way the labor movement—that is, the federation—views its function is in the *central* place now assigned to broad public policy. If the union spokesmen were to use the words of the economists they would say their collective bargaining efforts today can have only a "micro" effect. But the vexing problems of insecurity can be dealt with only through "macro" techniques. As the unions see it, only the Federal Government in the complex economy has the capacity to deal with these problems on a macro economic basis.

The broadening scope of labor's public policy interest is suggested by an observation of Andrew J. Biemiller, director of legislative activities of the AFL-CIO. (He is talking about the 1960 campaign.) "As a practical matter there was no 'labor issue'—you will note that I am using the singular—in this campaign. There was no attempt on the part of the labor movement to make a rallying-point or a *cause celebre* out of the Landrum-Griffin act; nor was there any disposition on the part of our opponents to make the labor movement a special target. . . . President Meany and most of the labor people felt that in terms of the national interest, many other matters were of far greater importance— and in all candor, likely to be far more effective campaign issues." [5] This emphasis on public policy is not idle talk. Day in and day out in both federal and state forums the labor movement acts as a major (if not *the* major) pressure group for the broad range of welfare legislation.

The movement has thus traveled a long way from classical Gompersian voluntarism. Unions today take the hardheaded view that political action is an essential concomitant of collective bargaining. And in some degree the federation has sought to assert a more conscious *public* interest in its policy judgments, even where conceivably this public interest may run counter to the interests of specific affiliates. This is most notable in the federation's positions on international trade.

The representative function of the federation has another purpose: asserting labor's role in the power structure of the national and the local communities. This is symbolized, even if not always realized, in the matter-of-course involvement of a federation spokesman in almost every labor-related committee and agency established at all levels of government and community organization.

Measured by the proportion of income spent, one of the most important of the federation's representative functions is its role in the international labor movement and international affairs generally. The importance of the federation's international role can be gauged also by the serious involvement of the officers and influential members of the executive council and by the diversity of opinion which it induces. The international role has two interrelated facets for the federation: (1) the maintenance of a strong American position in the International Confederation of Free Trade Unions, related international bodies, and the world labor movement, and (2) a continuing evaluation of United States foreign policy positions.

Organizing as a federation function is a difficult concept for the older AFL unions to accept, since the AFL rarely undertook to organize on its own. This aspect of the present federation's functioning is descended from the CIO, which was an organizing committee in origin. Only the federation's agricultural workers' organizing campaign resembles in concept the old CIO campaigns of the 1930's, and this has had an unsettled history. Federation organizers have been used mostly to aid

organizing efforts of specific unions and to assist unions in their challenge to organizations expelled from the federation on grounds of corruption. At first organizing efforts sponsored by the federation could
proceed only if conflicting jurisdictional claims of internationals were
adjusted—and they hardly ever were. In attempts to accelerate federation organizing the AFL-CIO is disallowing "paper" jurisdiction claims,
and is further experimenting with coordinated drives on a multiunion
basis in specific areas. A standing committee on organization has been
established to consult with the chief officers and the organization director "to develop programs and policies to assure a more effective and
adequate effort in meeting the challenge of organizing the unorganized." [6]

The federation performs a limited service function for the internationals in developing educational programs and materials and providing
research assistance. The most recent innovation here is an investment
department to encourage affiliates to invest pension, welfare, and trade
union funds in the housing field. The service function is somewhat
more extensive for the directly affiliated unions and the central bodies.

IV

The regulative function of the federation in relation to the internationals is derived from the constitutional provision that affiliated
unions shall be free from communism, corruption, and discrimination.
The federation has developed mechanisms to enforce these prohibi-
tions. An Ethical Practices Committee has been the medium for formulating specific ethical practices codes dealing with the issuance of local
union charters, health and welfare fund administration, racketeering,
infiltration, "conflict of interest" business investments, financial practices, and democratic processes. The committee has also acted as the
investigating arm of the federation in dealing with allegations of violations of the constitution and the codes.

The ethical practices purposes have been enforced in various ways:
by expulsion of offending unions, by putting offending unions on proba-
tion, by installing federation monitors, or by chartering and aiding rival
unions to some of the expelled unions. The aggressive ethical practices
program of the federation has been slowed down for two main reasons
probably: the enactment of the Landrum-Griffin law and the ability

of the Teamsters to survive expulsion, though others like the expelled Laundry Workers and Bakery Workers have been seriously hurt by expulsion.

The ethical practices interest of the federation constitutes the sharpest breach in the conception of national union autonomy within the federation. But even so the ethical practices provisions constitute a codification of the AFL's action in expelling the Longshoremen in 1953, and an expression that the established autonomy principle is no bar to proceeding against corrupt practices by affiliates.

Communist penetration into national unions has not been a serious problem recently, although in at least one case the federation executive council held up approval of merger pending examination of the charges of Communist infiltration by one of the union parties to the merger. In another case the issue of Communist penetration into an affiliate was considered but no action taken. The anti-Communist phase of the regulative function is traceable to the action of the CIO in expelling 11 Communist-dominated unions in 1949 and 1950.

The constitution contains a provision "encourag[ing] all workers without regard to race, creed, color, national origin or ancestry to share equally in the full benefits of union organizations," [7] and a section establishing enforcement through a Committee on Civil Rights. In enforcing the ethical practices and anti-Communist/antifascist provisions, suspension by the executive council is explicitly mentioned. There is no explicit reference to sanctions in the constitution against violators of the civil rights objective. The critics of the federation's performance in dealing with discriminatory practices by affiliates have urged strong disciplinary action and have deprecated what they consider to be the "kid glove" methods of the federation's Civil Rights Committee. Mr. Meany has distinguished between corruption and discrimination as grounds for expulsion of affiliates.

... Corruption—like communism—seizes the leadership of a union and works down to lower levels by perverting the union's democratic procedures. The rank-and-file members are not consciously affected in their daily lives. They don't know what's going on, and they tend to dismiss published charges against the leadership as just another attack by a normally hostile press. Expulsion was the only way to convince the membership of this domination by corrupt elements. In most cases the members then rallied to new, clean unions or have overthrown the old leadership.

But there is a big difference between corruption and discrimination. Discrimination is resisted at the top but perpetrated below. Discrimination represents the wrong-headedness of rank-and-file members; it is often maintained by unimpeachably democratic processes.

Would we be better off to cast out these misguided members and remove them from the influence of the mainstream of the labor movement; meanwhile expelling in the same action the national leaders who deplore and fight discrimination? I think not. I think we can do more toward educating them if they're in the federation, with their own leaders getting broad AFL-CIO support toward the same end.[8]

The judicial function of the AFL-CIO is exercised in disputes among affiliates, colloquially termed "jurisdictional disputes." Rival unionism is actually of two basic sorts: a dispute as to whose members, or whose *employer,* shall perform the work—this is the classic jurisdictional dispute; or a dispute as to which union shall represent the workers—this is a representation dispute.

Whatever merits the concept of exclusive jurisdiction may have in theory, it is impossible to apply as the sole test of legitimacy for reasons which go deep in history; changing technology, looseness in the wording of jurisdictional statements, and union "imperialism" are probably the chief reasons. The entry of government tribunals, most notably the National Labor Relations Board, into the labor-management area has further complicated the jurisdiction situation. Vested jurisdictional legitimacy is not a main consideration for the NLRB in determining questions of representation and in the process finding the appropriate bargaining unit.

The concept of exclusive jurisdiction is thus virtually inoperative as a basis for legitimating the claims of one union against another. There is a serious question, moreover, as to whether the concept ever had sufficient concreteness to be enforceable. The merger between the AFL and the CIO could not have taken place if it had had to wait on the settlement of rival claims. In fact, unity was entered into with constitutional recognition that multiple jurisdictions did in fact exist.

Before formal unity between the AFL and CIO was consummated a trial relationship was set up in the form of a no-raiding agreement which pledged each signatory to respect "the established bargaining relationship" of every other signatory of the other federation. Later the concept of "established bargaining relationship" was incorporated in the AFL-CIO constitution, and although the word "jurisdiction" is used in the constitution it is given no operative function.

The attempt to find a viable formula for achieving amity among individual affiliates had a long history in the AFL—the problem arose in the old CIO but it never had quite the same thrust—and has been a source of controversy and irritation within the AFL-CIO from the very inception. In some respects feeling over the situation worsened just as fratricidal warfare usually cuts more deeply than warfare among strangers.

The 1961 convention adopted a new Article XXI of its constitution incorporating procedures for the settlement of internal disputes. The new article sets up two principles of legitimacy: "the established collective bargaining relationship" and "the established work relationship." The established bargaining relationship is defined as "any situation in which an affiliate, or any local or other subordinate body thereof, has either (a) been recognized by the employer (including any governmental agency) as the collective bargaining representative for the employees involved for a period of one year or more, or (b) been certified by the National Labor Relations Board or other federal or state agency as the collective bargaining representative for the employees." An established work relationship is defined as "any work of the kind which the members of an organization have customarily performed at a particular plant or work site whether their employer is the plant operator, a contractor, or other employer." Affiliates are bound to respect and refrain from undermining these established relationships. There are valid defenses which if they stand up a union can use to justify a violation: transgression of a "basic concept of union morality," the "constitutional objectives of the AFL-CIO," or "accepted trade union work standards." The executive council if it sustains the defenses by two-thirds vote can excuse an attack on the established relationship. The article seems to protect only *established* relationships and not to apply to new organizing except that the latter is suggested in the prohibition against affiliates "circulating or engaging in activities designed to bring another affiliate into public disrepute."

The resolution of internal disputes is to follow a four-stage sequence after complaint: (1) mediation by members of a panel from within the labor movement; (2) if this mediation fails, a determination by an impartial umpire, i.e. from outside of the labor movement, selected from a predetermined panel; (3) an appeal from the umpire's determination to an executive council subcommittee; and (4) if the subcommittee grants certiorari, as it were, appeal may run to the whole executive council. If the subcommittee disallows the appeal the determination of the umpire is final. Otherwise the decision of the executive council is final. If after complaint the subcommittee finds that there has been noncompliance, a variety of penalties ensue, including loss of standing as a complainant in a federation proceeding, federation assistance to organizations resisting the violation, publicizing of noncompliance, and other penalties covered by "any other authority vested in the executive council under this constitution." These methods are intended to constitute "the sole and exclusive method for settlement and determination of [a] dispute." Resort to court or "other legal proceedings" is expressly prohibited.[9]

The internal disputes procedure outlined is part of a network of internal disputes mechanisms including the National Joint Board for Settlement of Jurisdictional Disputes in the Building and Construction Industry, administered on the union side through the Building and Construction Trades Department; a number of bilateral union pacts; and the Organizational Disputes Agreement, administered by the Industrial Union Department, which contains the most sweeping prohibition against interunion conflict ranging from disputes over new organizing to raids on established relationships. With the exception of the bilateral pacts all of these mechanisms involve the regular use of "outsiders" in the labor movement's processes. This routine acceptance of outside intervention marks another historic departure even though this has been an evolutionary change.

V

The politics of the AFL-CIO as a federation is generated by specific leaders and by well-defined blocs. The varieties in federation leadership are symbolized in four men: George Meany, Walter Reuther, James Hoffa, and A. Philip Randolph—in addition to a number of supporting players.

The dominant personality in the federation has been its president, George Meany. It was Meany who put unity on the track by undertaking to deal with the CIO as an equal rather than as a supplicant. It was Meany who bulled unity through the AFL in the face of a remarkable lack of enthusiasm in most of the AFL. It is Meany who has put the federation uncompromisingly against readmission of a Teamsters' union headed by Hoffa, and behind the ethical practices power of the federation. The internal disputes agreement at the 1961 convention is a Meany achievement.

Mr. Meany's exercise of federation authority is in the CIO style of John L. Lewis and Philip Murray. Samuel Gompers achieved what he achieved by sagacity, not by strong-willed action. The federation as a movement in its own right had little meaning to William Green. Mr. Meany's influence and effect derive from the sheer force of a strong personality which is an interesting amalgam of personal presence and a deceptively clothed intellectual power.

The other great figure in the federation is Walter P. Reuther, head of the Automobile Workers' union, president of the Industrial Union Department of the AFL-CIO, and before merger, president of the CIO. Mr. Reuther is unusual among labor leaders of importance in his emphasis on the role of program as opposed to improvisation. His influence has been materially felt in the content and character of the federation's public policy stands. He has brought to the federation his well-known conviction that the modern labor organization must function responsibly both in the collective bargaining sector and in the public policy sector. The absence of program has been the basis of Mr. Reuther's criticism of the federation's organizing performance. In the internal affairs of the federation he has led the "industrial union" forces in criticism of the building trades' rival union tactics and in pressing for a system of settling internal disputes.

Mr. Reuther's critical stance has probably been influenced by what appears to be a continually abrasive relationship with Mr. Meany. It is difficult for an outsider to make out what the basic source of conflict between the two men is. It is not ideological, since Reuther and Meany share common approaches to the economic problems of the country and of the world. To be sure, they have had different accents on the role of the federation in the international labor movement, but these, I believe, have not been of a fundamental character. The difference is probably a temperamental one.

A third man whose figure looms important in these proceedings is not now a leader of an AFL-CIO union: namely James R. Hoffa, the president of the Teamsters' union. Mr. Hoffa's significance for the federation's power structure stems in the first instance from the importance of the Teamster's union in the complex of interunion relations, but also, I think, from Hoffa as a symbol of success in spite of expulsion.

Hoffa's capacities have become enveloped in a good deal of imagery and it is not easy to make out where reality begins and ends and imagery and impression take over. Little is really known about Hoffa's capabilities as a union leader. Such appeal as he has within the labor movement is not derived, as far as is known, from extraordinary achievements or demonstrated sagacity in collective bargaining. It is derived primarily, I believe, from the "smell of success" with which the media of public opinion have surrounded Mr. Hoffa and which he has not dispelled, and from the frustrations of other union leaders who sometimes feel that virtue is not necessarily its own reward, as witness —they may say—Mr. Hoffa's rewards without the conventional virtues. Without Mr. Meany's commanding position the Teamsters would probably be readmitted into the federation with Hoffa as the president. The price of Teamster readmission which Mr. Meany is reputed to be asking is the elimination of Mr. Hoffa from the union's presidency. The building trades union leaders have not hidden their feeling that the Teamsters belong back in the federation. Nor have former CIO leaders such as Joseph Curran of the Maritime Union and Michael Quill of the Transport Workers hidden their favorable sentiments toward Mr. Hoffa.

Finally among the influential leaders has been A. Philip Randolph, the president of the Brotherhood of Sleeping Car Porters. Mr. Randolph's importance in the federation does not stem from the power of the Sleeping Car Porters' union but because in this generation he has been the foremost critic of the labor movement's discriminatory practices against Negroes, first in the AFL and now within the AFL-CIO. Even though there has been a substantial improvement in the labor movement's treatment and awareness of the Negro worker, Randolph has refused to be "reasonable," jabbing the raw nerves of the federation's performance in this field on every occasion he can find in and out of federation forums. He has, in addition, been instrumental in the formation of the Negro American Labor Council as a pressure group to prod the federation. In this stage Mr. Randolph is probably not insensitive to the powerful stirrings within the Negro community in the wake of the Supreme Court's antisegregation decision and the turmoil in Africa. Randolph's attacks combined with that of the NAACP have impelled the federation to confront the discriminatory practices of its affiliates in a more concrete way, including strengthening of the Civil Rights Committee.

Several leaders have been important as "mediators" in the federation's internal conflicts: notably George Harrison of the Railway Clerks, Al Hayes of the Machinists, David Dubinsky of the Ladies' Garment Workers' union, and Joseph Keenan of the International Brotherhood of Electrical Workers—heads of former AFL unions. With the exception of Dubinsky, their backgrounds are impeccably and authentically AFL, but their attitudes toward the former CIO unions are moderate and this moderateness, as well as their good personal relationship with President Meany, makes them admirably suited for mediating roles. Among the former CIO union leadership Joseph Beirne, president of the Communications Workers, seems to have established himself in this capacity.

Of major influence among the federation's nonelected leadership has been Arthur J. Goldberg. With Mr. Meany, Mr. Goldberg stands as a coarchitect of AFL-CIO unity. As general counsel of the CIO and later as AFL-CIO special counsel and IUD general counsel, Mr. Goldberg was of critical importance in finding acceptable grounds for dealing with no-raiding pacts, merger, and ethical practices. His role involved professional talent of a high order, but even more the federation's political leaders valued his sense of fairness and his sureness of touch in moderating conflict. Another sort of important "nonelected" leadership in a somewhat narrower scope is observed in Mr. Jay Lovestone. Mr. Lovestone holds the bland title of director of international publications in the Department of International Affairs. He has, nevertheless, been extremely influential first in the resurgence of AFL interest in international affairs and later as President Meany's international adviser in the AFL-CIO.

VI

Personal leadership is interrelated with interest blocs in structuring the political atmosphere of the federation. The dominant blocs are the building trades and the industrial unions, with their respective departments providing the organizational vehicles through which the issues in controversy are debated. Although the departments are constitutionally subordinate bodies they lead virtually independent political lives, taking on other departments and even the federation as adversaries.

The issue that gives the cutting edge to the debate between the building trades and the industrial unions is essentially a job issue with various faces. As a jurisdiction issue it turns on whether certain types of work—usually maintenance—shall be performed by employees working for a factory employer or by employees working for an outside subcontractor. In the former case, members of the industrial union will do the work; in the latter the members of a building trades union are likely to do the work. The industrial unionists have charged that the efforts of the building trades unions to secure this work have flagrantly exceeded the bounds of union morality, including boycotts and strike-breaking. The building trades counter by asserting that the industrial unionists' criticisms have given aid and comfort to antiunion elements.

The differences between the groups have legislative applications, particularly in proposed amendments to the Taft-Hartley Act, where the building trades have been pressing for an amendment which would legalize union picketing at multiemployer construction job sites. The IUD sought additional amendments legalizing such picketing for their unions as well, which the building trades interpreted as preventing passage of *their* bill. Even the discrimination issue has a building trades–industrial union face, in that the main thrust of the Negro discrimination charge is directed against the construction unions and the failure of the federation to secure compliance from the building trades unions with discrimination bans.

It is not, however, an ideological craft vs. industrial union battle that is being waged here, since virtually all of the building trades unions have substantial factory worker memberships and function in these situations as industrial unions. However "industrialized" the construction unions have become, some of the feeling of the battles of the 'thirties still remains. Despite the fact that the former "Young Turks" of the CIO are now in their forties and fifties with a record of twenty to twenty-five years of experience, the building trades leaders still look upon many of these men as upstarts. The main onus is reserved for Walter Reuther, who epitomizes to them all of the radical—in the special sense in which they use the term—qualities of his breed: his interest in program, his anti-Miami asceticism, his concern with causes, and his lack of the amenities of companionship. For the industrial unionists, the building trades leaders symbolize the decadent "business agent" mentality which they associate with lack of idealism and of dedication.

Merger has proved incomparably more difficult for many of the state and city central bodies than it has for the national federation, and several important mergers had to be forced by the parent federation.

To be sure, the central bodies are technically subordinate to the national federation. In practice, however, they are power centers in their own right, and unless they run into head-on conflict with a vital interest of the federation there is almost no centralized direction of their affairs. This situation does not seem to have been modified appreciably by the recent appointment of a "coordinator of state and local central bodies."

The state and local central bodies are important labor movement agencies in their areas. They are the faces of the labor movement to their communities legislatively and politically; and in almost every state and in every city of any size (irrespective of political complexion) the labor movement has an established and invariably powerful—even if not necessarily decisive—place in the power structure. The central body is likely to provide one of the forums to which local unions may bring contending claims, and in well-established labor communities the approval of the central body is a very important asset in a jurisdictional controversy or in an organizing drive. The leaders of the central bodies have been men of power and influence in their respective communities and in their respective central bodies; merger unsettled the situation. In many communities the backbone of the AFL central body has been the building trades unions, and the building trades–industrial union debate brought an added abrasiveness to the local merger problem; in some respects the merger issue has been still another expression of the "craft"–industrial union argument. If the federation, and particularly President Meany, had not asserted forceful leadership, dual central bodies would have functioned indefinitely in several important areas —a situation probably preferred by many of the parties themselves.

It is at the central body level that the ouster of the Teamsters has in many respects been most deeply felt. Teamster aid is always helpful to a union on strike. A Teamster was invariably a high officer of the central body; the Teamsters figured prominently in its strategic councils; the size of Teamster membership made them an important financial mainstay. Despite the Teamsters' ouster, fraternization between the AFL-CIO establishment and the Teamster element is still an important fact in the labor movements of many areas.

VII

The present federation government and its problems represent both historic continuities and historic contrasts. The most striking contrast is the greater power of the federation vis-à-vis the constituent national unions and the greater personal force of the current president of the federation. Neither the AFL-CIO nor Mr. Meany is as powerful, however, as were the CIO and its leaders in the formative years; but then the former are dealing with well-established affiliates while the CIO affiliates were, with a few exceptions, dependent on the CIO.

In addition to the quality of Mr. Meany's leadership the greater influence of the federation is also derived from the larger numbers in the labor movement. The federation means more today because it *is* more. At the deepest roots of this situation are the centralizing tendencies in economic life and the consequent need for organizational instrumentalities that have the capabilities to respond effectively to these tendencies. The commanding position of international issues on the agenda of public policy also acts to enhance central governmental power and therewith central trade union power.

Another break with the historic past is the virtual disappearance of an organized radical left. As Arthur Koestler has said in another context, the Communists, to the extent that they function in the American labor movement, are "east," not "left." The American labor movement is in the unusual position of being the only national labor center in which an organized socialist left, either in control or in opposition, is totally absent.

What might have been a non-Communist left, namely the industrial unions, have in general accepted the fundamental values of an enterprise-welfare state system because they have done very well under this system. And just as the potential radical, non-Communist left has moved to the right, so the force of circumstances pressured the "right" in the labor movement—the building trades, the craft unions—toward the left. The importance of government in construction, and of construction in economic policy, has propelled the "craft aristocracy" toward left of center. This is not, I think, out of ideological conviction but out of job interest, which now goes beyond the work site into the halls of the Federal Government.

The main historic continuity is the unchallenged position of the nationals in the spheres of collective bargaining and internal union management. Collective bargaining has been touched not at all by the increased power of the federation. In contrast to the CIO relationship, there may even be something of a recision in federation power in this sphere. The federation is rarely involved in collective bargaining except in moral support. (It is, of course, involved for the dwindling number of directly affiliated unions.) Its influence on the internal management of unions has been marginal, affecting the ethical practices problem and the Negro civil rights admission practices—but the routine of union administration is untouched by the federation.

What assessment can one make of the federation's performance as a government? The federation's major accomplishment is that it has survived in the face of internal and external forces acting to disjoin it. But more than survival has been achieved, I think. The federation has addressed itself firmly to the sorts of questions that the evidence of history suggests are the proper concern of a federation, even as there are sharp differences over the answers (or the absence of answers) which the questions have yielded.

The interests that divide the federation internally are real; the issues involved are matters of substance, not slogans or pure ideology. The issue, for example, as to how far an association of unions—which in the last analysis is a voluntary association—can go in using the sanction of expulsion to enforce its commandments is a serious one. What sanctions short of expulsion or including expulsion may be utilized to enforce the standards which the federation has committed itself to? If the ultimate sanction is not utilized in cases of clear-cut violation the constitutional commitment has a hollow ring. On the other hand, if it is utilized the expelled affiliate is free to carry on the proscribed conduct outside the federation.

There has been ingenious experimentation with forms, processes, and theories suitable to the government of a labor *movement*. I would single out (1) the idea of due process as demonstrated in the use of outside arbitrators to afford a fair determination of internal issues in controversy, (2) the "subautonomies," notably the trade and industrial departments within the federation that inhibit the federation from becoming a monolith, and (3) the expertise of its technical secretariat in dealing with complex issues of public policy, which constitutes an important reservoir of knowledge outside of the government.

The federation has functioned as a responsible member of the national and the world community. The federation has not abdicated its responsibility to take responsible positions on matters that affect the whole society importantly. On frequent occasions it has had the courage to take positions which were unpopular with many of its constituents, as for example support of a liberal trade policy. It has also shown courage in taking a position in favor of government regulation of corrupt practices and civil rights in unions. No other group in comparable circumstances, I think, has demonstrated such detachment.

Notes

1 American Federation of Labor and Congress of Industrial Organizations, *Constitution,* Dec. 1957, Art. X, Sec. 3.
2 David Dubinsky, quoted in Benjamin Stolberg, *Tailor's Progress* (New York, Doubleday, Doran, 1944), p. 276.
3 Robert F. Hoxie, *Trade Unionism in the United States* (2d ed. New York, Appleton, 1923), p. 262.
4 See discussion between Philip Taft and Leo Troy, "Local Independent Unions and the American Labor Movement," *Industrial and Labor Relations Review,* Oct. 1961.
5 Andrew J. Biemiller, "Labor Issues in the 1960 Political Campaign: A Labor View," *Proceedings of the Thirteenth Annual Meeting,* Industrial Relations Research Association, 1960 (Madison, Wisc., 1961), p. 218.
6 Report of the AFL-CIO Executive Council, 1961 Convention, pp. 46–47.
7 AFL–CIO, *Constitution,* Art. II, Sec. 4.
8 "Statement of George Meany," President, American Federation of Labor and Congress of Industrial Organizations, before the Special Subcommittee on Labor of the House Committee on Education and Labor, on the Equal Employment Opportunities Bill, Jan. 24, 1962, p. 6. Mimeographed.
9 "Text of New Internal Disputes Plan," *AFL-CIO News,* Washington. D.C. (Dec. 23, 1961), p. 6.

Sources

Much of this paper is derived from personal knowledge and experience. For documentary sources see the *Reports of the AFL-CIO Executive Council* to the biennial conventions as well as the *Proceedings* of the conventions. The founding constitution of the AFL-CIO and the premerger documents are conveniently collected in Arthur J. Goldberg, *AFL-CIO—Labor United,* New York, McGraw-Hill, 1956. For the best running report on events as they occurred see the *New York Times, Business Week, Monthly Labor Review* (U. S. Department of Labor), *AFL-CIO News,* and A. H. Raskin's frequent articles in the *New York Times Magazine.* The *American Federationist* (the AFL-CIO monthly) is the best regular source for the federation's public policy analyses. For the labor press consult University of Michigan, Bureau of Industrial Relations, *Index to Labor Union Periodicals.* In addition see the following:

AFL-CIO, *Decisions and Recommendations of the AFL-CIO Impartial Umpire,* Vol. 1, 1954–1958 (Washington, D. C., n.d.); *This Is the AFL-CIO,* revised Jan. 1962. Pamphlet.

Jack Barbash, *Labor's Grass Roots,* New York, Harper, 1961; *The Practice of Unionism,* New York, Harper, 1956; "The Union Response to the Hard

Line," *Jour. Indus. Rels.* Berkeley, Univ. of California, 1961; "The Jurisdictional Dispute," *Indust. Bul.*, N. Y. State Department of Labor, Nov. 1957.

George Barnett, "The Dominance of the National Union in American Labor Organization," *Quart. Jour. Econ.*, Vol. 28 (1913), reprinted in John R. Commons, *Trade Unionism and Labor Problems*, 2d series (Boston, Ginn, 1921), pp. 387–88.

Robert R. Bendiner, "What's Wrong in the House of Labor," *The Reporter*, Oct. 12, 1961.

Irving Bernstein, "Union Growth and Structural Cycles," *1955 Proceedings*, Industrial Relations Research Association.

Warner Bloomberg, Jr., Joel Seidman, Victor Hoffman, "The State of the Unions, Chapter II," *The New Republic*, n.d. Reprint of series of articles written in 1959.

Tom Brooks, "Negro Militants, Jewish Liberals, and the Unions," *Commentary*, Sept. 1961.

Will Chasan, "American Labor Attacks Its Own Segregation," *The Reporter*, May 1, 1958.

Henry M. Christman, ed., *Walter P. Reuther, Selected Papers*, New York. Macmillan, 1962.

David L. Cole, "Interrelationships in the Settlement of Jurisdictional Disputes," *1959 Spring Proceedings*, Industrial Relations Research Association.

Alice H. Cook, "Labor's Search for Its Place in the Community," *Jour. Educ. Sociol.*, Vol. 29, No. 4; "Education of Workers for Public Responsibility in Community and Political Affairs," *Labor's Public Responsibility*, National Institute of Labor Education, 1960.

Archibald Cox, "The Role of Law in Preserving Union Democracy," in *Labor in a Free Society* (Berkeley, Univ. of California Press, 1950), pp. 56–57.

John T. Dunlop, "Structural Changes in the American Labor Movement," *1956 Proceedings*, Industrial Relations Research Association.

Harry Fleischman, "Labor and Civil Rights," *The New Leader*, April 19, 1960.

Walter Galenson, *The CIO Challenge to the AFL*, Cambridge, Harvard Univ. Press, 1960.

Herbert Hill, "Labor Unions and the Negro," *Commentary*, Dec. 1959.

John Hutchinson, "The Constitution and Government of the AFL-CIO," *California Law Review*, Dec. 1958.

"The AFL-CIO Merger," *Industrial and Labor Relations Review*, April 1956.

Joseph Krislov, "The No-Raiding Agreements, Progress Report for 1955," in *1955 Proceedings*, Industrial Relations Research Association.

Seymour H. Lehrer, "The CIO Jurisdictional Disputes Settlement Experience," unpublished Master's thesis, Ithaca, N. Y., Cornell Univ., N. Y. State School of Industrial and Labor Relations, 1957.

William M. Leiserson, *American Trade Union Democracy*, New York. Columbia Univ. Press, 1959.

Edward Levinson, *Labor on the March*, reprinted with intro. by Walter Reuther and foreword by James T. Farrell, New York, University Books, 1956.

Lewis L. Lorwin and Jean A. Flexner, *The American Federation of Labor:*

History, Policies and Prospects, Washington, Brookings Institution, 1933.

Jay Lovestone, "American Labor and the World Crisis," *1956 Proceedings,* Industrial Relations Research Association.

James O. Morris, *Conflict within the AFL,* Ithaca, Cornell Univ., 1958.

National Association for the Advancement of Colored People, *Racism within Organized Labor,* 1961. Mimeographed.

Louis Sherman, "The National Joint Board for Settlement of Jurisdictional Disputes in the Building and Construction Industry," *Spring 1959 Proceedings,* Industrial Relations Research Association.

David Stowe, "The Organizational Disputes Agreement, Industrial Union Department, AFL-CIO," *Spring 1959 Proceedings,* Industrial Relations Research Association.

Philip Taft, *The AFL in the Time of Gompers,* New York, Harper, 1957; *The AFL from the Death of Gompers to the Merger,* New York, Harper, 1959; *The Structure and Government of American Labor,* Cambridge, Harvard Univ. Press, 1954; "The Responses of the Bakers, Longshoremen, and Teamsters to Public Exposure," *Quart. Jour. Econ.,* Aug. 1960.

U. S. Congress, Senate Select Committee on Improper Activities in the Labor or Management Field, *Investigation of Improper Activities in the Labor or Management Field.*

John P. Windmuller, "ICFTU after Ten Years: Problems and Prospects," *Industrial and Labor Relations Review,* Jan. 1961.

5

NATHAN P. FEINSINGER

Law and the Public Interest in
Labor-Management Relations

The role of law is to employ the resources, if need be the force, of the state to regulate conflicting interests in society with a view to maintaining order and ensuring a reasonable and just result, through due process. Society, said Commons, "is a metaphysical entity which those in the midst of conflict identify with their own class, wage, profit, or rent interests." In seeking to resolve conflict much depends, he observed, "on politics and the accidents of personality in the executive, legislative and judicial branches of government." Reasonableness, he believed, "is idealism limited by practicability." Due process, as he read the views of the Supreme Court, means " 'substantial justice' under changing conditions, and . . . justice [is] equivalent to reasonableness." [1]

A good part of Commons' life, within and outside the field of labor-management relations, was devoted to establishing the foundation for a legal determination of reasonableness by securing an advance accommodation of conflicting interests through voluntary agreement. This was Commons' concept of "collective bargaining." The essential point of collective bargaining, or the "Representation of Conflicting Interests," he observed, is "the elimination, as far as possible, of a third party, the arbitrator—whether King, legislature, governor or dictator, handing down rules and regulations from above—and the substitution of rules agreed upon collectively, by conciliation." [2]

Since Commons expressed these ideas there has been, in the field of labor-management relations, at least one notable instance of federal law derived from agreement of the competing parties: the Railway Labor Act of 1926 and the 1934 amendment to it. [3] During World War II and the Korean crisis representatives of labor and management, under the guidance of "public neutrals" proceeding "by conciliation," were entrusted with the responsibility of developing national wage policies and resolving labor disputes, their actions being given the effect of law. In the main, however, since Commons wrote, the law regulating labor-management relations has not awaited agreement of the parties. Rather it has developed on the basis of the legislative idea of the public interest which emerged after consideration of conflicting interests separately advanced and reflected in legislative debate. From the 1930's to the 1960's the dominant legislative concept in this area has been free collective bargaining between management and organized labor, as the most effective means of promoting the public interest.

Until recently, the public interest has been deemed sufficiently served by the making and maintaining between labor and management of collective bargaining agreements designed to promote industrial peace and stability. Except in the two periods of emergency controls mentioned above, Congress has not concerned itself with the merits of the economic bargain reached, any more than it has with prices established by employers unilaterally. Labor and management have been free to bargain in their self-interest. Recent developments, however, indicate a new and more difficult role for the collective bargaining process. In brief, labor and management are being urged to take the public interest into account in negotiating the terms of their private agreements. [4] [To this end,] President Kennedy has established a tripartite Advisory Committee on Labor-Management Policy, which has undertaken to define the issues in which the public interest is involved and to establish guidelines for the determination of such issues in collective bargaining negotiations.

Whether the institution of collective bargaining, under its present custodians, will be equal to the new role assigned to it remains to be seen. Thus far only the executive branch has acted to promote that role. What is certain is that in the 1960's collective bargaining will be subjected to greater demands in the public interest than simply the peaceful accommodation of competing private interests, important though that result may be. The future role of the lawmakers in shaping those demands is not certain. Some reflection on how the lawmakers have acted in the past in regulating the conduct of labor-management relations with a view to protecting and promoting the public interest may be helpful in anticipating the course of future events.

A major difficulty of analysis in any field of law is the lack of agreed-upon criteria for determining "the public interest" in a particular situation at a given time. Thus, the constitutional guarantee of free speech has been judicially interpreted as stopping short of protection of expressions of views when such expressions create a "clear and present danger" of causing conditions which the legislature is authorized to prevent or forbid. In whose view, and by what test? Legislatively, by the view of a majority of those voting, following committee hearings and debate in which varying arguments, motivated by self-interest or by inner conviction, have been heard and considered. Judicially, by the view, in the final analysis, of a majority of the nine members of the Supreme Court, each of whom is free to choose between opposing arguments of counsel and to decide, in a close case, according to the dictates of his individual conscience and the scale of public values as he reads them.

These general observations apply to the role of law in the regulation of labor-management relations, in which the interests of the individual worker, the workers as a group, the union representing the group, the employer, and the general public may come into conflict. When weighing such conflicts, the lawmakers are called upon to make a choice or to strike a balance among various courses of action, according to their conception of the public interest. In most cases the result is a balancing of interests rather than a clear choice. This is understandable, since a single private interest seldom has all the "right" on its side, and "the public interest" may or may not coincide with one or more of the private interests involved.

Let us take, for example, the familiar issue of union security, or compulsory unionism, and consider the manner in which "the law on the books" has sought to adjust the conflicting interests involved. First, what are those interests? At the risk of oversimplification, one might describe them as follows. A union demanding a union shop or some variant of it, under which employees, as a condition of employment, are required to join the union, seeks thereby to strengthen its organization as a means of protecting and advancing its standards of wages, hours, and conditions of employment. An employer opposing the demand seeks, aside from any inner conviction as to the interests of his employees as individuals, to contain the bargaining strength of the union or perhaps to exclude or eliminate the union entirely. Nonunion employees opposing the demand seek thereby to avoid paying dues to an organization not of their own choosing, or being subject to its discipline. The public, to the extent that it is concerned at all, is divided in its sentiments as one argument or another captures its favor. This division of public sentiment, or perhaps public indifference, may be what has given the law its leeway in dealing with the issue.

How has the law attempted to resolve the issue? The matter first arose in the courts. *Plant* v. *Woods,*[5] a Massachusetts Supreme Court case of 1900 in which a union struck to obtain a closed shop, is revealing. Justice Hammond, who spoke for the majority of the court, could see no economic or other justification for the strike. Recognizing the conflict of interests involved, he nevertheless concluded: "In this as in every other case of equal rights the right of each individual is to be exercised with due regard to the similar right of all others, and the right of one be said to end where that of another begins. The right involved is the right to dispose of one's labor with full freedom. This is a legal right, and it is entitled to legal protection."

Contrast the reasoning of then Chief Justice Holmes. In his dissenting opinion, he begins with the premise that a strike for the purpose of obtaining higher wages and the like is lawful, and concludes: "I differ from my brethren in thinking that the threats [of strike and boycott] were as lawful for this preliminary purpose [obtaining a closed shop] as for the final one to which strengthening the union was a means."

Holmes recognized, of course, that the issue was not black or white but one of public policy as to the conditions under which injury may be justified where one interest must suffer if another is to prevail.

Plant v. *Woods* involved the issue of what constitutes a lawful *objective.* In *Vegelahn* v. *Guntner,*[6] an earlier case involving the legality of peaceful picketing as a *means* of pursuing a legitimate objective, Holmes stated:

. . . [I]n numberless instances the law warrants the intentional infliction of temporal damage, because it regards it as justified. It is on the question of what shall amount to a justification, and more especially on the nature of the considerations which really determine or ought to determine the answer to that question, that judicial reasoning seems to me often to be inadequate. The true grounds of decision are considerations of policy and of social advantage, and it is vain to suppose that solutions can be attained merely by logic and general propositions of law which nobody disputes. Propositions as to public policy rarely are unanimously accepted, and still more rarely, if ever, are capable of unanswerable proof. They require a special training to enable any one even to form an intelligent opinion about them. In the early stages of law, at least, they generally are acted on rather as inarticulate instincts than as definite ideas, for which a rational defense is ready.

How striking, in contrast to Holmes' concern with the difficulty of decision making in the realm of public policy, is the assurance with which a federal district judge declared, some nine years later: "There can be no such thing as peaceful picketing, any more than there can be chaste vulgarity, or peaceful mobbing, or lawful lynching." [7]

While the courts continued to struggle with the policy problems involved, the closed shop issue was brought to the attention of Congress in the debates preceding the enactment of the National Labor Relations (Wagner) Act of 1935. The result was a seeming paradox. In the act as finally adopted, the employer was forbidden generally either to "encourage or discourage" membership in a union. At the same time, however, he was permitted to enter into a closed shop agreement with a union representing a majority of his employees; his employees would then be not merely encouraged but compelled to join the union and maintain membership in good standing, or face discharge by the employer at the request of the union. One rationale for the new rule was that it limited the right, where it had previously existed, to execute a closed shop agreement with a union which had only a minority of members or none among the employees, and that the formula adopted was a fair compromise. The inconsistency remains, however, and is followed by similar inconsistencies in the subsequent development of the law, as will be seen.

The 1935 law permitted but did not require the closed shop. The union had only the right to propose that the employer agree to a closed shop provision. Agreement was difficult for the unions to obtain. The demand for a closed shop often provoked a strong emotional negative response. For example, such a demand on the part of the United Mine

Workers in 1941, and the coal mining industry's resistance to it, caused the demise of the National Defense Mediation Board. The issue was resolved in that case when the coal industry, under the prodding of President Roosevelt, agreed to arbitration, which resulted in an affirmative award. The issue arose again when, in 1941, President Roosevelt designated a tripartite group of public, labor, and management representatives to confer on a wartime program for handling labor disputes. When the conferees reported to the President that they agreed on all points except the authority of the National War Labor Board to direct a closed shop, the President, it is said, penciled a red line through the latter part of the report, implying that he was not interested in areas of disagreement. The War Labor Board could not so easily ignore the disagreement. After much travail, it succeeded in evolving and obtaining acceptance of a standard formula known as "maintenance of membership." Under this formula no employee was required to join a union against his will, but an employee who voluntarily joined or had joined a union was required to maintain his membership in good standing for the life of the labor agreement. The public need in this instance was clear, namely for a formula—*any* formula—which labor and management would accept as a solution for the duration of the war, to resolve an explosive issue threatening the war effort.

In 1947 Congress was again faced with the closed shop issue as part of a widespread demand for restraints on labor unions, an aftermath of a wave of postwar strikes in the mass production industries. The legislators were in a mood to outlaw compulsory unionism altogether. This time help came to the unions from an unexpected quarter. Senator Robert Taft, though opposed to compulsory union membership in principle, was also impressed by the "free rider" argument, i.e. that employees enjoying the benefits of collective bargaining owed an obligation to contribute to the financial support of the bargaining agent. The compromise he proceeded to engineer was ingenious. Under his formula, though the closed shop as such was outlawed, a union might still demand an agreement from the employer requiring all employees in a bargaining unit to become members of the union, or to contribute to its support in an amount equal to its initiation fees and dues. The union might terminate membership for various reasons. But it could not, on that ground, demand that the employer discharge an employee so long as he continued to tender the equivalent of his initiation fees and dues.

At the same moment Congress, while continuing the exclusive jurisdiction of the National Labor Relations Board over all other aspects of
its functions, authorized the states in their discretion to prohibit union
security agreements. By thus opening the door to state legislation,
Congress revived the union security issue and undermined the very
formula by which it had hoped to put this troublesome matter at rest.
All of the traditional arguments pro and con have since been dusted
off for possible debate in fifty legislative forums instead of one. A
number of states have already adopted constitutional amendments or
statutes, generally described as "right to work" laws, prohibiting agreements requiring employees to join unions. These laws are found mainly
in agricultural states or in states seeking to attract industry by the
assurance against "labor troubles" implicit in such laws. This is not
to say that many legislators may not have supported such laws because
of an inner conviction that they are needed to protect the liberties of
the individual worker. But it is difficult to assume that the inner convictions on that score of a majority of legislators in some states can
differ so markedly from the inner convictions of a majority of legislators in other states. The contrast can be accounted for only by a difference in the various states in the degree of acceptance of unions as an
integral part of the economic structure.

The most recent development in this area is the Supreme Court's
holding in *International Association of Machinists* v. *Street* [8] that a
union may not use dues collected pursuant to a union security clause
to support political causes over the objection of a contributing employee. Here is an illustration of policy making by the courts, in the
process of interpreting legislation, in contrast with their shaping of
public policy through the common law.

I have chosen to discuss the union security or compulsory unionism
issue as an example of the role which judges, legislatures, and the
executive and administrative agencies may play in the field of labor-
management relations, in seeking to reconcile conflicting private interests in the over-all interest of the public. The anomalous feature of
this example is the fact that at the moment the law, in the form of
Congressional action, had succeeded in producing a formula likely to
resolve the conflict, it sowed the seeds for renewed conflict by permitting a new interest, a form of "states rights," to be injected into the
formula. Thus it cannot be said that "the law" even today reflects a
clear feeling as to where the public interest lies. The issue is therefore

likely to continue to irritate labor-management relations in this country indefinitely.

The major issues of labor-management relations are tied to the conflict between employers and organized groups of employees. Conflict is inevitable even when unions are fully accepted. Speaking in 1896, Holmes philosophized:

> I have seen the suggestion made that the conflict between employers and employed was not competition, but I venture to assume that none of my brethren would rely on that suggestion. If the policy on which our law is founded is too narrowly expressed in the term "free competition," we may substitute "free struggle for life." Certainly, the policy is not limited to struggles between persons of the same class, competing for the same end. It applies to all conflicts of temporal interests.

> . . . .

> One of the eternal conflicts out of which life is made up is that between the effort of every man to get the most he can for his services, and that of society, disguised under the name of capital, to get his services for the least possible return. Combination on the one side is patent and powerful. Combination on the other is the necessary and desirable counterpart, if the battle is to be carried on in a fair and equal way.[9]

In 1921 the Supreme Court, in *Duplex Printing Press Co.* v. *Deering*,[10] held that the federal antitrust laws were violated by boycott or a product manufactured by a concern which a union sought to organize in order to protect the employment standards of competing concerns it had previously organized. In his dissenting opinion in that case Mr. Justice Brandeis carried Holmes' proposition one step further. Failing to find any legislative intent to outlaw the boycott in question, he stated:

> Because I have come to the conclusion that both the common law of a state and a statute of the United States declare the right of industrial combatants to push their struggle to the limits of the justification of self-interest, I do not wish to be understood as attaching any constitutional or moral sanction to that right. All rights are derived from the purposes of the society in which they exist; above all rights rises duty to the community. The conditions developed in industry may be such that those engaged in it cannot continue their struggle without danger to the community. But it is not for judges to determine whether such conditions exist, nor is it their function to set the limits of permissible contest and to declare the duties which the new situation demands. This is the function of the legislature which, while

limiting individual and group rights of aggression and defense, may substitute processes of justice for the more primitive method of trial by combat.

Shortly after Brandeis had spoken, Congress began to assert leadership in spelling out, in terms of the permissible "ends" and "means" of combat, the "duty to the community" owed by labor and management as "industrial combatants." The basic premise of its action was that industrial democracy and industrial peace and stability are matters of public concern, and that these goals can best be achieved through free collective bargaining between employers and unions freely designated by a majority of employees in an appropriate bargaining unit. This is the premise on which are based the Railway Labor Act of 1926 as amended in 1934,[11] the Norris–La Guardia of 1932,[12] the National Labor Relations (Wagner) Act of 1935 as amended by the Labor-Management relations (Taft-Hartley) Act of 1947, and the Labor-Management Reporting and Disclosure (Landrum-Griffin) Act of 1959.[13] The assumption is that in face-to-face dealings the representatives of labor and management come to understand each other's problems, and that an effort made in good faith to reconcile such differences is likely to succeed; thus the risk of resort to a test of strength is lessened.

The formula of bargaining in good faith was not to extend to requiring agreement or influencing the terms of the bargain. In instances where an impasse might develop, the parties were to be free to flex their economic muscles, the employer by adhering to his "no" and the union by resorting to strikes, picketing or boycott in an effort to change his mind. In emergency situations created by a strike or threat of strike on a railroad or airline, the President might, as provided by the Railway Labor Act, appoint an "Emergency Board" with authority to make recommendations for settlement.[14] In strikes found to affect "the national health or safety" the President might, as provided by the Taft-Hartley Act, initiate an application for an antistrike injunction for eighty days and in the process appoint a fact-finding board, called a "Board of Inquiry," with no authority, however, to make recommendations.[15] Aside from the usual processes of mediation, or the appointment of ad hoc boards or commissions by the President, in the exercise of his executive authority, to investigate and make recommendations for settlement, government was not to intervene further in labor disputes. In the case of so-called "minor disputes" on railroads, however, that is, disputes "growing out of grievances or out of the interpretation or application of agreements concerning rates of pay, rules, or working conditions," provision was made by preagreement of the carriers and their unions for compulsory, final, and binding arbitration.[16] Arbitration of similar disputes in industry generally was also endorsed, but not made compulsory.[17]

In the remainder of this paper, I intend to deal in the main with three questions. First, how has the statutory scheme of law worked? Second, what changes are needed in the public interest or are likely to occur? Third, what role, if any, will the law play in bringing about such changes? The answers depend in part on the level of labor-management relations, in terms of the degree of accommodation of conflicting interests, achieved by the parties concerned. There are at least three such levels to consider.

At one level is the union seeking to organize and the employer seeking to resist organization. At this level "the law on the books," as pronounced by the courts and administrative agencies in interpreting the legislative intent, is of paramount importance in guiding the conduct of the parties. Each side presses toward its objective as far as its lawyer advises that it is safe to go, and continuously pressures Congress to provide it with additional weapons of combat. In the later effort, the employers have recently been more successful than the unions. For example, since 1935 Congress has enlarged employers' freedom to combat organizational drives, particularly through the "free speech" amendment,[18] and has circumscribed use of the unions' traditional organizing weapons—strikes, picketing, and boycotts—by reviving the "ends" and "means" tests; [19] this is in spite of the fact that in enacting the Norris-La Guardia Act of 1932 Congress had disavowed such tests for judicial use in consideration of labor disputes.[20]

The free speech amendment, designed to permit an employer to make antiunion speeches so long as they contain "no threat of reprisal or force or promise of benefit," appears to represent a significant shift from the philosophy of active encouragement of unionism by the government to a policy of neutrality, and in effect converts an organizational drive into a contest between the employer and the union for the loyalty of the employees.[21] The legal limitations on the unions' use of their traditional weapons further handicap them in their organizational efforts. On the one hand, these limitations prevent them from bringing pressure to bear on "neutral" employers as an aid in organizing other employers. On the other hand, they prevent the unions from bringing pressure on the "primary" employer if the effect is to put pressure on employees to join a union, in derogation of their statutory right "to refrain from" union activities. The constitutionality of these limitations as infringements on workers' "free speech," for example, has yet to be finally determined; but in the light of a series of recent Supreme Court decisions upholding restrictions on peaceful picketing where the picketing is used for a purpose deemed by a legislature or court to be contrary to public policy,[22] the likelihood of adverse judicial decision is small.

At this first level of labor-management relations, we are not likely to witness a cessation of economic warfare. With membership shrinking as a result of automation, the shift in work assignments from "blue collar" to "white collar" workers, and the movement of industry to areas relatively hostile to unions, unions are not likely to reconcile themselves to the present state of the law. Relief from Congress will be difficult to achieve, as a matter of practical politics, since the steady trend of legislation would have to be reversed. Unions will no doubt look to the courts and the National Labor Relations Board for favorable rulings where the statute is vague, but such rulings at most could only ease, not eliminate, what the unions regard as an unfair handicap in the organizational struggle. Certainly at this level no assistance can be forthcoming from labor and management in the current effort to promote the public interest in the areas under consideration by the President's Advisory Committee.

At the second level of labor-management relations are those employers and unions which have adopted collective bargaining as a procedure but are not yet prepared to make full use of its potential as a means of self-government and mutual advancement. At this level also the "law on the books" plays a prominent role. The parties carefully observe the amenities of collective bargaining as defined by the law or as required by their contracts, relying on their lawyers, fresh from reading the advance sheets, for advice as to the measure of their rights and obligations. If one side has a practical problem which it seeks to correct at the bargaining table, the reaction of the other is likely to be, "Is this a mandatory or only a permissive subject of bargaining? [23] If the latter, we are not interested." At this level such questions arise as whether a union may engage in slowdowns and similar harassing tactics to bring pressure on the employer.[24] Similarly, in the day-to-day functioning of the contract grievance procedure, the parties, instead of looking a problem in the face, tend to concentrate on the letter of the agreement, to appraise their chances of winning a dispute before an arbitrator and, particularly in the case of management, to ask the lawyers for an opinion as to whether the arbitrator's jurisdiction can be successfully attacked in court. There is little, if anything, that Congress, the courts, the National Labor Relations Board, or the arbitrators can do to hasten the maturing of such relationships. Nor can the parties who operate at this level be expected to contribute greatly to the achievement of the objectives of the President's Advisory Committee.

At the third level are those labor-management relationships in which the parties have wholeheartedly accepted collective bargaining as an institution of self-government, with full realization of the interdependence of their interests.* At this level reason, rather than law or contract,[25] is the determining factor in the process of adjustment of competing interests. The "law on the books" is not regarded as the sole measure of the basic obligations of the parties to each other. Seldom, if ever, do their problems reach the courts or the National Labor Relations Board. In disposing of grievances, they may make extensive use of the process of voluntary arbitration for its "therapeutic value," but in proportion to the grievances settled directly, such use is minimal. Matters of concern to either party are recognized as problems to be resolved rather than battles to be won. References to "management prerogative" or "union prerogative" are taboo; the talk is of management and union "responsibility." Yet in such a relationship management may have, in fact, greater freedom to manage, and the union more real security, than in a relationship where the preservation of "preroga-

---

* See, for example, the following introduction to the General Motors-UAW, AFL-CIO Agreement:

"The management of General Motors recognizes that it can not get along without labor any more than labor can get along without the management. Both are in the same business and the success of that business is vital to all concerned. This requires that both management and the employees work together to the end that the quality and cost of the product will prove increasingly satisfactory and attractive so that the business will be continuously successful.

"General Motors holds that the basic interests of employers and employes are the same. However, at times employes and the management have different ideas on various matters affecting their relationship. The management of General Motors is convinced that there is no reason why these differences cannot be peacefully and satisfactorily adjusted by sincere and patient effort on both sides."

See also "The Case for Collective Bargaining," address by Earl R. Bramblett, Director of Labor Relations, General Motors, before the Mid-winter Personnel Conference, American Management Association, Chicago, Ill., Feb. 16, 1962.

tives" continues as the main concern of the parties. It is at this level that hope exists for an adaptation of the collective bargaining process to serve the public interest in effectuating the program of the President's Advisory Committee.

Labor and management in autos and steel, for example, have come a long way since the "Battle of the Overpass" and the "Saint Valentine's Day Massacre." In the twenty-seven years since the adoption of collective bargaining as our national policy, we have seen an increasing number of labor-management relationships progress from an era of mutual hostility through an era of mutual toleration to an era of mutual respect and constructive cooperation in solving problems. Even to the most mature relationships, however, the 1960's present a new challenge, the nature of which is becoming increasingly clear. The response of the "industrial statesmen" on both sides of the table to the challenge is not yet certain.

Until recently we have tended to measure "industrial statesmanship" by the ability of the leaders of labor and management to resolve their disputes peacefully. The test of "the public interest" has been a negative one: the avoidance or curtailment of strikes. The new challenge superimposes a more positive and much more difficult test. Briefly stated, it is whether labor and management, through mutual self-restraint in some instances and the exercise of bold imagination in others, are capable of cooperating with government on a voluntary basis, rather than by compulsion, with a view to resolving the increasingly serious and complex social and economic problems which confront our nation—problems which government alone cannot resolve without resort to legislation, such as compulsory arbitration, which would jeopardize the values of a free society and reverse the tradition of a free enterprise economy.

The nature of the challenge becomes plain when we catalogue the problems of the 1960's. For this purpose, we may refer to the list of subjects or areas selected for study by President Kennedy's tripartite Advisory Committee on Labor-Management Policy, chaired by the secretaries of Labor and Commerce. These subjects are

1. Free and responsible collective bargaining and industrial peace.

2. Economic growth and unemployment.

3. Automation, technological advance, industrial productivity, and higher standards of living.

4. Policies designed to ensure that American products are competitive in world markets.

5. Sound wage and price policies.

As Undersecretary [now Secretary] of Labor W. Willard Wirtz has stated, if labor and management are now prepared to gear their negotiations to tackle problems of this magnitude, then "Collective bargaining has suddenly become identified as integrally related to the broadest processes of national and international decision making." [26] This is not to say that labor and management have not heretofore discussed one or another of these problems. But such discussions have usually been limited to intermittent periods of crisis bargaining in a particular industry, during which each side has tended to adopt or adapt economic theories or statistics calculated to provide a semblance of scientific support for predetermined and self-serving positions. All too often the public interest has been confused with self-interest. Labor and management are now being challenged to conduct their bargaining outside of a crisis atmosphere and with a sense of common purpose to advance the national interest.[27]

In a recent speech discussing the work of the committee and its goals, former Secretary of Labor [now Mr. Justice] Goldberg stated:

> The President's committee was not established to pass resolutions. We do not intend that it should attempt to obtain or enforce a rigid and pale unanimity of opinion. Rather, the purpose of the committee is to permit an interchange of views between labor and management and to articulate a consensus of these views.
>
> .   .   .   .
>
> The attainment of these goals is clearly in the national interests. The implications for labor and management seem equally clear, especially in terms of the abandonment of restrictive policies that impair efficiency in the exercise of statesmanship in meeting the social consequences of change and in the formulation of wage and price policies.
>
> It remains to be seen whether these things can be done.
>
> Our aim must be to attain these objectives without sacrificing the free operation of private bargaining. Under no circumstances can we afford to lose sight of the fact that collective bargaining is an integral element of all our freedoms, an institution essential to a free society.[28]

It is too early to appraise the reaction of labor and management to this new concept of their responsibilities. At the very least, however, when bargaining issues are approached by the parties in terms of what the national economic and social welfare requires, the reports of the committee will provide some guidelines for rational and purposeful discussion. For example, in its first and only report thus far, entitled "The Benefits and Problems Incident to Automation and Other Technological Advances," the committee recommended to organized labor that it support technological change despite short-run hardships to individuals currently employed, and that it not seek a general reduction in hours to offset those hardships; rather all interests should cooperate in achieving both full employment and a full work week. At the same time the committee recommended that management take certain specified actions designed to cushion the impact of technological change on the work force. These included

timing and coordinating technological changes to the extent possible, with expansion of operations and the normal turnover in the work force, so that displacement will be minimized;

notifying and cooperating with employees, their representatives, and the public employment service in efforts to meet displacement problems;

enabling workers threatened with displacement to qualify for new jobs at the same plant;

facilitating relocation of displaced workers to other plants of the same firm, with accumulated seniority and pension rights where feasible;

providing severance pay in appropriate circumstances for those displaced.

In a related development, the President's Council of Economic Advisers has proposed certain guideposts for wage and price adjustments. Those guideposts, in their broad form, are stated as follows:

The general guide for noninflationary wage behavior is that the rate of increase in wage rates (including fringe benefits) in each industry be equal to the trend rate of over-all productivity increase. General acceptance of this guide would maintain stability of labor cost per unit of output for the economy as a whole—though not of course for individual industries.

The general guide for noninflationary price behavior calls for price reduction if the industry's rate of productivity increase exceeds the over-all rate —for this would mean declining labor costs; it calls for an appropriate increase in price if the opposite relationship prevails; and it calls for stable prices if the two rates of productivity increase are equal.[29]

The most recent negotiations in the steel industry, in which every issue under consideration by the President's Advisory Committee is involved, will provide a test of the effectiveness of the new approach to collective bargaining now being urged by the Administration.* Speaking of those negotiations, President Kennedy has commented:

The best way to achieve a desirable settlement in *the public interest* is through free and responsible collective bargaining.

An early labor settlement consistent with price stability in steel would be in *the public interest as well as in the interests of the parties themselves.*

The nation as a whole, I am sure, shares my conviction that such an agreement would materially strengthen our economy and country . . . .

These companies are free and the unions are free. All we can try to do is to indicate to them *the public interest* which is there. After all, the public interest is the sum of the private interests, or perhaps it's even sometimes a little more.

In fact, it is a little more.

But the Federal Government has no power in these negotiations, unless there was a strike which threatened *the national health and safety,* and that would be sometime late in the summer.

So all we can do is attempt to persuade the parties to go around the bargaining table and point out to them how vitally *the public interest* is involved.

In the first place, this is a basic industry. We are in a period of recovery which we want to maintain. This is going to be regarded symbolically as a test of our ability to manage our economy in a competitive world.

It will be looked on in Europe. I think this is—*the public interest is*—so involved, I think there's enough *community of interest between the company and union* after their '59 experience that I am hopeful they can reach an accord, and I'm hopeful when they go back in March that they will do it.

But we are limited by the Constitution and statutes and proprieties to the areas which I've discussed. But this—I hope they work it out, because it's in *their interests* as well as the Federal Government['s].[30] [Emphasis added.]

---

* Since this manuscript was prepared—August 1962, the parties reached an early settlement generally considered as "noninflationary." Subsequently, on April 10, 1962, U. S. Steel announced a price increase. Other steel producers, but not all, followed. The Administration and Congressional committees moved swiftly on several fronts to investigate. One proposal was to establish a commission of neutrals to appraise the need for a price increase. On April 13 the announced increase was rescinded. This action, while due in part to the decision of two steel producers to "hold the line," was also due in part to adverse public reaction, stimulated by presidential comment. This incident is without parallel in history, so far as I know. The success of the President in mobilizing public opinion in this instance may have significant implications for the future. Among other things, the episode suggests that public opinion may itself operate as "law" in the sense of protecting the public interest without the need, which has usually been the case, for a legislative follow up.

The present Administration's undertaking, particularly the work of the Advisory Committee, embraces Commons' concept of collective bargaining as an effort to accommodate conflicting group interests by "rules agreed upon collectively, by conciliation." One important difference is that Commons sought agreement through "joint committees" as a guide for legislation or administration,[31] whereas the Kennedy Administration's emphasis is not on legislation but on establishing guidelines for voluntary action. The spirit of Commons' approach was, however, essentially the same. For example, in referring to the work of the Wisconsin Industrial Commission and its advisory committees in the promulgation of various codes, he wrote: [32] " 'Reasonableness' was ... deemed to be ascertained, not by conflicting arguments and pleadings in court or legislature, nor by legal precedents, nor by ordinary custom, nor by opinions of judges, but by collective action of leading representatives of conflicting interests in the advisory committees." Holding such a view, Commons would surely have approved —and joined wholeheartedly in—the undertaking of President Kennedy's Advisory Committee.

The new challenge to which I have referred involved (1) participation by labor and management in the development of national economic and social policy and (2) adaptation of the collective bargaining process to implement that policy. Neither of these ideas is entirely new. During World War II and the Korean crisis a tripartite board of public, labor, and management representatives formulated and administered national wage policy with a view to curbing inflation. During World War II also, and to a lesser extent during the Korean crisis, such boards undertook to settle labor disputes with a view to maintaining uninterrupted production. In both areas the deliberations of the boards were conducted in an atmosphere, and to a large extent followed the procedures, of collective bargaining; the public members served as catalysts. During World War II in particular, labor and management shared a common purpose, the winning of the war, and needed no prodding to foster that purpose or to recognize the public need as the controlling consideration in all things. The end of the crisis brought a revulsion on the part of both against government control of wages and prices and regulation of the collective bargaining process. For a time the general public appeared to share that feeling. In recent years, however, people have become increasingly concerned with what they regard as excessive wage increases and unjustified price increases, as well as with strikes in essential industries. The public, so far as can be judged, continues to view wage-price controls and compulsory arbitration in lieu of strikes with suspicion; but there appears to be a mounting demand for some action to fill the vacuum between complete laissez faire and direct government regulation. In a word, we would like to preserve our free enterprise economy but we are concerned when it appears merely to drift. The new challenge assumes a need to revitalize that economy by giving it a sense of purpose and direction and to enlist the collective bargaining process in that endeavor. Meeting the challenge will be more difficult for labor and management than the World War II or the Korean War experience, because the setting is not so dramatic. But the need is as great if not greater, the collective bargaining process in my opinion is adequate to the need or can be made so, and labor and management have leaders with the capacity to make the effort successful, if they will recognize the need. The 116-day-long steel strike of 1959 and the public reaction to it have tended, I believe, to hasten that recognition.

My comment that the collective bargaining process is adequate or can be made adequate to meet the demands of the 1960's relates to certain significant adaptations of the process which have occurred in recent years. These adaptations are most likely to occur in those labor-management relations which have reached what I have called the third level, in which the parties have accepted collective bargaining as a joint cooperative venture rather than as a forum for the exchange of demands. One development is the increasing use of "private neutrals" in various ways to assist labor and management in particular cases in resolving especially complex or difficult problems that have a distinctly public aspect. These individuals are private in the sense that they are not regularly employed by government. They are neutral in the sense that they are not committed to the viewpoint of either labor or management; while concerned with the interests of both, they are able to inject into the relationship a willingness to consider the public interest as they sense it from observation and experience. Most of them are men in academic life. They are typically alumni of the War Labor Board or the Wage Stabilization Board or both, where they developed perforce some expertise in the synthesis of considerations of private and public interest and in the process of mediation. They have generally had wide and intensive experience as grievance arbitrators, through which they have acquired an understanding of the realities of industrial life. As one of these private neutrals, now in government, has described this development: "A number of companies and unions are experimenting today with new methods of using reason as an alternative to force through greater reliance on neutrals—not only as arbitrators, but as participants in the negotiating process itself, or even in its pre-negotiation phases. These neutrals help to identify problems and to examine them free of the myopia of the negotiating sessions. They also provide the parties with a sample of the public reaction to their positions." [33]

Two outstanding examples of the use of private neutrals in facilitating the collective bargaining process are the Armour–Meat Packing Union's study committee on automation and the Kaiser–United Steelworkers' study committee on how equitably to distribute productivity gains among investors, employees, and the public.[34] In these cases the private neutrals were appointed directly by the parties concerned. Differing somewhat in structure but performing essentially the same function are the President's tripartite railroad study commission, established to make recommendations on such perennial issues as work rules, and the President's "all-public" airlines study commission, established to make recommendations on the troublesome issues of job security, crew complement, and related representation rights involving two competing unions and a number of major air carriers, issues which resulted from the introduction of jet aircraft. In common with the Kaiser, Armour, and similar undertakings, these commissions have as their goal the resolution of basic problems rather than makeshift settlements.

One important feature of this development, particularly in the case of the wholly voluntary type of arrangement, is the wide range of procedures available to the parties. This flexibility, I am sure, is all to the good. I do not think it material whether the assistance of the neutrals is given in the form of observation, study, mediation (before, during, or after formal negotiations), fact finding with or without recommendations, arbitration, or any variant or combination of these procedures. The important consideration is that the parties have available the assistance, in whatever form they choose, of disinterested, knowledgeable persons in whose judgment they have confidence, and in whose success they have a stake if for no other reason than that they have freely invited the individuals concerned to join them in a common undertaking. Speaking from personal experience as well as observation, I am certain that the chances of success of such a voluntary joining of forces are considerably greater than if the help were to be forced upon the parties, even through the normal channels of government mediation. This is not to belittle the effectiveness of the latter process. It is simply stating the fact.

Some of the experiments referred to have already produced results. The others, while promising, are not yet completed. It may be worthwhile to explore the possible extension of the underlying principle, at least to those industries which are commonly regarded as essential. It would be most desirable, of course, if the extension were to come naturally, as in the case of grievance arbitration before private neutrals, after important employers and unions had taken the plunge and found the water to their liking. The fact is, however, that most employers and unions distinguish between contract making and contract interpretation, in the use of "outsiders," and are reluctant to seek private assistance of any kind in the former area. It must be remembered also that despite an improved climate of labor-management relations the government must still be prepared for large-scale strikes. Various steps have been suggested as alternatives to or to supplement the "national emergency" injunction as a means of avoiding or terminating such strikes. In case legislation should be felt necessary for this purpose, it may be worthwhile to explore here the possible use of the "private neutral" concept.

What I should like to suggest, in broad outline, is legislation that would require labor and management, in any enterprise in which a strike might be thought of sufficient public concern, to incorporate in their collective bargaining agreement a "labor peace formula." This formula would provide for a "labor peace agency" which had whatever authority the parties chose to give it and included among its members at least one neutral selected jointly by the parties. For the purpose of testing its workability, the President might experiment with the idea through executive action with respect to important enterprises which hold government contracts. This formula, of all that have been advanced involving some form of government compulsion, seems perhaps the most consistent with our basic concept of free collective bargaining and with the needs and trend of the times.

The use of "outsiders" to perform the role of keeper of the "public conscience" is not limited to the labor-management relationship. Recently, for example, a large electrical manufacturer, having been criticized for collusive bidding and similar unconscionable activities, secured the services of a law school dean to perform a policing function. In another instance, a college president was persuaded to serve as a member of a corporate board of directors, for the same purpose. In a related development, the Institute of Humanistic Studies of Aspen, Colorado, conducts seminars each summer for top executives under the guidance of distinguished moderators and special guests, with a view to instilling an understanding of the problems of modern American society and of the opportunities and responsibilities of the corporation to assist in giving purposeful direction to the search for their solution. The AFL-CIO in recent years has adopted codes of ethics embracing the concept of accountability of the labor movement to the public. Most recently, the AFL-CIO has adopted a procedure for resolving jurisdictional disputes that involves the use of private neutrals. The Public Review Board of the United Automobile Workers and similar boards of the Upholsterers and of the Packinghouse Workers, which are designed to ensure the rights of individuals vis-à-vis their union and all involve the use of private neutrals, appear to be part of the same development. In these instances, the unions may have acted in response to restrictive legislation or to forestall it. Regardless of motive, however, such moves are significant as part of a definite trend toward consideration of the public interest as a guiding factor in institutional behavior, in the area of labor-management relations.

In a world of tension, in which the rule of reason seems not always to be effective, we tend to look to increased legal restraints to allay our fears. It is difficult to point to any significant area of public concern in which government, through law, is not intervening with increasing frequency and scope in order to safeguard the national interest and security. In the area of labor-management relations the law has also played a prominent role from time to time. In this area, however, the law has definite limitations, of which Congress, in particular, appears to be instinctively aware. Congress has wisely concentrated its efforts on establishing the basic conditions for industrial freedom, permitting the parties meeting those conditions to develop their own institutions of self-government. By adopting collective bargaining as a national policy, but leaving the content of the bargain in the main to the parties concerned, Congress has made it possible for labor and management to develop those institutions within the framework of a free enterprise economy and a free society.

Until recently, collective bargaining has centered around the immediate interests of the respective groups. In that period, the public interest was thought to be sufficiently fulfilled if the parties could manage to live together in relative peace. The interplay of competitive forces in the collective bargaining process was deemed adequate to produce sound economic and social results. Unfortunately, the traditional processes of collective bargaining have left unsolved economic and social problems of increasing concern to the public. In some instances the processes have created new problems.

We are now entering an era in which labor and management are being asked to lift their sights and to direct their joint efforts, in cooperation with government rather than in response to governmental fiat, to the solution of old and new problems which demand an answer. In a very real sense, labor and management are being urged and given the opportunity to help shape our national economic and social future. The alternative is increased governmental intervention, legislative or executive, supported by public opinion. One may hope that labor and management will recognize that the moment for decision has come and make the right choice. The fate of free collective bargaining may hang in the balance.

Notes

1   John R. Commons, *Myself* (New York, Macmillan, 1934), pp. 87–88, 124, 156, 160.
2   Ibid., pp. 72–73.
3   See International Association of Machinists v. Street, 367 U.S. 740, 758 (1961); Brotherhood of Railroad Trainmen v. Chicago River & Indiana Railroad Co., 363 U.S. 30, 37 (1956).
4   See address by Undersecretary [now Secretary] of Labor W. Willard Wirtz before the Mid-winter Personnel Conference, American Management Association, Chicago, Ill., Feb. 14, 1962; address by Secretary of Labor [now Mr. Justice] Arthur J. Goldberg before the officers and directors of the Executives' Club, Chicago, Ill., Feb. 23, 1962.
5   176 Mass. 492, 57 N.W. 1011 (1900).
6   167 Mass. 92, 44 N.E. 1077 (1896).
7   McPherson, J., in Atchison, T. & S. F. Ry Co. v. Gee, 139 Fed. 582, 584 (Cir. Ct. Iowa, 1905).
8   Supra, n. 3.

9   Vegelahn v. Guntner, supra, n. 6.

10 254 U.S. 443, 65 L. Ed. 349 (1921).

11 U. S. Code, Title 45, chap. 8.

12 Act of March 23, 1932, 47 Stat. 70, 29 U.S.C.A. Sec. 101 et seq.

13 49 Stat. 449 as amended by 61 Stat. 136 and 73 Stat. 136 and 73 Stat. 519, 29 U.S.C.A. Sec. 141 et seq.

14 Sec. 10, Railway Labor Act, supra, n. 11.

15 Labor-Management Relations (Taft-Hartley) Act of 1947, Public Law 101, 80th Cong., 1st Sess., 29 U.S.C.A. Sec. 19 Title II, Secs. 206–210.

16 Sec. 3, Railway Labor Act, supra, n. 11. See Chicago River case, supra, n. 3.

17 Sec. 203 (d), Labor-Management Relations Act of 1947, supra, n. 15.

18 Sec. 8 (c), National Labor Relations Act, as amended in 1947, supra, n. 13. "The expressing of any views, argument, or opinion, or the dissemination thereof, whether in written, printed, graphic, or visual form, shall not constitute or be evidence of an unfair labor practice under any of the provisions of this Act, if such expression contains no threat of reprisal or force or promise of benefit."

19 Most recently, through the Labor-Management Reporting and Disclosure Act of 1959, 73 Stat. 519, amending Sec. 8 (b) (4) of the National Labor Relations Act of 1935, as amended in 1947, and by adding thereto Secs. 8 (b) (7) and 8 (e).

20 See United States v. Hutcheson, 312 U.S. 219, 61 S. Ct. 463.

21 See Wirtz, the New National Labor Relations Board: Herein of "Employer Persuasion," 49 Northwestern Univ. L. Rev. 594 (1954).

22 See International Brotherhood of Teamsters v. Vogt, 354 U.S. 284, 77 S. Ct. 1166 (1947) and cases cited therein.

23 See NLRB v. Wooster Division of Borg-Warner Corp., 356 U.S. 342 78 S. Ct. 718 (1958). See Cox, "The Duty to Bargain in Good Faith," 71 Harv. L. Rev. 1401 (1958); Feinsinger, "The National Labor Relations Act and Collective Bargaining," 57 Mich. L. Rev. 807 (1959).

24 See NLRB v. Insurance Agents' International Union, 361 U.S. 477, 80 S. Ct. 419 (1960).

25 See Shulman, Reason, Contract and Law in Labor Relations, 68 Harv. L. Rev. 999 (1955).

26 P. 4 of address cited in n. 4 above.

27 The steel negotiations are an example.

28 Pp. 6 and 8 of address cited in n. 4 above.

29 For complete text see 49 LRR 306, Jan. 28, 1962.

30 *New York Times*, March 8, 1962, p. 14.

31 See Commons, *Myself*, pp. 157 ff., espec. p. 174.

32 Ibid., p. 159.

33 P. 6 of Wirtz' address cited in n. 4 above.

34 See remarks of Chamberlain, Cole, Dunlop, Fleming, Ross, and Taylor in a symposium entitled "Neutral Consultants in Collective Bargaining," conducted on January 25, 1962, by the National Academy of Arbitrators. It will be printed as part of the Academy's *Annual Proceedings*.

III THE LABOR MARKET AND SOCIAL LEGISLATION

6 ARTHUR J. ALTMEYER

The Development and Status
of Social Security in America

The Influence of Commons

John R. Commons did not actually participate in the drafting of the Social Security Act or in the research leading to the recommendations upon which the act is based, yet his teachings and general philosophy of social legislation had a profound influence upon those who were charged with the responsibility for developing a social security program for this nation. The President of the United States, members of his Cabinet, and the technical staff upon which they relied were all familiar with the contributions that Professor Commons had made in the field of social legislation, particularly labor legislation. Indeed, a number of Commons' former students served as senior advisers to the President and his Cabinet Committee on Economic Security, which made the recommendations upon which the Social Security Act is based. They were selected for the very reason that they were known to have worked with Professor Commons in the drafting and administration of social insurance laws which were precursors of the social insurance provisions of the Social Security Act.

Commons had participated in the drafting and administration of the Wisconsin Workmen's Compensation Act of 1911, which was the first state law of its kind to go into effect in this country. Workmen's compensation was the first and only form of social insurance in this country until 1932, when the Wisconsin Unemployment Compensation Act was passed. This law was the outgrowth of ten years of effort by Commons and his students in drafting bills which were introduced in successive sessions of the legislature.

In its original form the Wisconsin Unemployment Compensation Act, strictly speaking, was not an unemployment insurance law, since each employer's liability for the payment of unemployment benefits to his employees was limited to the amount of his own reserve fund. However, immediately after benefits first became payable (1936) the law was amended to provide for partial pooling of funds so that, while each employer's rate of contribution continued to be determined by the amount in his particular reserve account, unemployed workers were paid the full amount of benefits to which they were entitled regardless of the amount of an employer's reserve.

In addition to having actually played an important role in the enactment of the Wisconsin Workmen's Compensation Act and the Wisconsin Unemployment Compensation Act, Professor Commons was an early advocate of other forms of social insurance, such as health insurance, old age and invalidity insurance, and widows' and orphans' insurance. He devoted to this subject 111 out of 464 pages of *Principles of Labor Legislation*, the book he wrote in collaboration with John B. Andrews.[1] In that book he called the message of Emperor William I to the German Reichstag in 1881 the beginning of "a great new movement in labor legislation." It is important to note that the origin in this country of what we now call social security will thus be found more largely in our labor legislation than in our poor relief laws. This is in sharp contrast to Great Britain, where the development was influenced more largely by dissatisfaction with its Poor Law. This difference in the relative influence of labor legislation and poor relief legislation accounts for many of the basic differences to be found in the social security systems of these two countries.

It is not too much to say that the philosophy underlying the Social Security Act is the same philosophy which Professor Commons expounded to his students throughout the years. It was a philosophy he traced to a group of French economists known as the Solidarity School, which came into prominence at the turn of the century. Commons had been much impressed by the writings of Léon Bourgeois, who undertook to clarify the concept of solidarity, which had previously been used in a rather metaphysical sense. Bourgeois employed the term "solidarity" to designate a kind of quasi contract. This legal gloss contributed greatly to the success of his theory, and appealed to Commons.

But probably more important was the fact that Bourgeois believed, as Commons believed, that solidarity (sometimes referred to as solidarism) was a substitute for both unrestrained individualism and complete socialism. Moreover, they both believed that solidarism found its practical expression in association based upon a mutuality of interests, and that this mutuality of interests transcended or at least reconciled conflict of interests. Thus Commons could say, in commenting on a court decision upholding the constitutionality of a workmen's compensation law: "Partnership of capital and labor, solidarity of individuals within a class, group responsibility of employers, becomes a theory of jurisprudence to a limited extent, in place of the theory of individual responsibility." [2]

Both men recognized two forms of solidarism: nongovernmental and governmental. Both believed that a maximum of nongovernmental collective action was desirable, but that this needed to be buttressed by collective action in the form of social legislation. As early as 1916 Commons wrote: "Thus social insurance accomplishes what, in France, is called solidarism, as a correction of individualism. . . . The solidarism of social insurance enforces the joint responsibility of employer, employee, and the community." [3] "Group insurance and welfare systems are coming," he predicted, "because, like accident compensation, they fill the next largest gap in the struggle of capital and labor. . . . The drawback is that they cannot make it universal. The backward, indifferent, incompetent or small employer should be brought up to the level of these pioneers. Only compulsory insurance can bring this about. . . . But this argument of solidarity . . . cannot be carried too far. . . . Carried to the extreme it is socialism, just as individualism carried to its extreme is anarchism." [4]

The Enactment of the Social Security Act

During the years Commons was active in the development of social insurance legislation, it was assumed that the power to enact social legislation, if it existed at all, resided solely in the states. Two federal child labor laws, one based on the power of the Federal Government to regulate interstate commerce and the other based on the taxing power, had been declared unconstitutional. The doubt this aroused as to the constitutionality of federal social legislation was of great concern to President Franklin Roosevelt's Cabinet Committee on Economic Security, since the President wished to place chief reliance on a nationwide comprehensive system of social insurance for the prevention of destitution and to rely on public assistance only to the extent necessary because social insurance benefits were inadequate or were not payable in individual cases.

The two forms of social insurance that the President wished to have enacted immediately were unemployment insurance and old-age insurance. As regards unemployment insurance, he had already endorsed a bill introduced by Senator Wagner of New York and Congressman Lewis of Maryland. This bill levied a federal tax on payrolls and allowed an offset against this tax for contributions that employers made under state unemployment insurance laws. Even if the President had not indicated his preference for a federal-state plan such as this instead of a straight federal system, it is probable that his Cabinet Committee would have recommended such a system for two reasons. One reason was that this plan had the advantage that it stood the best chance of being upheld by the U. S. Supreme Court. This was because it followed the precedent established by the Federal Estate Tax Act, which allowed an offset against this tax for payments made under state inheritance tax laws. Furthermore, if the federal law should be declared unconstitutional it was likely that many state laws would continue to function because they were self-sustaining. The other reason was that there was bitter disagreement among the advocates of unemployment insurance as to what the substantive provisions of the law should be. Under a straight federal system decisions would have to be made as regards these substantive matters for the entire country without the advantage of any experience and without an opportunity to experiment on a state-by-state basis with differing provisions.

There had been much argument among the advocates of unemployment insurance as to whether there should be a straight federal system or a federal-state system, probably a majority favoring a straight federal system, although they could not agree on the substantive provisions. Those who favored a straight federal system urged that if a federal-state system was adopted it should be of what was called the subsidy type instead of the tax offset type. They favored the subsidy type (which would have provided a 100% federal grant-in-aid to the states) because they believed it would be possible to establish stronger federal requirements as regards the benefit provisions of state unemployment insurance laws.

Of course, the same difficulty would have been experienced in securing agreement on these substantive provisions as under a straight federal system. Moreover, legal authorities were agreed that the more federal requirements there were under either the subsidy type or the tax offset type of system the greater was the danger of the federal law being declared unconstitutional.

As it turned out the Congress would probably have been unwilling to include very stringent federal requirements since it eliminated a very important one that the Committee on Economic Security had recommended. This was that each state unemployment insurance law must provide that at least 1% on each employer's payroll subject to the law must be paid into a pooled state fund. The states however would be free to adopt either an individual employer reserve type of law or a 100% pooled fund type of law under which all of the employers' contributions would be pooled. If Congress had accepted this recommendation it would probably have resulted in a more adequate general level of benefits, for reasons that will be discussed later.

The President had indicated to his Cabinet Committee on Economic Security that, while he wanted a nationwide system of social security, he felt it desirable to rely upon the states to the maximum extent in the actual operation of the system. The Cabinet Committee first explored the possibility of operating an old-age insurance system on a state-by-state basis. The actuaries consulted were unanimous in advising the committee against this. They pointed out that the great movement of workers across state lines made it impossible to estimate the future age composition of each state or the length of time that individual workers would be working in a particular state before retiring. The actuaries were of the opinion that this difficulty could be mitigated but not entirely overcome if each state was required to adopt a uniform system and to transfer records, wage credits, and contributions of workers who moved from one state to another.

The committee was convinced that the constitutionality of such a system was open to as much doubt as a straight federal system. It was also appalled at the administrative difficulties that would be involved. Hence it decided to recommend a straight federal system. There was not much difficulty in reaching agreement on substantive provisions, with the exception of financing. The Secretary of the Treasury insisted that the system be completely self-sustaining for all time to come. The rest of the committee was of the opinion that there should be a relatively small subsidy out of general revenues. The President supported the position taken by the Secretary of the Treasury.

The committee considered very carefully the desirability of also recommending a system of health insurance. Its staff devoted considerable time to a study of this form of social insurance. Likewise, this subject was studied intensively by a medical advisory committee appointed by the Cabinet Committee. However, this medical advisory committee could not reach an agreement. It appeared that the furthest the representatives of the American Medical Association on this medical advisory committee might go would be to consider insurance against "catastrophic illness."

The Cabinet Committee concluded that it would be better to defer making a specific recommendation until after Congress had acted upon its other recommendations, which were less controversial.

Besides recommending the two forms of social insurance, unemployment insurance and old-age insurance, the Cabinet Committee also recommended two forms of public assistance: old-age assistance and aid to dependent children. Both of these forms of public assistance would be based on individual need, as distinguished from social insurance, which provided benefits related to wage loss without any showing of individual need. The committee recommended that these forms of assistance be provided under state law and that the states be given federal grants-in-aid to help finance the cost.

Lastly, the Cabinet Committee recommended federal grants-in-aid to help the states finance maternal and child health and welfare services. It also recommended that more federal funds be made available to the U. S. Public Health Service and the Federal Office of Vocational Rehabilitation to provide more liberal grants-in-aid to the states for public health work and vocational rehabilitation.

Thus it may be said that the program recommended by the Committee on Economic Security consisted of three parts. As a first line of defense against destitution the committee recommended two forms of social insurance. As a second line of defense against destitution it recommended two forms of public assistance. Thirdly, in addition to these income maintenance programs, it recommended certain health and welfare services. The Congress accepted these threefold recommendations and added to them assistance to the blind as another form of public assistance. However, the Congress changed the name of the legislation from economic security to social security as being more appropriate to its varied and far-reaching character.

On August 14, 1935, President Roosevelt signed the bill, calling it "a cornerstone in a structure which is being built but is by no means complete"—and the Social Security Act became a part of the law of the land and a part of the American way of life.

The 1939 Changes in the Law

The Social Security Board in 1937, in cooperation with the Senate Finance Committee, appointed an advisory committee to recommend changes in the old-age insurance system; the research staff of the Board served this committee as well as the Board. There was particular need to consider changes in the old-age insurance system. It had been called a "fraud" and "a cruel hoax" during the presidential campaign of 1936. This attack continued after the campaign was over and was centered on its financing provisions.

The criticism was that the large reserve which would accumulate in the early years was unnecessary, would encourage extravagant demands for increased benefits, and was fictitious because it would consist only of worthless IOU's, meaning U. S. Government bonds.

The Board suggested that the terms of reference of this advisory committee be made broad enough to include consideration of changes in benefits as well as of the method of financing. Benefit changes, the Board believed, not only were desirable per se but would reduce the size of the reserve. The advisory committee's recommendations, submitted in December 1938, coincided on the whole with the recommendations the chairman of the Social Security Board had made in 1937 to the President. Congress accepted the old-age insurance changes and amended the Social Security Act in 1939. These changes had the effect not only of liberalizing retirement benefits during the early years of operation of the system but of placing them on a family basis. In addition they provided what really amounted to life insurance for widows and orphans. The face value of this "life insurance" equals the face value of all private life insurance written in this country. All of this was accomplished without increasing the long-range cost. This seeming miracle was performed by lowering the amount of benefits payable to single workers who would retire many years hence, and eliminating refunds to estates of deceased workers who had not drawn benefits equal to 3½ % of the wages upon which contributions had been paid.

In the field of unemployment insurance, the Board recommended and Congress agreed that the maximum annual earnings subject to the federal unemployment tax be fixed at $3,000, as under the old-age insurance system. Very little importance was attached to this change at the time. In retrospect it is clear that it would have been far better to have amended the old-age insurance title to remove the limitation of $3,000. The effect of a maximum limitation in both unemployment insurance and old-age insurance (now old-age, survivors, and disability insurance) has been to create a serious lag in the adjustment of benefits to take account of the steeply increasing general wage level.

In the field of public assistance Congress accepted the recommendation of the Board that public assistance records be kept confidential. It also accepted the Board's recommendation that state public assistance agencies (and state unemployment insurance agencies) be required to employ their staffs in accordance with a merit system. The Congress thus validated the policies previously adopted by the Board without specific legislative authority.

Another recommendation of the Board which Congress accepted should also be mentioned. It was that the public assistance titles be amended to make it crystal clear that public assistance could be provided only on the basis of individual need. This was important because the Townsend flat pension plan was still a hot political issue. Still another recommendation by the Board which was accepted by the Congress was that the federal grant for aid to dependent children be raised 33⅓ to 50%, as it already was for old-age assistance and blind assistance.

However, one important recommendation of the Board was not accepted. The Board had recommended that the federal grant for public assistance be related to the fiscal capacity of each state instead of being a uniform 50%. It was not until nineteen years later (1958) that Congress accepted this principle.

The Period 1940-49

After the 1939 amendments, there was little permanent federal legislation in the field of social security until 1950. This was largely because of the nation's preoccupation with the war and postwar problems. At his first press conference following the attack on Pearl Harbor on December 7, 1941, President Roosevelt announced that "Old Dr. New Deal" had to be replaced by "Dr. Win-the-War." But in spite of his concern with the war, the President continued to urge the expansion of social security. President Truman also repeatedly urged expansion of the system. The National Resources Planning Board made an extensive report in 1943 on *Security, Work, and Relief Policies* which included recommendations for improvement of the social security program. In spite of all this, and the further fact that Lord Beveridge's famous report on *Social Insurance and Allied Services* had received widespread publicity in this country, there was little actual legislation.

Aside from an amendment in 1946 making survivors of veterans who die within three years of their discharge eligible for survivors' benefits, the only amendments to the old-age and survivors insurance system during the decade of the 'forties were those restricting its coverage and freezing the scheduled increases in the contribution rate. The so-called Gearhart Amendment of 1948 narrowed the definition of "employee" so as to exclude an estimated 600,000 persons. President Truman made this an important issue in the presidential campaign of that year. The initial contribution rate of 1% each by employers and employees based upon wages up to a maximum of $3,000 a year was frozen six times during the period 1939–50. Under the 1935 law it had been scheduled to rise to 3% each by 1950.

In unemployment insurance a temporary provision for federal loans to state funds was in effect from 1944 to 1949, but no state found itself obliged to apply for such loans. In 1944 state unemployment agencies acted as agents of the Federal Government in paying readjustment allowances to unemployed veterans. In 1946 maritime workers were brought into the system. And in 1948 the definition of "employee" was narrowed as in the case of old-age and survivors insurance.

In public assistance, federal grants were liberalized on three occasions. The Congress did not accept the Board's recommendation that the percentage of federal matching be related to the fiscal capacity of each state as measured by its per capita income. Instead, it adopted a matching formula which was only roughly related to fiscal capacity.

Failure to extend the coverage of the old-age and survivors insurance system and to increase monthly benefits to take account of the rising wage level and increasing cost of living meant that benefits became more and more inadequate. This created the anomaly that as late as 1950 more aged persons were receiving on the average higher monthly payments under old-age assistance than under the insurance system.

So far as the federal-state unemployment insurance system was concerned, the failure of the states to increase weekly benefits to take account of rising wage levels resulted in a steady decline in the ratio of the average weekly benefit to the average weekly wage. In 1939 the average benefit was 41% of the average weekly wage; in 1950 it was 35%. The maximum duration of benefits had been increased, yet 1,800,000 unemployed workers exhausted their benefit rights before they could find other jobs. This represented more than one-third of all beneficiaries.

The Period since 1949

In January of 1949 President Truman in his Budget Message and his Message on the State of the Union repeated his previous recommendations. He followed this by handing the chairman of the Ways and Means Committee two draft bills prepared by the commissioner for Social Security. One of the bills covered old-age and survivors insurance and the other covered public assistance.

After many months of hearings, the Ways and Means Committee approved extensive changes in the Social Security Act, most of which were accepted by the Senate Finance Committee and became law in 1950. The most important amendments affecting the old-age and survivors insurance system were the following:

1. The coverage of the law was extended to include farm workers and domestic workers as well as urban self-employed persons.

2. The eligibility requirements were greatly liberalized.

3. The monthly benefits were almost doubled.

4. An increase in the monthly benefit for each year a worker had been insured was eliminated.

5. The contribution rate was increased from 1 to 1½% each for employers and employees for the first time since the law was passed in 1935.

The most important amendments affecting public assistance were:

1. The addition of another title providing for federal grants to the states to help finance assistance to needy persons who were permanently and totally disabled.

2. The liberalization of aid to dependent children to permit the states to include the needs of the caretaker as well as the children.

3. The liberalization of aid to the needy aged, blind, and disabled to permit the states to include in their disbursements which were eligible for federal matching both cash assistance to individuals in medical institutions and direct payments to doctors and hospitals.

One very important amendment which the Ways and Means Committee accepted but the Senate Finance Committee rejected was the expansion of the old-age and survivors insurance system to include monthly benefits for permanent total disability.

The general significance of the 1950 amendments was that they extended the coverage of the old-age and survivors insurance, and liberalized both the benefits and the eligibility requirements, so that for the first time the number of aged persons receiving public assistance began to decline.

It was not at all certain before the 1950 amendments that this contributory social insurance system with both benefits and contributions related to past wages would survive. Thus the Ways and Means Committee said in its report: "There are indications that if the insurance program is not strengthened and expanded, the old age assistance program may develop into a very costly and ill-advised system of non-contributory pensions, payable not only to the needy but to all individuals at or above retirement age who are no longer employed." [5]

In 1952 there was some further liberalization in both old-age and survivors insurance benefits and in old-age assistance. One amendment to the old-age and survivors insurance system appears on the face of it inexplicable; it gave a permanently and totally disabled person the right to have his benefit rights frozen as of the time his disability began, although no benefits would be paid until he reached the minimum retirement age of 65, or unless he died. Without such a provision his average wage upon which benefits are calculated would decline because the period during which he could not earn wages would be included in the divisor. However, he could not make application for freezing his benefit rights before July 1, 1953, and the amendment became ineffective June 30, 1953!

The reason for this curious provision was that the Senate Finance Committee would not agree to the freezing amendment as adopted by the Ways and Means Committee and the House of Representatives. It was only possible to get this sort of agreement, which would be abortive unless affirmative legislation was passed before July 1, 1953.

It was also provided that the determination of whether a person was permanently and totally disabled would have to be made by a state agency, and that the federal agency administering the law could reverse the state agency's decision only if it was favorable to the applicant. It could not reverse it if it was unfavorable. All of this strange arrangement was due to the combined opposition of lobbyists for the American Medical Association, private insurance companies, and employers' organizations.

In 1954 Congress amended the old-age and survivors system in several important respects. It made the disibility "freeze" provision actually effective. It extended the coverage to include farm operators and most professional self-employed persons, and it also liberalized the benefits.

Regarding unemployment insurance, the first major extension of its coverage was made in 1954, by including federal employees under the state laws and by reducing from 8 to 4 the number of employees which would make an employer subject to the federal unemployment tax. Another 1954 amendment provided for setting up a federal loan fund of $200,000,000 to assist states whose reserves had become depleted.

In 1956 there were two major changes in the old-age and survivors insurance system. Benefits were made payable for permanent total disability after 50 years of age. Retirement benefits were made payable to women at age 62, with an actuarial reduction in the monthly amount because of retirement before age 65. However, surviving widows could draw benefits at age 62 without any reduction. Both of these changes were strongly opposed by the Administration, particularly the payment of disability benefits. Members of the armed forces and all professional self-employed persons except doctors were covered without opposition.

There were no 1956 changes in the unemployment insurance law. However, federal grants to the states for public assistance were liberalized.

In 1958 the old-age, survivors, and disability insurance benefits were further liberalized, and dependents of permanently and totally disabled workers were given the same benefits as dependents of retired workers. In unemployment insurance, provision was made for loans to states to cover the cost of extending the duration of benefits. Federal grants to the states for public assistance were further liberalized, and for the first time the federal grant was related to the fiscal ability of each state, as measured by its per capita income.

In 1960 the major change in the old-age, survivors, and disability insurance system was to make disability benefits payable at any age. The only change in unemployment insurance was to raise the federal unemployment tax by $\frac{1}{10}$ of 1% to provide additional federal funds for grants to the states for administrative expenses and loans to states with depleted reserves.

An extremely important change was made in public assistance by what is known as the Kerr-Mills bill. A new section was added to the old-age assistance title of the Social Security Act which provided federal matching of the cost of medical care for persons over 65 years of age who were not sufficiently needy to qualify for cash assistance to cover their ordinary expenses but who were unable to pay their medical expenses. The percentage of the total cost met by the federal grant ranges from 50 to 80%, depending upon the per capita income of a state. The federal matching of cost of medical care provided for recipients of cash old-age assistance was correspondingly liberalized.

In 1961 the old-age, survivors, and disability insurance was liberalized in a number of respects: men were allowed to qualify for monthly benefits at age 62 with the same actuarial reduction as women; the minimum monthly benefit amount was increased; the monthly benefit payable to adult survivors was increased; the eligibility requirement was liberalized; and the amount a beneficiary could continue to earn without affecting his monthly benefit was increased.

A Temporary Extended Unemployment Compensation Act was passed that year which provided for outright grants (instead of loans as in 1958) to the states to extend the duration of benefits for workers who exhausted their benefit rights and were still unemployed. This act was financed by an increase of $\frac{4}{10}$ of 1% in the federal unemployment tax.

In public assistance there was further liberalization in the federal sharing of the cost. There were also two other very significant changes in the program for aid to dependent children. However, both are temporary. One (effective until 1967) is an amendment which makes eligible those children who are needy because their parents are unemployed. The other (effective until 1964) is an amendment which provides federal grants to assist the states in paying the cost of foster family care for needy children who must be removed from their own homes because of the inability of the parents to provide properly for their welfare.

This historical summary has dealt so far only with the changes made in the provisions of the Social Security Act, and has not mentioned other important social legislation in the field of social security. The first form of social insurance in this country was workmen's compensation covering employment injuries; federal employees were covered as early as 1908. As already stated, Wisconsin's Workmen's Compensation Act of 1911, which Professor Commons helped draft, was the first state law to go into effect. Today all states have similar laws, in addition to federal laws which now cover not only federal employees but also longshoremen and harbor workers, and private employees in the District of Columbia.

There are also federal social insurance laws protecting railroad workers. The Railroad Retirement Act, originally passed in 1934, was declared unconstitutional while the Social Security Act was still under consideration. In 1937 another Railroad Retirement Act was passed which has been in effect ever since, and provides not only retirement benefits but also benefits in case of permanent total disability. In 1938 a Railroad Unemployment Insurance Act was passed which was amended in 1946 to provide not only unemployment benefits but also cash sickness benefits.

Four states also passed laws during the period 1942–49 providing for cash sickness benefits to compensate for wage loss.

Legislation on veterans' benefits should also be mentioned. This provides cash benefits under certain conditions, as well as extensive medical care for both service- and non-service-connected disabilities. In many countries that have comprehensive social security systems, military benefits are more closely coordinated with the general social security system than in this country. Although members of the armed forces were brought under the old-age, survivors, and disability insurance system in 1956, benefits are still payable for service-connected disability and death, and retirement pay is provided, in addition to the social insurance benefits.

Appraisal of the Present Social Security System

The foregoing historical discussion has described how our social security system has developed throughout the years. However, in order to appraise our present social security system properly it is not enough to know about its historical development. It is essential that we examine more closely the purpose to be served by a social security system in a country such as ours, and determine the extent to which we have achieved that purpose.

One hundred and twenty-five countries throughout the world now have some form of what we call social security. Some of these countries have a relatively high-level economy, some a relatively low-level economy. Distinctive social and political differences exist among them. Although there has been a tendency for nations to copy from each other, the various social security systems necessarily reflect these differences.

Since the United States has a high-level economy, the first question that must be considered is whether there is enough economic insecurity to require the establishment of a social security system. This question answered itself during the Great Depression of the 'thirties. But our per capita gross national product—after the change in the price level has been taken into consideration—has trebled since then.

There is no question that the proportion of our population which suffers from actual poverty, regardless of how that term may be defined, is much less than it was thirty years ago. President Roosevelt in his second inaugural address said: "I see one-third of a nation ill-housed, ill-clad, ill-nourished." But even today we must acknowledge the inescapable fact that much poverty still exists in the midst of the most affluent society in history. Robert J. Lampman, in his study for the Joint Economic Committee of Congress, estimated that in 1957 19% of our people were in what he termed "low-income status." This he defined as a minimum income ranging from $1,157 for a single person to $3,750 for a family of seven or more.

But the proportion of our total population in low-income status does not tell the whole story about economic insecurity. Much of our poverty is concentrated in certain areas of our country and in certain groups of our population, such as the aged, the disabled, the widowed and orphaned. Moreover, practically our entire population is exposed to major economic hazards which may plunge them into poverty at any time. These economic hazards are inherent in a system of free enterprise characterized by increasing industrialization, urbanization, technological changes, and changes in consumer demand. All of these changes have led to a less self-sufficient family group and greater dependence upon an uninterrupted paycheck for continuing security.

It is true that increased wage levels have resulted in increased savings, private insurance, and home ownership. However, the adequacy of such protection is less, relative to the wage loss that occurs when a worker's income is interrupted through unemployment, sickness, permanent disability, old age, or death. Thus we find that in our high-level economy the major cause of economic insecurity is interruption of wage income rather than inadequate income while working.

The interrelationship of mass production, mass consumption, mass advertising, mass installment buying, and social security was once described as follows by Charles E. Wilson, at one time president of General Motors Corporation, and later Secretary of Defense: "I do not consider that federal pensions fully paid for by employer and employee are in any sense contrary to free enterprise, but amount to an extension of the principle of group insurance. . . . We have millions of salesmen abroad in our country trying to persuade these same people to spend the last dollar they can get their hands on. We have radio, television and all forms of advertising programs designed to entice them to spend their money, and with the best of intentions they are likely to arrive at their old age without on their own initiative having accumulated adequate personal savings." [6]

The generally accepted primary purpose of social security in this country is to assure through a governmental program minimum basic protection against major personal economic hazards which are likely to cause widespread destitution. In some other countries a good deal of emphasis has been placed on social security as a means of effecting a redistribution of income. In the United States the emphasis so far as redistribution of income is concerned is to redistribute a worker's income over periods of nonearning as well as of earning.

Another purpose served by social security is the maintenance of mass purchasing power. In the early days of our social security system, when we were still suffering from the Great Depression, social security was regarded by some as a panacea for restoring and maintaining general prosperity. Some economists then and now, while not regarding social security as a panacea, have advocated manipulating social security benefits in a specific manner to serve as a contracyclical force to a greater extent than they do normally.

As late as the advent of World War II some economists were advocating uniform old-age pensions financed to a considerable extent out of general revenues rather than by payroll taxes. They favored increasing the size of the monthly pension during periods of recession and decreasing it during periods of business expansion. Today there is one well-known economist, Kenneth Galbraith, who advocates that unemployment benefits be similarly increased and decreased depending upon the phase of the business cycle.

It seems to the present writer that carrying out such proposals would impair the fundamental social purpose of providing security for individual human beings, out of all proportion to what their effect might be on maintaining general economic stability. Certainly the individuals actually experiencing economic loss due to old age or unemployment continue to have the same need for protection regardless of the various phases of the business cycle. Unfortunately the Congress of the United States itself has failed to realize this fact, as will be pointed out later in the discussion of unemployment insurance.

In appraising the extent to which our social security system has achieved its primary purpose of assuring a minimum basic protection against major economic hazards, we need to consider not only the magnitude of these hazards and the adequacy of the protection but also whether the maximum amount of protection is provided at a minimum cost, in accordance with a consistent principle, and in proper relationship to our economic, social, and political institutions.

The magnitude of these hazards, the adequacy and cost of the protection afforded can best be discussed in quantitative terms in connection with each phase of social security. However, at this point a word should be said regarding the determination of the consistent principle to be observed and the determination of the proper relationship to our economic, social, and political institutions, since these are pervasive considerations which must be kept in mind throughout. Actually, they are questions of public policy which only our elected representatives can finally resolve. Thus, our federal and state legislatures have concluded that established individual need shall be the principle to be followed in providing public assistance, and that loss of wages shall be the principle in determining the amount of social insurance benefits. They have also determined that social insurance is preferable to public assistance as a protection against destitution. They have not accepted the principle of "equal shares," as it is called in Great Britain, which underlies the payment of uniform benefits unrelated to either individual need or wage loss. Likewise, Congress has decided, some phases of social security can best be administered by the Federal Government and others by state governments. The implementation and the effect of these public policy decisions will be covered in the discussion which follows.

Workmen's Compensation

Another contributor to this volume is discussing workmen's compensation in detail. However, since it was the first form of social insurance to emerge in this country and since it influenced the development of later forms, particularly unemployment insurance, it should be discussed here generally. Unfortunately when we consider what has happened to workmen's compensation during the more than half century it has been in effect in this country, we find a discouraging record of failure to live up to its high purpose of providing prompt and adequate compensation to injured workers. The early laws, which were admittedly crude, inadequate, and experimental, have not been materially improved in many states. Indeed, in many states benefits today are even less adequate in terms of the wage loss sustained. Litigation has delayed prompt payment, and administrators have failed to protect the rights of injured workers.

The percentage of wage loss which these state laws specify shall be paid sounds good, running all the way from 50 to $97\frac{1}{2}\%$. But the low weekly maximum dollar-amounts result in most states in only about a third of the actual wage loss being paid in cases of temporary disability. In cases of permanent disability the situation is far worse, because there are also limitations on the number of weeks that compensation can be paid and on the total amount. In cases of death the situation is still worse. Only nine states provide for weekly payments to a widow for life or until remarriage and for minor children until a specified age is reached. Therefore it is fortunate that the federal old-age, survivors, and disability insurance system now provides widows' and orphans' benefits and permanent total disability benefits.

Occupational diseases are not covered at all in two states, and in twenty states only certain specified occupational diseases are covered. Even the amount of medical care that must be provided in case of injury is limited in seventeen states.

If we take into account all the limitations placed upon the amount of benefits a worker and his dependents can receive, it is doubtful whether these benefits cover even as much as one-third of the wage loss sustained. And after all these years only about 80% of the wage and salary earners of this country are covered. Some of these laws cover only what are termed "hazardous employments"—although it is small comfort to a worker to learn that he is not entitled to compensation because he was injured in a nonhazardous employment. Moreover, most of the state laws do not cover small employers or domestic or agricultural employment.

The main reason that legislatures do not include small employers and domestic or agricultural employment is the high cost of an insurance policy. Less than two-thirds of the premiums paid to private insurance companies is returned in benefits.

There are other reasons for this sad state of affairs in workmen's compensation. Some people ascribe it to the fact that state legislatures are impressed by the argument which is often advanced, that the increased cost to employers would drive business out of the state. Actually, the aggregate benefit payments now made are equivalent to less than two-thirds of 1% of covered payrolls. But this sort of argument has led the AFL-CIO to call for the enactment of a national workmen's compensation law.

A fundamental proposal such as this can be considered only in relation to what changes are made in social insurance generally, particularly in compensation for nonoccupational sickness and disability. However, unless wholly new factors are introduced into the situation, we are not likely to see any more improvement in state laws in the next fifty years than we have seen in the last fifty. Therefore, assuming a continuance of the present state-by-state system, this writer believes that injured workers should be given the right not only to receive their benefits under the state workmen's compensation law but also to sue their employers for damages if they believe they can prove their injury was due to negligence on the part of the employer. The employer should not be allowed to plead contributory negligence on the part of the employee. In return for employees being guaranteed their benefits under the workmen's compensation law, the measure of damages in a suit against the employer should be restricted to wage loss, actual and prospective, with no allowance for pain and suffering and other noneconomic factors that are usually taken into consideration for nonoccupational injuries.

Employers with government contracts are already required to observe the wage and hour provisions of the Federal Fair Labor Standards Act. If they were also required to pay workmen's compensation benefits in accordance with the provisions of the U. S. Employees' Compensation Act, the resulting disparity of benefits payable to employees, depending upon whether or not they worked on government contracts, might induce the states to improve their workmen's compensation laws. Whether or not workmen's compensation continues to be a responsibility of the states, any fundamental solution would necessarily involve superimposing workmen's compensation benefits upon the general social insurance system in a rational manner. These supplementary workmen's compensation benefits would be in recognition of the special obligation resting upon employers in the case of work injuries. This is the solution arrived at in Great Britain and in a number of other countries.

Unemployment Insurance

The U. S. Supreme Court, in upholding the constitutionality of the Federal Unemployment Tax Act, specifically recognized that its fundamental purpose was the relief of unemployment. How adequately has the law achieved this purpose? It has, of course, induced all states to enact unemployment insurance laws so that their employers could claim an offset of 2.7% against the federal payroll tax. However, the federal law does not lay down any minimum benefit requirements that must be met by the state laws. Let us therefore examine these state laws and their operation during the last quarter century to determine whether the fundamental purpose of the federal law had been achieved.

Because of the complete lack of experience upon which to base estimates of unemployment insurance costs, the Social Security Board in 1935 recommended very conservative provisions both for the percentage of weekly wage to be paid and for the duration of benefits. It was contemplated that benefits would average at least 50% of the wage loss. However, as wages have increased, the states have failed to increase sufficiently the maximum amount that can be paid, with the result that benefits now average only 35% of wage loss as compared with 41% in 1939.

While the duration of benefits has been increased under most of the state laws, more than one out of four of all beneficiaries have exhausted their benefits during recent years. Moreover, 13,500,000 workers are employed by employers who have not been made subject to these laws. The result is that at this writing only about half of the workers who are unemployed are actually drawing any benefits under these laws, and those who do are receiving benefits averaging hardly more than a third of their wage loss. So actually only about 20% of the total wage loss due to unemployment throughout the nation is compensated.

There has been an increase in the amount of wages and the length of employment necessary to qualify for benefits. But more disturbing are the increasingly harsh disqualification provisions. Of course, since it is the purpose of unemployment insurance to provide protection in periods of involuntary unemployment, there should be some provision disqualifying a person who voluntarily quits his job without good cause, is discharged for misconduct, or refuses to accept suitable work. But twenty states disqualify a worker even though he has been obliged to quit his job for admittedly good personal cause, such as the fact that the conditions of employment are undermining his health, or he is obliged to move to another locality, or he has been offered a steadier job or another job at better pay.

Certainly in a system of free enterprise workers should be free to exercise their right to move from one job to another in the interest of making the greatest use of their skills and bettering their standard of living. Yet these states disqualify unemployed workers who have quit for any of these reasons, because their laws require the worker to prove that he quit for good cause attributable to his employer.

It is not too much to say that these disqualification provisions indicate that the state unemployment insurance laws have moved away from providing protection at times of involuntary unemployment, in the direction of providing such protection only if the unemployed worker can prove not only that he is involuntarily unemployed but also that his unemployment was the fault of his previous employer.

This situation has developed largely because the federal law does not protect employers in states that may desire to have an adequate unemployment insurance law from unfair competition by employers in other states that have inadequate laws. There is no question that it was the intent of the law to protect them. At first thought it might be concluded that the imposition of a uniform federal unemployment tax of 3% would prevent unfair interstate competition. However, the actual average contribution rate based on taxable wages varies widely from one state to another. In 1960 the range was .54 to 2.96%, because the law includes a provision which permits employers to claim the 2.7% offset against this tax not only for contributions they have actually paid under a state unemployment insurance law but also for those they have been excused from paying because of their favorable experience with respect to unemployment or to the payment of unemployment compensation to their employees. This is known as employer experience rating. It has sometimes been asserted that only the advocates of the Wisconsin type of unemployment insurance law favored employer experience rating, but actually the advocates of other types also favored some form of experience rating.

When the Social Security Act was under consideration, the main argument made for this provision was that it would give individual employers an incentive to stabilize their employment, thus preventing unemployment. In the course of time, more emphasis came to be placed on the argument that this sort of provision properly allocates the "social cost" of unemployment. According to this argument, the cost of unemployment should be included in the employer's cost of production of goods and services, like the cost of wages and materials and other expenses, in order to arrive at the true cost of production.

This change of emphasis may have come about because there is no statistical evidence that employer experience rating has had any general effect in stabilizing employment. However, individual employers have said that they took steps to stabilize their employment because of this incentive.

It was, of course, recognized that the effect of employer experience rating would be that employers in different states, like those in different parts of the same state, would pay different rates of contribution. But it was assumed that those with the same unemployment experience would pay substantially the same rates. Unfortunately this has not proved to be the case; they may pay widely differing rates.

This is caused partly by the differences in the basic type of employer experience rating system that is included in the various state laws. It is also partly due to the fact that some states charge all the benefits received by an unemployed worker to the recent employer; some charge them to past employers in inverse chronological order; and some charge them to past employers in proportion to the past wages paid by these employers.

Only five states use the decline in an employer's payroll as a measure of his experience. In all the rest the sole measure is the amount of benefits paid to his former employees. This direct relationship between an employer's contribution rate and the amount of benefits paid to his former employees naturally creates an incentive not only to stabilize his labor force and oppose improper claims but also to keep the level of benefits low and eligibility conditions high.

Much of the variation in the average contribution rate for all employers from state to state is due to variations in the volume of unemployment. But much of it is also due to variations in the relative adequacy of the state laws. Thus nine of the twelve states with the lowest ratio of employers' contributions to total payroll (ranging from .36 to .76% had either lower benefit rates or higher exhaustion rates in 1960 than the average of all states. Six of the nine had both lower benefit rates and higher exhaustion rates than the average of all states.

Hence it has come about that unemployment insurance in this country has been considered too much as a tax program and too little as a program intended to pay adequate benefits to unemployed workers. The specter of interstate competition has been present in attempts to improve benefits, just as in the case of workmen's compensation, although the Federal Unemployment Tax Act was intended to prevent this. However, instead of achieving reasonable uniformity it has resulted in employers with the same employment experience being charged widely varying rates, and workers with the same employment history being entitled to widely varying benefits in the various states.

It seems to this writer imperative that the Federal Government assume greater responsibility in the field of unemployment insurance. There can be no question but that the Federal Unemployment Tax Act was responsible for the very existence of the state laws. Certainly the causes and cure for unemployment are for the most part beyond the control of the individual states.

The Congress recognized the necessity for a government move when it enacted what is known as the Temporary Extended Unemployment Compensation Act of 1961, which paid benefits out of the Federal Treasury to workers who continued unemployed after exhausting the benefits which state unemployment insurance laws allowed them. This law, as its name indicates, expired on June 30, 1962, and, as a committee report says, was intended only to help offset the effects of the current recession. A number of states have also passed laws providing for an extended duration of benefits only when the percentage of insured unemployment rises to a specified rate.

The President has recommended permanent federal legislation of this character. However, helpful as this legislation can be in providing compensation for long-term unemployment during a period of recession, it does not provide any protection to workers who remain unemployed after their benefit rights expire during periods when the general rate of unemployment is lower. There is a considerable amount of long-term unemployment at all times in most states from such causes as automation and chronically depressed industries and areas. And of course such legislation does nothing to assure that the weekly benefit compensates for a reasonable proportion of the wage loss.

This writer believes that Congress should enact permanent legislation incorporating minimum benefit standards in the Federal Unemployment Tax Act and providing that the Federal Government share in the cost of benefits. The federal unemployment tax in 1961 was 3.5%, of which .8% was retained by the Federal Government. Half of this .8% was intended to finance federal grants to the states to cover the entire cost of administration of the state unemployment insurance laws, and half was intended to cover the cost of the Temporary Extended Unemployment Compensation Act. If minimum benefit standards were incorporated in the federal law, the temporary increase of .4% in the federal rate should be restored and used to reimburse the states for a large proportion of the cost of benefits above a specified level of total payroll. This would not only help to spread some of the risk of unemployment over the entire nation but also provide a positive incentive to the states to make their laws more adequate.

A more fundamental change would be to substitute for the present complicated federal tax offset plan a simple system of federal grants of 50% of benefit payments and administrative expenses payable out of a straight federal payroll tax. This approach would result in still greater spreading of the risk as between states and would also offer still greater encouragement to the states to make their laws more adequate.

The most important of the minimum standards that should be incorporated in the Federal Unemployment Tax Act would of course be the weekly benefit rate and the duration of benefits. The rate should not be less than that recommended by both President Eisenhower and

President Kennedy: high enough so that the great majority of insured workers would be eligible for weekly benefits equal to at least half of their average weekly wage. The maximum duration should be at least as high as that contemplated in the Temporary Extended Unemployment Compensation Act, namely 39 weeks.

The coverage of the Federal Unemployment Tax Act should be extended to include all the kinds of employment covered by the federal old-age, survivors, and disability insurance system. It should apply to all employers who have employed one or more employees during twenty or more weeks. This would automatically result in the states extending the coverage of their unemployment insurance laws to correspond.

The maximum earnings of $3,000 per employee which are subject to the employer's tax should be raised at least to the level of the maximum subject to the payroll tax under the old-age, survivors, and disability insurance system, which is now $4,800. On the average, only 60% of an employer's total payroll is now taxed. Therefore the tax rate could be reduced correspondingly, and the total yield would remain the same. This change would not only simplify employers' reports but reduce the tax burden on small employers, whose proportion of high-wage earners is usually smaller.

The Old-Age, Survivors, and Disability Insurance System

The other social insurance program contained in the Social Security Act, namely the federal old-age, survivors, and disability insurance system, presents a brighter picture. As its name implies, this system provides not only retirement benefits but also benefits for permanent total disability and benefits to widows, orphans, and dependent parents when an insured person dies. The face value of this survivors' insurance protection is now $550 billion.

At the present time 95% of all employees and self-employed persons are covered under this system or some other public retirement system, as compared with 65% in 1937. Eighteen million persons are now receiving monthly benefits amounting to $15 billion a year. The chief groups without any protection are the less regularly employed agricultural and domestic workers. This gigantic social insurance system, which has been called "the largest insurance company in the world," is administered at a cost of 2%.

As has already been mentioned, the benefit formula has been liberalized a number of times. Because of that fact and because of the rising wage level throughout the years, the average monthly benefit of a retired worker without dependents has increased from $22.10, when monthly benefits first became payable in 1940, to $76.16 in September 1962. This increase in the average benefit represents about the same proportionate increase as the increase in the average annual earnings of insured workers. However, this average benefit represents only about 25% of the average monthly wage being earned by insured workers. This rather low percentage is due to a considerable degree to the very liberal eligibility requirements that were put in the law in 1950 and liberalized still further in 1960 and 1961. The result has been that millions of workers with very little past employment in insured employment were able to qualify for at least the minimum benefits. The effect of these liberalized minimum requirements on the average benefit is demonstrated by the fact that the average monthly benefit being paid to disabled workers, who have to meet more stringent requirements, was $89.84 in September 1962. This represented 30% of the average monthly wage being earned by insured workers.

Of course, the addition of dependents' benefits results in a retired worker with a wife who has also reached the minimum retirement age receiving a 50% increase in his monthly benefit. Survivors' benefits have also been added since the original law was enacted. So the total benefits can amount to as much as $254 a month, depending upon the average wage of the insured worker and the number of eligible dependents. But even so the benefit level should be raised at least 33⅓%. This should be accomplished by liberalizing the benefit formula and by raising the maximum amount of annual earnings taken into account in calculating the benefit.

The benefits payable to low-wage earners have been liberalized more than those payable to high-wage earners. Thus the minimum monthly benefit payable to a retired worker without dependents has been quadrupled and is now $40, instead of $10, as it was in the beginning. However, the maximum monthly benefit payable to a retired worker has increased only 50% and is now $127, instead of $85, as it was in the original act.

Compensation for a larger proportion of the wage loss suffered by a low-wage earner is desirable from a social standpoint since his need is presumably greater than that of a high-wage earner. However, it is also necessary to make certain that individual equity is also maintained. Even though high-wage earners receive a smaller proportion of their wage loss as a benefit, they still receive far more protection than they could purchase from a private insurance company with the contributions they have made. This will continue to be so for employees dying or retiring during the next twenty years and for self-employed persons during the next fifteen years.

But eventually, as the scheduled rate of increase in the contribution rate goes into effect, there will be some high-wage earners without dependents who will not receive their money's worth. Before that time is reached, the law should be amended so that the contribution rate for both employees and self-employed persons will not be permitted to increase beyond the level which assures that they do receive their money's worth.

The reduction in the scheduled increases in the contribution rate of employees and self-employed persons could be offset by applying the employers' contribution rate to their total payroll instead of only up to the maximum individual earnings taken into account for the calculation of the individual worker's contribution and benefit. At the present time the maximum annual earnings taken into account are $4,800. This results in only 80% of the total payroll of employers subject to the law being taxed.

The benefits now payable for permanent total disability should be payable for all disabilities continuing beyond six months. Determining whether a disability is both total and permanent is often difficult. Moreover such a determination is destructive of a worker's morale and hampers rehabilitation efforts. In addition to paying benefits for extended disability, the present cumbersome, confusing, and illiberal arrangement between federal and state officials for determining disability should be abandoned.

Besides improving both the benefit provisions and financing provisions, the system should be extended to cover the 5% of workers not now protected under any public insurance system.

*Insurance against Wage Loss
Due to Nonoccupational Temporary Disability*

Two other kinds of contributory social insurance usually found in social security systems are not contained in the present Social Security

Act: insurance to cover wage loss due to temporary disability and insurance to cover the cost of medical care. The Railroad Unemployment Insurance Act insures against wage loss due to unemployment caused by disability as well as by lack of work. The entire cost is borne by the employers. Also, four states have temporary disability laws, which cover more than 11,000,000 employees—almost one-fourth of those employed in private industry.

A clear distinction should be made between insurance to cover wage loss due to disability and insurance to cover the cost of medical care. Thus the American Medical Association, which opposes compulsory health insurance, in 1938 passed a resolution approving its committee report that it unreservedly endorsed insurance against loss of wages during sickness as it has distinct influence toward recovery and tends to reduce permanent disability.

The accident and health insurance companies, of course, have always opposed this kind of social insurance. Unfortunately they protect less than 10% of the ten-billion-dollar annual loss of income due to sickness. Moreover, the companies writing individual policies pay back to these policyholders in benefits only half of every dollar they collect in premiums.

If we add to the protection provided by commercial accident and health insurance policies the protection provided under the laws already mentioned and that provided under formal paid sick leave plans covering both private and public employees, 28% of the total wage loss is compensated. It is interesting to note that half of this protection is provided under government auspices, that is, under the laws mentioned and through sick leave granted to federal, state, and local government employees.

Not only does existing protection cover only a small proportion of the total wage loss due to sickness but it largely fails to cover low-wage earners working for small employers in both rural and urban areas, the very groups who most need it. Therefore the extension of social insurance to provide cash indemnity for a part of the wage loss due to sickness is essential.

A nationwide system of protection against wage loss due to non-occupational disability might be provided in either of two ways: adding it to the protection provided under the federal-state unemployment insurance system or to the protection provided under the federal old-age, survivors, and disability insurance system. If it were added to unemployment insurance, the Federal Unemployment Tax Act should require the states to pay benefits for unemployment due to temporary disability as a condition for their employers receiving the 2.7% offset against this tax.

Three of the four states which now have temporary disability insurance laws link them to unemployment insurance. At one time, it seemed that many more states would do this. However, no state has adopted a temporary disability insurance law since 1949. Therefore there is no likelihood of many states acting soon unless the Federal Unemployment Tax Act is amended as suggested. There are various arguments pro and con as regards the desirability of linking temporary disability insurance to unemployment insurance. To this writer, the most important argument against doing so is the fact that the states have shown so little interest and have failed to enact reasonably adequate unemployment insurance laws.

The advantage of providing this protection under the federal old-age, survivors, and disability insurance system is that it could be related closely to the existing protection for wage loss due to permanent total disability. Thus a disabled worker would receive his benefits for wage loss due to temporary disability during the first six months of his disability. Before the end of that time a determination could be made as to whether he was permanently and totally disabled, and if he was he would continue to receive his benefits without interruption. Of course if the law, instead of requiring a determination of permanent total disability, were amended to compensate for total disability extending beyond six months, the relationship would be even closer.

Health Insurance

Only a general appraisal of the need for health insurance, as seen by this writer, will be undertaken here. It is well known that the cost of medical care has risen more steeply than other main items entering into the cost of living. The Consumer Price Index prepared by the Bureau of Labor Statistics shows that since 1949 all medical costs have increased twice as much, and hospital costs four times as much, as the index of all consumer prices.

Even with this increase, expenditures for private medical care are only 4% of the gross national product and 5.6% of the total personal income of the American people. The real problem is how to spread the cost of medical care. Fifty-two other countries have chosen social insurance.

Social insurance to cover the cost of medical care, usually called "health insurance," is simply a method of spreading the cost of medical care. The result is that instead of those individuals who are unfortunate enough to be sick being obliged to bear the whole cost, at a time when they can least afford to do so, the cost is borne by everybody through a system of prepayment into a common fund.

Health insurance, of course, is not socialized medicine. Under socialized medicine, medical services are provided by physicians employed by the government and in hospitals owned by the government. Under health insurance medical services are provided by private practitioners who are reimbursed from the insurance fund for the services they render.

As a matter of fact, we do have considerable socialized medicine in this country today. The federal, state, and local governments own and operate three-quarters of all the hospital beds in the United States. In government hospitals and with doctors on the public payroll in whole or in part, the taxpayers finance full medical care for all members of the armed forces, for all veterans with service-connected disabilities, and for many veterans with non-service-connected disabilities. The government also provides complete care for tubercular and mental patients.

In addition, the various units of government are paying out larger and larger amounts for medical care to the indigent. The Federal Government also pays for the medical care of dependents of members of the armed forces. From all the foregoing, it is apparent that the various units of government are paying a large portion of the medical bill of this country.

Those who oppose government health insurance believe that private health insurance can be depended on to help people meet the cost of medical care. This is now the position of the American Medical Association. This represents a change in the position that it took in 1932. At that time it officially approved a report which stated: "It seems clear then that if we must adopt in this country either of the methods tried out in Europe, the sensible or logical plan would be to adopt the method to which European countries have come through experience, that is a compulsory plan under governmental control." [7]

Much has been said about the growth of private health insurance plans. But all forms of private insurance to cover the cost of medical care, including all nonprofit plans such as Blue Cross and Blue Shield, as well as all commercial insurance, in total cover only 22% of the 24-billion-dollar annual medical bill of this country, which is less than the percentage paid out of public funds. Moreover, most of the persons protected by private insurance are in the middle and higher income brackets and live in the larger cities. As in the case of insurance against wage loss due to temporary disability, the commercial insurance companies writing individual policies pay back to these policyholders in benefits only half of every dollar they collect in premiums.

Therefore it seems to this writer that some form of governmental health insurance is necessary. As a matter of fact, we already have in operation in every state in the nation a system of health insurance applicable to occupational accidents and diseases, namely workmen's compensation. Health insurance is simply more inclusive and covers nonoccupational accidents and diseases.

It would be possible for Congress either to enact legislation that would create a strong inducement for the states to pass health insurance laws, or to enact a wholly federal health insurance law. In either case the administration would have to be decentralized, so that the necessary arrangements with doctors and hospitals could be subject to adjustment on a local basis. The local doctors and hospitals should be permitted to choose the method of remuneration they desire. There should also be free choice of physicians and free choice of patients. Voluntary nonprofit organizations that provide or pay for health services should be reimbursed for services rendered.

The 18,000,000 retired workers and their wives, disabled workers, and widows and orphans now drawing monthly cash benefits under the federal old-age, survivors, and disability insurance system are in particular need of protection against the cost of medical care. Retired workers are in an exceptionally difficult situation since their average income is much less than that of younger persons but their medical costs are far greater.

Only through collecting a small contribution based upon the wages of insured workers during their working years can health insurance be financed to protect them when they become old or disabled or when they die leaving dependents. It is then too late to collect a premium because their wage income has ceased.

This writer believes that it would be desirable to provide immediate insurance protection to these groups against major medical costs, such as the cost of hospital care, surgical and medical care provided in hospitals, and diagnostic services to hospital outpatients. Protection should also be provided as rapidly as possible for nursing home care and for visiting nurses' services.

The cost of administering these benefits would be small. The centralized system of record keeping and the nationwide network of local offices of the old-age, survivors, and disability insurance system would of course be utilized for determining eligibility. Likewise, non-profit, cooperative, prepayment medical care plans would be utilized to the fullest extent. This would strengthen and stimulate the growth of nonprofit plans, which are now confronted with the necessity of rejecting low-income high-cost families, or charging them higher rates than they can afford to pay, or attempting to spread the cost over all contributors. Commercial insurance companies have for the most part chosen the first two alternatives. Therefore they would be little affected since they have not found it feasible or profitable to insure these groups.

Those who oppose providing protection against the medical costs of persons already entitled to cash benefits under the old-age, survivors, and disability insurance system advocate that this protection be provided only to "medically needy" persons—that is to persons who are self-supporting except for medical costs. This approach was adopted by Congress when it passed what is known as the Kerr-Mills bill in 1960.

As already explained, this bill amended the old-age assistance title of the Social Security Act to provide federal matching to the states for the medical costs of persons whose property and income made them ineligible for cash assistance. However, these persons still must meet a somewhat more liberal income and resources test administered by a public welfare agency.

Since this approach is a form of public assistance, we should consider here the basic public policy which is involved. This is whether we shall rely primarily upon contributory social insurance in order to prevent destitution before it occurs or upon public assistance to relieve destitution after it occurs.

As has already been stated, President Roosevelt and his Cabinet Committee were convinced that social insurance was preferable, and contemplated the eventual establishment of a comprehensive system of social insurance which would prevent all but exceptional cases of destitution. Contributory social insurance, they believed, not only sustains but promotes a system of free enterprise because it utilizes well-known principles of insurance to achieve both social adequacy and individual equity. They consider that its specific advantages, as compared with public assistance, were that (1) benefits were based on presumptive need measured by wage loss instead of on investigated need; (2) costs were covered by contributions made by or on behalf of the beneficiaries instead of out of general taxes. This writer believes that experience has demonstrated the soundness of these views.

The approach in the Kerr-Mills bill is contrary to the basic policy underlying the original Social Security Act, since it accepts public assistance as a satisfactory substitute for contributory social insurance instead of as only supplementary. It also assumes that our present public assistance system is adequately meeting the needs of persons who are wholly destitute and that the states can meet their share of the cost of medical care for persons who are not destitute. Therefore let us look at the actual functioning of our public assistance system.

Public Assistance

At the present time 7,500,000 destitute persons in this country are receiving cash public assistance and 6,000,000 are receiving surplus food or food stamps. There is of course a very large overlap in these figures. Of the 7,500,000 persons receiving cash public assistance, 6,500,000 are in the categories for which the Federal Government makes grants under the Social Security Act: 2,350,000 needy aged, 3,650,000 dependent children, 400,000 needy persons who are permanently and totally disabled, and 100,000 needy blind. In addition 1,000,000 are receiving what is called general assistance, for which federal grants are not available. People receiving general assistance include the needy unemployed, the seriously disabled, older persons who have not yet reached the age of 65 which would qualify them for old-age assistance, mothers who cannot qualify for aid to dependent children because the children are over 18.

Our failure to develop an adequate and comprehensive system of social insurance during the last quarter century is the principal reason that the Federal Government and the states have been obliged to rely upon public assistance to a far greater extent than was ever contemplated. But while a large proportion of these millions of needy persons would not have been obliged to apply for public assistance if a more adequate social insurance system had been in effect, it would be a mistake to assume that this could prevent all destitution. There are hazards causing destitution that social insurance cannot insure at all or cannot insure adequately. Thus, two-thirds of the children receiving aid to dependent children are in need because of the breakdown of the family, resulting in divorce, separation, or desertion of a parent, or because the mother was unwed. Only the third who are needy because of the death or disability of a parent could have been protected under social insurance. A large number of those receiving public assistance are low-wage earners or irregularly employed. Social insurance which provides benefits related to wage loss cannot be a substitute for adequate wages and stable employment.

Therefore it is essential that we have an adequate and humane system of public assistance. Unfortunately our present system does not achieve this objective. According to the Report of the Advisory Council on Public Assistance submitted in 1960, three-fourths of the states do not meet the full needs in one or more of the federally aided categories, the needs of recipients being determined by the states' own standards. The situation in general assistance, which, as already stated, is not federally aided, is far worse. For example, the national average monthly payment per recipient is $26.47, as compared with $68.78 for old-age assistance.

The failure of the states to provide adequate public assistance is due in considerable degree to their limited capacity to do so, even though the Federal Government pays as much as 80% of the cost in some states. In many states public attitudes toward needy people are responsible for inadequate appropriations. This is clearly the primary reason in a number of high- and middle-income states.

A number of changes in the federal law are necessary to improve our public assistance system. Certainly the Federal Government should share in the cost of "general assistance." It was thought at the time the Social Security Act was passed that the persons not covered by the specific categories would constitute a small residual group which the states and localities could take care of. However, the number receiving general assistance has been as high as 1,600,000 in recent months.

Congress has recently recognized that the states need federal aid in meeting the needs of unemployed workers with children who have been obliged to apply for general assistance. It passed a temporary law, expiring June 30, 1967, which broadened the definition of "dependent child" to include children who are needy because of the unemployment of a parent. This law helps the states meet the increased costs of general assistance due to unemployment during a period of recession. However, even in years of high employment there have been 375,000 of these persons receiving general assistance and countless hundreds of thousands more who are in need but receiving no assistance. For instance, seventeen states have laws which make families with an employable member ineligible for assistance even though no work is available.

The federal aid for the existing four categories is more liberal for the needy aged, blind, and disabled than it is for aid to dependent children. The matching formula is roughly related to the per capita income of the states. If it were more strictly related, so that high-income states received a smaller proportion of the total federal aid, there would be no increase in cost to the Federal Government for providing aid to the states for all needy persons regardless of whether or not they fell within specifically defined categories.

Besides simplifying the federal matching formula and making it more equitable, the federal law should require the states to meet 100% of the need of applicants for public assistance. The states should be required to establish a standard budget which they certify is sufficient to provide reasonable subsistence compatible with decency and health. Undoubtedly, the standard budget of each state will be affected by the standard of living of self-supporting workers, so that low-income states will have a lower standard than high-income states. The only solution to this dilemma is to undertake the development of programs which will raise the per capita income of these low-income states.

The federal law should also require the states to eliminate residence qualifications. The reason the Federal Government is bearing 60% of the total cost of public assistance for the country as a whole is to protect needy Americans regardless of where they happen to live in the United States of America. This is essential since every year 5,000,000 Americans move from one state to another.

Besides improving the federal law to assure that public assistance is made more adequate in meeting the needs of destitute persons, it is highly important that the Federal Government provide more funds to the states for financing constructive social services of all kinds. At present the Federal Government shares on a far less liberal basis in the cost of administration of public assistance than in the cost of the assistance given to needy persons. Congress apparently has looked upon administration as simply overhead expense, failing to recognize that proper administration of public assistance involves rendering vital social services to recipients and to applicants. The entire process of determining eligibility and extent of need should be carried on in a manner that helps restore self-confidence, encourages the desire to become self-supporting, and promotes stronger family responsibility. Specialized services also need to be provided to accomplish these purposes.

Not only should general administrative costs be reimbursed by the Federal Government on as liberal a basis as the cost of assistance, but specialized services designed to prevent or reduce dependency should be reimbursed on a still more liberal basis. Moreover, federal funds should be made available for the education and training of persons equipped to provide these services.

The Cost of Social Security

In a very real sense, social security is not an added expense to the nation but a social mechanism whereby existing costs are met in a more equitable and less burdensome manner. The loss of family income—due to unemployment, sickness, permanent disability, economic old age, and death—is a fact, whether or not protection is provided against it. The cost of medical care is a fact, whether or not protection is provided against it. What contributory social insurance does is to spread workers' income to cover periods of nonearning and to enable workers to pay for medical expenses while they are well instead of when they are sick.

It is true of course that social security represents an allocation of a certain proportion of our gross national product. But it must be borne in mind that to the extent social security reduces dependency and stabilizes purchasing power it increases the gross national product.

At present we are using 6% of our gross national product for social welfare, including social insurance, public assistance, public health and public medical services (but not including veterans' programs, which amount to 1%). This is about the same percentage as when the Social Security Act was enacted. Of course, within this 6% there has been a large increase in the proportion going into social insurance and a large decrease in the proportion going to relief and work relief.

All of the improvements suggested here in both the social insurances and public assistance, including medical care for the beneficiaries under the old-age, survivors, and disability insurance system, would increase the percentage of our gross national product devoted to social welfare to 8%. A universal comprehensive health insurance system would require the allocation of another 3%.

Devoting this proportion of the gross national product to social welfare would provide the American people a basic protection upon which they could build more effectively a higher degree of well-being through savings, private insurance, home ownership, and industrial welfare plans. It would not mean that everyone would be guaranteed all the good things of life without any effort on his part. It would not mean a redistribution of wealth but a redistribution of welfare. What it would mean is more genuinely equal opportunity in a free society. Thus, it would be a validation of Professor Commons' philosophy of social solidarity expounded to his students a half century ago.

Notes

1 *Principles of Labor Legislation*, New York, Harper, 1916.
2 *Industrial Goodwill* (New York, McGraw-Hill, 1919), p. 56.
3 *Principles of Labor Legislation* (rev. ed., 1920), p. 499.
4 *Industrial Goodwill*, pp. 89–90, 102.
5 U. S. House of Representatives, Report No. 1300, Social Security Amendments of 1949, 81st Cong., 1st Sess., p. 2.
6 Charles E. Wilson, speech before the Chicago Executives' Club, January 6, 1950, entitled "Economic Factors of Collective Bargaining."
7 *Medical Care for the American People: Final Report of the Committee on the Costs of Medical Care, Adopted October 31, 1932* (Chicago, Univ. of Chicago Press, 1932), pp. 164–65.

7

ABNER BRODIE

The Adequacy of Workmen's Compensation as Social Insurance: A Review of Developments and Proposals

A version of this paper appeared as an article in the Wisconsin Law Review, *January 1963.*

In the twentieth century, legislation and the administrative process have shaped law and the economy to the demands of an industrial society. Two principal features of legislative policy have been, as Ernst Freund said, "the steady growth in the value placed upon individual human personality and the shifting of the idea of the public good from the security of the state and established order to the welfare of the mass of the people. The growth of social legislation combines those two. . . ." [1] And so does the conception of social insurance.

The adaptation of the insurance principle to those hazards of economic insecurity which are so pervasive as to be of concern to the whole society and demand social action is a modern development brought about by conditions of technology and large-scale industrialization. The United States, although today the greatest of all industrial societies, has been neither innovator nor pioneer in developing and utilizing social insurance principles and mechanisms to answer the demands of an industrial society. This is as true of workmen's compensation to protect against the consequences of industrial injuries and diseases as of other forms of social insurance. Workmen's compensation here followed by almost a generation its adoption by Germany and other continental nations, and by more than a decade England's first act.

In England and the United States the changes wrought by the factory system and modern industry strained beyond their capacity for adaptation common law doctrines developed to meet the needs of a simpler economy. Common law rules of liability embody principles of indemnity based upon notions of fault. And under the doctrine of respondeat superior an employer may be vicariously responsible for harm to third persons caused by employees' acts or omissions within the scope of employment. This is variously rationalized as flowing from the employer's right to control the employees' work, as a method of shifting the risk to one who stands to profit and can pass on the cost, and as furnishing an incentive to reduce the hazard.[2]

Neither the early cases in which the principle of respondeat superior developed, nor the policies it reflected, precluded its application to an employee injured through a fellow worker's negligence. But the courts, alarmed by the possible consequences of permitting an employee to recover from his employer for a fellow worker's neglect, added to the employer's existing defense of contributory negligence the defenses of fellow servant's fault and assumed risk.[3]

An economic rationalization for these narrow views, but unsupported by facts, was the notion that a man's pay reflects the hazards of the job, hence the consuming public, and not the worker, ultimately bears the burden of the risk through the price paid for the product.[4] What is more likely, however, is that the courts considered needs of developing industry to have priority over needs of injured workers.[5]

Judicial decisions and employers' liability acts which cut down defenses and mitigated the common law's strictness gave little relief to injured workers; they still had to prove the employer at fault. But the machine processes which increased industrial accidents and their severity at the same time multiplied the number in which no fault could be proved.[6] A new remedy was needed for injuries to employees caused by work.

Great Britain adopted such a remedy, workmen's compensation, in 1897, moved by dissatisfaction with the common law and employers' liability acts and by the example of the successful compensation law which Germany adopted in 1884. Like the German law, the first British act applied only to specified hazardous industries. Until 1906 there was no general coverage in Britain. Unlike the German law, Britain's did not require security for compensation. And it left enforcement to court action by the injured worker; no administrative agency was established.

Experience in the United States under the common law and employers' liability acts resembled England's. Recovery by injured employees was uncertain. Damages, when recovered, were often short of the wage loss suffered. Inadequate settlements were common. The system was wasteful; less than half the money employers paid out because of industrial accidents reached the injured workers. The industrial accident cases which clogged court calendars raised the cost of administering courts and prejudiced other judicial business. The system bred hostility between employers and employees. Workmen's compensation was recommended to protect injured workers and their dependents against wage loss with a minimum of delay, litigation, and expense, and with benefits sufficient to maintain living standards near established levels.[7]

In 1910 New York became the first state to adopt a workmen's compensation act of general application, compulsory for certain especially hazardous jobs, otherwise optional.[8] The compulsory law did not survive a constitutional challenge in *Ives* v. *South Buffalo Ry. Co.*[9] The New York Court of Appeals held that it violated the state's due process clause, a clause similar to that of the Fourteenth Amendment. New York's constitution was quickly amended and a new law enacted in 1913. But the Ives case influenced other state legislatures to enact optional statutes.[10] Only the State of Washington bucked the tide with a mandatory act, which its court sustained;[11] but this influenced few other states. In 1917, when the U. S. Supreme Court dispelled all doubts about the validity of workmen's compensation under the Fourteenth Amendment,[12] a pattern of elective statutes had already become established.

Workmen's compensation may have appeared radical to a court dominated by what Commons called "the classical economic and the common-law theory of individual responsibility, and its correlative, 'no responsibility without fault,'"[13] which the Ives case elevated to a constitutional principle. But the pioneer American workmen's compensation laws were only cautious, tentative steps toward social responsibility. This is scarcely remarkable. The social insurance principle was but newly arrived on these shores. New York's highest court had raised grave doubts of its legitimacy. While social legislation was not a novelty, *Lochner* v. *New York*[14] was notice from the Supreme Court that "the right of free contract" as to labor could be a strong check on exuberant legislatures. Labor was not an organized political force; trade unions numbered among their members less than 7 percent of the nation's total of gainful workers and less than 10 percent of nonfarm gainful workers. More than a fifth of that small segment was outside the American Federation of Labor.[15] Under prodding from President Theodore Roosevelt, Congress in 1908 had enacted a workmen's compensation law for federal employees; but general federal labor legislation under the commerce clause was a quarter of a century away.[16] The Supreme Court's narrow view of the commerce power [17] assured that that could not support a federal workmen's compensation law for private industry. Only state laws were possible. And so whatever the advantages of experimentation by the several states, there were to be expected disparate treatment, uneven and haphazard development, and the depressing influence of interstate competition for industry on workmen's compensation standards.

Most of the pioneer American compensation laws followed the English model of 1897. Only Washington's and Ohio's acts resembled Germany's law, under which employers discharged their obligations by payments to a state insurance fund responsible to workers for compensation. These early laws provided no more than a rudimentary form of social insurance. In most of the states with workmen's compensation acts neither the law's application nor security or insurance for compensation was mandatory. A new substantive condition of liability was established; that was all. To be sure, there were inducements to elect to come under the statute; common law defenses to employee tort actions were either modified or withdrawn. But these inducements were not irresistible, especially where workmen's compensation had to be affirmatively elected rather than negatived.[18]

Coverage of the early laws was limited; even when elective, most acts applied only to specified hazardous industries. None covered all classes of employees. Agricultural workers, domestic help, and casual workers were most commonly excluded. Only a few acts applied to public employment. In general, compensation laws limited indemnity benefits to maximum total amounts, even for permanent disability or death. Cash benefits were usually stated as a percentage of wages at the time of injury, 50 percent being the most common, although a few acts provided for about two-thirds of wages, subject to statutory maximum compensation ranging from $10 weekly in several states up to $15. Several states made no provision at all for medical benefits. Where provided, they were limited in duration or amount or both. Wisconsin provided medical benefits for 90 days, with no amount fixed; this was the most liberal provision. Others ranged from two weeks with $100 maximum to eight weeks and $200.

The English revision of 1906 covered occupational disease, but none of the early American acts did so expressly. Statutes which provided compensation for "injury" could be interpreted to apply to disability from disease as well as from accident. The other acts were expressly limited to "injury by accident."

All except Washington's act required uncompensated waiting periods of one to two weeks, although some did provide retroactive benefits for disabilities lasting longer than a prescribed period.[19]

Workmen's compensation laws caused changes in industrial safety laws and their administration. Earlier safety statutes typically were enforced by criminal sanctions and by employees' recovery of damages for personal injuries. Proof of violation of the statute made out a case of negligence by the employer. Workmen's compensation acts ended enforcement of safety laws through personal injury suits; the compensation remedy for injured employees was exclusive. States established administrative agencies to enforce safety, many with power to make rules to implement general statutory standards.[20]

A notable example of administrative safety regulation was Wisconsin's, under the leadership of Commons. Commons drafted the state's Industrial Commission law and served from 1911 to 1913 as a member of the Commission. "The Industrial Commission law of 1911 had consolidated under one commission the enforcement of the accident compensation law and the drafting and enforcement of safety rules to prevent accidents." Safety committees were organized "consisting of employers and employees with a deputy of the Commission as secretary, for the purpose of drafting rules and regulations to be afterwards given the force of law as 'orders' issued by the state Commission. These orders took the place of the many complicated and detailed statutes enacted by successive legislatures and fought over by lobbies which usually consisted of legal representatives of the conflicting interests. The 'orders' ... were drafted by joint action of employers and employees.... They could be changed, with further experience, by the same committees that had formulated them originally ... [and] they were workable and acceptable to both the employers and employees." There was thus established "not only the administrative system of developing the safety spirit and the educational system of preventing accidents, but also the joint bargaining system between representatives of opposing organized interests, with the state government acting as a conciliator. . . ." [21]

There were few compensation claims during the first two years of the new system, because employers had to elect to be covered; when the law was changed to presume coverage unless employers rejected it, many more workers came under the law. Commons describes how Wisconsin used the first two years to advantage: "The commission turned its energies towards 'accident prevention,' rather than 'accident compensation.' The former 'big stick' factory inspectors, attempting to enforce by criminal prosecutions the impracticable statutory safety laws, were converted into 'safety experts' to advise employers how to reduce accidents. . . . Employers showed that they could do much more voluntarily to prevent accidents than could the state by compulsion. . . ." [22] One of the few aspects of workmen's compensation about which there is no disagreement is the impetus it gave to accident prevention and safety.

It took almost forty years for workmen's compensation to cover every state. The initial momentum carried some forty states by 1920. But twenty-eight years more were needed to cover the rest; it was not until 1948 that the last state, Mississippi, joined the march. Workmen's compensation acts also cover the District of Columbia, Puerto Rico, and employees of the United States. The Longshoremen's and Harbor Workers' Act provides workmen's compensation for maritime workers (other than seamen) who are barred by a vagary of interpretation of the admiralty clause of the Constitution from the reach of state laws.[23] Railroad employees whose work furthers or affects interstate commerce are covered by the Federal Employers' Liability Act; they are also barred from state workmen's compensation.[24]

Early advocates of workmen's compensation looked upon it as a simple and speedy remedy which would reduce litigation over industrial injuries. Their hopes were not realized. While the legal standards of compensable harm are simple—the existence of an employment relation, injury, and a causal connection between the employment and the injury—their application was found not to be.

A relation of employment is central to most social insurance and social legislation. Whether it exists in a given situation is one of the most puzzling problems before English and American courts, and has been for generations. This is because almost numberless variables are inherent in the factual circumstances in which it is asserted services have been performed. Statutes to protect employees have compounded the difficulties by adding to the incentives to disguise the employment relation so that employers will be free of the burdens of regulation or taxation which such statutes impose.[25]

Workmen's compensation has suffered a large share of these confusions. Early compensation cases established criteria for the employment relation derived from the common law master-servant relation and its antithetical independent contractor status which courts developed for purposes of applying principles of respondeat superior and vicarious liability. The crucial issue in those cases was the employer's right to control the employee in the performance of the details of the work.[26]

While the right to control the details of the work may be relevant in deciding who should bear the risk of injuries to a third party, it should have little or no bearing on the issue of liability for the worker's injuries. Unless a person can pass on his risk of injury as a cost of doing business, there seems little reason for workmen's compensation not to cover him as an employee of the enterprise he serves and depends on for his living.

New York's Court of Appeals recognized this a generation ago in *Glielmi* v. *Netherland Dairy Co.*[27] Despite a written "contract adroitly framed to suggest a different relation" by purporting to give a route "salesman" of milk and cream discretion as to prices and terms on which defendant's products could be sold, the court decided that he was an employee entitled to workmen's compensation for injuries suffered when thrown from the defendant's milk wagon he was driving. As Chief Judge Cardozo wrote, claimant "is bound hand and foot as long as he works the route at all, his freedom an illusion, and his independence but a name" because "If he does anything at variance with the will of his employer, its policy or preference, he knows that his contract of employment may be ended overnight." While the court framed its conclusion in terms of the employer's right to control the work, the underlying basis was the employee's lack of economic independence.

Later, and more explicitly, the U. S. Supreme Court also held that economic realities should be the test of an employment relation for purposes of social legislation, rather than "the same sort of technical legal refinement as has characterized the long evolution of the employee-independent contractor dichotomy in the courts for other purposes." [28] Congress later wrote a narrower definition of employment for the Social Security and National Labor Relations acts. But the Supreme Court's views influenced other courts, which have revealed a trend toward an evaluation of the economic realities, even while they continued to rationalize results in terms of a right to control.

Some state legislatures have also accepted economic dependence as a test of the employment relation for workmen's compensation act coverage. For example, Wisconsin provides that "Every independent contractor who does not maintain a separate business and who does not hold himself out to and render service to the public, . . . shall . . . be an employee of any employer . . . for whom he is performing service . . . at the time of injury." [29]

It would be fatuous to assume that the "technical legal refinement . . . of the employee-independent contractor dichotomy" no longer bars workmen's compensation to injured workers. But though the course of judicial decision reveals generally a more realistic view of the employment relation in accord with the purposes of workmen's compensation, courts of course cannot extend workmen's compensation to occupational groups which are excluded by the terms of statutes from their coverage.

What constitutes harm for which workmen's compensation will be awarded, given the requisite employment connection, also has been a much-litigated question. In defining compensable harm most American compensation acts adopted language similar to the English statute's and referred to "personal injury by accident." Quite early it was decided that "injury by accident" meant an unexpected event or mishap, the date and place of which could be definitely fixed. Many early decisions and some later ones rejected the view that an unexpected consequence of an event which was not abnormal might also be "accident." [30] They stressed cause, and not effect, in deciding whether there was compensable harm. Hence many courts denied compensation for "heart attacks," infections, heat prostration, injury from exposure to cold, and other disabilities caused by routine exertions and events, as well as for degenerative conditions and other disabilities which were gradual in their onset and could not be attributed to a clearly defined, unexpected event. [31]

When courts first broke out of the narrow boundaries of the concept of injury by accident, they often rationalized their results in terms of the older theories by finding, for example, that a clearly identifiable event, occurring over and over again, caused a condition of degeneration; [32] or that infection entering a body abnormally and as a result of circumstances which could be fixed at a definite time and place, satisfied a requirement of a traumatic injury; [33] or that it was the unusual or abnormal severity of exertions or conditions which caused injury.[34] It was an easy extension from these subtleties for courts to conclude that unexpected harm resulting from routine conditions met the statutory requirements.[35] And this is the direction in which more and more courts are going.

Legislative action in some states has contributed to these results by deleting "by accident" from the statutory description of compensable harm. Also, occupational disease coverage for disability which is the expected and characteristic consequence of a worker's occupation tends to make anomalous a denial of redress for a disability which is the unexpected consequence of routine conditions of the job.[36]

At the same time, along with their enlarged view of what constitutes accidents, courts have expanded their conception of what constitutes injury. Advances in psychology, psychiatry, and medical science have taught that emotional, nervous, and mental disturbances may cause serious disabilities even though there may be no objective organic injury or pathological symptoms. Many courts have accepted these teachings and upheld compensation to workers suffering from disabling neuroses and other emotional disturbances when the requisite connection with employment has existed.[37]

Fruitful of controversy as questions of employment and compensable disability have been, issues concerned with the causal relation of employment to disability have been far more prolific of controversy. This was foreseen. In 1912, when Bohlen wrote of the problem of drafting workmen's compensation laws and the need to prevent litigation, he suggested that "two things are required: First, that the act can be so construed as to supply definite rules and principles by which a given state of facts, when proved to exist, can be determined to fall within or outside its operations. Such principles must be capable of being formulated in advance so that they may furnish an existing standard by which the rights of the parties under the act can be ascertained. Secondly, such rules and principles should regard as decisive only such facts as are capable of definite and certain proof by witnesses.... Every effort should be made to exclude as decisive of the right of compensation those so-called issues of fact which are in reality matters of inference from physical facts proven to exist." [38]

Bohlen had "examined the decisions of the British courts which have construed and applied the phrase 'arising out of and in the course of employment,'" and concluded that "such general principles as have been formulated for the application of the phrase . . . are at best vague and indefinite save where they are purely arbitrary . . . [and that] there is even grave doubt as to whether any general principles do exist." He concluded that "it is indeed difficult to see how litigation is prevented rather than encouraged by its use," and cautioned against adopting the language of the British act, particularly "arising out of the employment," for "in the construction and the application of" those terms he found that "the greatest dangers exist." [39]

Most American legislatures, however, adopted the terms of the English statute or substantially similar language. A few states omitted "arising out of." The phrase "in the course of the employment" refers to the time, place, and circumstances of the injury. It has been described as less uncertain of interpretation and application than the phrase "arising out of." The latter refers to the origin or cause of the injury, and has been called "the litigious phrase." [40] Usually the time, place, and circumstances of an injury will embrace its cause, although not invariably. An injury which arises out of the employment will arise also in the course of the employment. Factors which at one time were treated as relating to the cause or origin of injury later have been considered to bear on the issue of deviation or departure from the course of employment, to avoid restrictive interpretations of cause or origin. [41] It is questionable whether the two conditions can be so clearly differentiated that the omission of "arising out of" from an act significantly affects the course of judicial decision or the volume of litigation. [42]

Decisions concerned with the course of employment have reflected a growing appreciation that work is a congeries of activities of which only a part is the actual, physical performance of the immediate duties of the job. Courts have found the course of employment to include activities on or near the employer's premises before work has actually started and after it has ended; [43] errands for the employer before and after working hours, even though the route traversed is the employee's normal route between home and place of work; [44] acts on the employer's premises, and sometimes off, for the employee's personal comfort, such as smoking, eating, getting refreshment, and going to the toilet; [45] recreational activities; [46] and horseplay and altercations. [47]

Treatment of the requirement that injury arise out of the employment has followed similar broadening trends. Early cases followed English precedents and sustained awards only if the injured worker could show that the employer's operations or the conditions of the employer's premises caused the injury, that is, that the employee was exposed to some peculiar or increased danger by the nature of his employment. As a corollary to this "peculiar risk" doctrine, compensation was denied if the employee's own conduct added to his danger and caused injury.[48]

The "peculiar risk" doctrine denied compensation to workers injured by exposure to hazards common to the community generally. For example, no compensation would be awarded for a worker struck by lightning while at work unless the presence of steel tools, or work in an isolated, elevated spot, or some other condition of the job increased the danger from lightning. Otherwise the hazard was deemed to be one which the injured worker shared with all members of the community, and the injury was not considered to arise out of the employment.[49] The same reasoning denied compensation to workers injured by hazards of the public streets to which all similarly situated were exposed in like degree;[50] and to employees who suffered heat prostration, or freezing, from natural climatic conditions.[51] And the "added peril" rule, which barred compensation when the employee's actions added to the hazard causing the injury, further limited recovery by importing into workmen's compensation a defense similar in nature to contributory negligence.

Later decisions overruled or modified most of these restrictive rules of causation. The "added peril" defense is now viewed as raising a question whether the worker left the course of his employment. As such, it depends upon the degree and nature of the deviation, and, in some instances, whether there was misconduct by the injured employee.[52] Well-considered modern cases reject "peculiar risk" as a criterion of recovery, and its corollary "common hazard" doctrine.[53] It may be enough that the employment provides the occasion for the injury, and the worker by reason of his job was in fact exposed, when injured, to the conditions which harmed him, whether or not those conditions originated in the business or entirely independently of it, so long as they were not entirely personal to the employee.[54]

In the same spirit, the fact that injury was the result of horseplay or an altercation may no longer be reason mechanically to deny workmen's compensation. As Justice Rutledge pointed out, there has been "a shift in the emphasis from the particular act and its tendency to forward the work to its part as a factor in the general working environment. The shift involved recognition that the environment includes associations as well as conditions, and that associations include the faults and derelictions of human beings as well as their virtues and obediences.... Momentary lapses from duty, as in horseplay, kidding and teasing, which often explode into bursts of temper and fighting ... [are] regarded, not as an isolated event, but as part and parcel of the working environment, whether related directly to the job or to something which is a by-product of the association." "The risks of such associations and conditions ... [are] risks of the employment." [55]

The treatment of occupational disease may not always reflect these trends toward a broad view of causation in workmen's compensation cases. Most states now cover all or some occupational diseases under their workmen's compensation acts. But their courts may not apply the same standards of causation in disease cases that they developed for industrial accidents. For example, in an occupational disease case the New York Court of Appeals expressed concern lest it "transform workmen's compensation into life and health insurance....

"An ailment does not become an occupational disease simply because it is contracted on the employer's premises. It must be one which is commonly regarded as natural to, inhering in, an incident and concomitant of the work in question. There must be a recognizable link between the disease and some distinctive feature of the claimant's job, common to all jobs of that sort.... the disease is not to be deemed occupational if the illness results from unexpected and unforeseen conditions of a job which, by its nature, is no more likely to cause the disease than any other kind of employment." [56]

This makes it difficult to prove that a disease which it is possible to contract in many places and under various circumstances was caused by the employment. Unlike the case of an industrial accident, it may not be enough that the employment provides the occasion for contracting the disease and the worker by reason of his job was in fact exposed to it.[57]

In the main, the trends in workmen's compensation decisions reflect progress. But confusion and uncertainty remain, and the volume of litigation is far from the ideal which was envisioned earlier. In 1912 Bohlen described the wastefulness of the mass of common law industrial accident litigation as "inseparable from any system which requires the proof of fault as a basis to liability and which, being based upon the essentially common law idea of antagonistic litigation, makes the right to recovery depend upon the proof of difficult and uncertain issues of fact." And with prophetic insight he cautioned that if workmen's compensation acts "accomplish no more than the extension of the field within which claims of workmen for compensation may be advanced with a chance of success, but within which the employer may hope equally to resist liability successfully, the waste of litigation instead of being diminished will be increased by widening the area in which it may occur. Such a result would satisfy no one." [58]

Litigation cannot be avoided entirely. Some facts must always be proved, and evidence of them may conflict. Only the litigation process can resolve the conflict and establish the facts. This of course will provide no precedents or general principles which will establish facts or resolve conflicts of evidence in other and different circumstances. And legislation cannot accomplish that either.

A major share of workmen's compensation litigation in the courts does not involve establishing facts or resolving conflicts in evidence. It concerns rather the interpretation and application of the statutory conditions of liability to facts which have been established, and involves issues which, as Bohlen says, "are in reality matters of inference." A question arises here whether this represents what Judge Friendly says is a "failure to develop standards sufficiently definite that decisions will be fairly predictable and that the reasons for them will be understood." [59]

Bohlen advised the framing of more definite statutory conditions of liability to avoid the "waste of litigation." Brown, a generation ago, in his landmark article " 'Arising out of and in the Course of the Employment' in Workmen's Compensation Acts," [60] found confusion rampant. He too suggested that legislatures try to draft more certain and predictable standards; and he offered his analysis to provide a basis for that. In the 1950's the work of Larson [61] provided a similar opportunity.

Legislatures have not responded, and statutory conditions of workmen's compensation liability remain essentially unchanged. This is so even in states like Wisconsin, where the Commons "joint bargaining" approach to labor legislation provides, in the Workmen's Compensation Advisory Committee composed of employer and labor representatives, a natural medium to work out a change.

There may be a more fundamental reason for the volume of workmen's compensation litigation than the failure of legislatures to enact more definite standards of liability. That is the nature of workmen's compensation, which breeds litigiousness just as did the common law of liability for industrial injuries. Workmen's compensation adopts, in one respect, an essentially common law approach to liability.[62] The financial burden is a charge upon the employer of the injured worker or the employer's insurer, affected by loss experience. While this provides an incentive to employers and insurers to promote safety, it also creates adverse pecuniary interests. In that respect it is "based upon the essentially common law idea of antagonistic litigation." The system purports to eliminate considerations of fault. One may question whether it only extends "the field within which claims of workmen for compensation may be advanced with a chance of success, but within which the employer may hope equally to resist liability successfully . . . ."

One should not consider, however, that workmen's compensation litigation has been a completely barren experience. Despite the volume of it, which has so disappointed expectations, and its failures to provide clear rules of liability, a half century of litigation has produced some fruit. The courts found the common law and its rules of tort liability and respondeat superior, which they had evolved, insufficiently plastic to be molded into an effective instrument to deal with problems of work injuries in an industrial society. In the process of resolving controversies over the interpretation and application of workmen's compensation, courts have been able to perform a creative function in moving the law of workmen's compensation toward standards of social insurance.

Legislatures also effected some progress. They reduced uncompensated waiting periods; and most states now provide for compensation retroactive to the date of injury for extended disabilities. They added some benefits, improved others, and of course increased dollar amounts payable. By covering occupational disease, legislation made workmen's compensation more nearly responsive to the needs of an industrial society, although restrictive rules of coverage and causation, both legislative and judge-made, limit progress here. Many states established second-injury funds to protect employers of handicapped workers who are later injured in their employ against greater disability than that caused by the job; and thus enhanced job opportunities for the disabled. The fund pays the difference between the employer's liability, which will be for the injury in his employ, and what the employer would otherwise have been liable for had the employee's entire disability been caused by his job and no part of it by prior disability contributing to it. All states but Louisiana now require insurance or security for compensation. Other advances were made.

But despite the progress from the modest beginnings of fifty years ago, employers and labor are both dissatisfied with workmen's compensation as it enters upon its second half century. Not unnaturally, their animadversions are differently focused. And their historic positions are almost reversed. Workers once looked to the state legislatures for relief from the rigid interpretations of the common law, which denied an effective remedy for industrial injuries. Today it is against state legislatures that labor's principal criticism is directed. Employers and their insurers, on the other hand, object chiefly to administrative and judicial decisions, especially broad judicial readings of injury, accident, and causation.

Concern about improvements which only legislation can achieve relates to coverage, benefits, and administrative provisions. In its economic context workmen's compensation is considered almost to have retrogressed. Once this country's sole example of social insurance, it is now but one item in a fairly comprehensive program of social insurance and negotiated welfare programs. Requirements and standards of adequacy are higher; so are expectations.

Thus, when workmen's compensation was new, only legislation by the separate states met constitutional tests. And differences among states provided opportunities to experiment. Today, differences among states may further interstate competition for industry, and that inhibits advances in the state laws. Rehabilitation of disabled workers was unheard of fifty years ago. Today it is one of the most significant aspects of workmen's compensation, concerned with restoring disabled workers to useful lives and using the labor force effectively. Constitutional doubts may once have justified elective compensation laws. But for forty-five years compulsory coverage has been consistent with the Fourteenth Amendment. The lack of administrative experience under workmen's compensation laws which once exempted employers with fewer than a minimum number of employees, and also excluded agricultural workers, was remedied long ago. Similarly, there has been sufficient experience with financing workmen's compensation to enable full medical benefits to be provided. Statutes of limitations which bar claims before a person can be charged with knowledge they exist are not adequate; nor is a workmen's compensation law which encourages employers not to hire handicapped workers.

The principal of universal coverage is inherent in the concept of social insurance. It may not always be possible to realize, but necessary compromises should not be directed away from the ideal. This latter direction, however, is the one taken by workmen's compensation acts. In no state today are all persons who work for wages covered. In more than half the states employers are exempt who employ fewer than a stated minimum number of employees, ranging from two in four states to fifteen in South Carolina.[63] Yet because they are likely to have lower wage rates, be unorganized, lack the protection of formal safety programs, and work for enterprises with meager financial resources, employees of small businesses probably need workmen's compensation protection even more than do those who work for large employers. Similar considerations apply also to casual workers and domestic help. There is now sufficient administrative experience to permit covering all these workers, even casual domestic help. The home is not free of danger, either to those who live there or to those who work there. About 40 percent of all accidental injuries occur in homes.[64] It should be possible to make adequate arrangements to protect casual domestic workers as well as other part-time workers without excessively burdening householders.

Agricultural workers form another group commonly denied workmen's compensation protection. There are various reasons for this, apart from the effective lobby which succeeds in exempting agriculture and agricultural employment from much social legislation. Traditions of the family farm, a belief that farm work is not hazardous, and notions that coverage of farm workers is not administratively feasible, as well as other factors, all play a part.

But today farming is in fact one of the most hazardous of all occupations. The injury rate for farming exceeds by far the average for all industries, as well as the rates for wholesale and retail trade, manufacturing, public utilities, and service industries. Only transportation, construction, and the mining industries have higher injury rates. The death rate in farming ranks even higher; it is exceeded only by construction and mining industries. Almost one-fourth of the total number of accidental deaths in American industry occur in agriculture; this is more than in any other industry classification.[65] Mechanization and lack of comprehensive safety codes and inspections for farming cause these high hazard rates.

Yet despite the hazards of farm work only eight state compensation acts apply alike to farm and other workers. About ten other states cover only specified agricultural work or farms employing more than a minimum number of workers. Well over half the states provide no coverage at all for farm workers except on a voluntary basis, rejection of which carries no disadvantage to the employer as it does under elective acts. A few states prohibit entirely workmen's compensation for farm workers.[66]

Almost half the states still retain elective laws.[67] Most of these laws, if not all, provide that workmen's compensation will apply unless a contrary election is made. Employers who elect against workmen's compensation are denied certain defenses to workers' tort actions; and employees who elect against coverage are subject to the common law defenses. Complete statistics of coverage are not available, but there is evidence that these inducements to accept workmen's compensation are not irresistible. To the degree that workmen's compensation is rejected, these elective laws can only be considered failures; if workmen's compensation is accepted, the availability of an election seems pointless. On either consideration the election provisions should be struck out and the laws made mandatory; elective acts offer temptations to gamble to the least responsible and least solvent employers.

There are still major gaps in coverage. More than one of every five wage and salary workers is not covered. The proportion covered, about 79 percent, has remained virtually constant since 1944. In 1960 there were about 12,000,000 wage and salary workers outside workmen's compensation.

Other social insurance programs, however, expanded substantially during the same period, 1944–60. The proportion of wage and salary workers under old-age, survivors, and disability insurance rose almost 13 points, from about 75 to almost 88 percent, while under unemployment insurance it rose 5 percent, from about 75 to about 80 percent.[68] Millions of workers came under collectively bargained benefit programs.

Many states limit protection in occupational disease cases in ways which do not apply to industrial accidents. Many compensation acts do not cover all industrial diseases or all harmful consequences of those covered, or do not provide benefits for covered harmful consequences of covered diseases equal to benefits for industrial accidents. Two states make no provision whatever for occupational diseases. About 18 provide compensation only for disability caused by diseases named in a statutory schedule. The remainder, and the District of Columbia, Puerto Rico, and the federal acts purport to provide full occupational disease coverage.[69] But even in some of the states providing full coverage of occupational diseases, as well as in some of the others, coverage may still depend on election.

Schedule coverage is subject to political processes; there must be legislation to expand a statutory schedule of covered diseases. That must overcome indifference and resistance to change, which is not likely until a bad situation becomes notorious, and then it may be too late to help early victims.

Even where there is full occupational disease coverage there may be limits on benefits which do not apply to industrial accidents. Benefits, both cash and medical, are lower in some states for disease than for accident. There are states in which compensation is awarded only for total disability from disease, not for partial. This applies especially in cases of silicosis and other dust diseases.[70] There are other restrictions in disease cases, such as exposure for a minimum number of years, or disability within a given period after the last exposure.

Some of these conditions derive from fears that enactment of occupational disease coverage will create an immediate heavy liability for antecedent disabilities. Others come from concern about difficulties in proving work connection. Onset of disease usually is gradual, and proof of the employment in which it began may be impossible. Passage of time either has proved fears of heavy liability for preexisting conditions exaggerated or has eliminated the possibility of liability for conditions existing before the law. Questions of causation are more difficult, and they expose the adversary character of workmen's compensation. But difficult questions of causation should not be solved or avoided at the expense of disabled employees. There is an element of arbitrariness in putting the full burden of disability on the last employer who contributed to it, but time and the operation of averages will equalize the burdens among the employers in the industry and their insurers.[71]

Requiring total disability as a condition to compensation for disease seems especially harsh. Exclusive remedy provisions of compensation statutes may bar a partially disabled employee from common law remedies against even a negligent employer, even though the worker is discharged because of his disability or transferred to a job carrying lower wages.[72] Better provisions exist in states which grant special benefits for employees who lose or change their jobs because of nondisabling disease.[73]

Occupational disease victims are in other ways less favorably treated than victims of industrial accidents. Time limits for filing claims, which run from date of injury, or last exposure, may bar claims for slowly developing diseases before it is known they exist. Such limitations create more concern as use of atomic energy increases hazards of radiation diseases which may take years to develop. Many states have extended their statutory limitations on claims for radiation diseases.[74] Extensions may not be adequate, however, if the time begins to run before it can be known that a claim exists. A statute of limitations for occupational diseases, and for accidental injuries as well, should not begin to run until the worker can be charged with knowledge of disability, its nature and relation to his employment; and it should provide adequate time thereafter for him to begin proceedings before it bars them.[75]

No workmen's compensation system is complete which fails to make adequate provision for rehabilitation of disabled workers to restore them to useful life and enhance their social and economic well-being. Advances in medical and related sciences make it possible to rehabilitate workers who would have been considered hopelessly disabled a few years ago. Concern of some states with problems of rehabilitation goes back almost to the beginning of workmen's compensation. Then, following World War I, Congress enacted the Vocational Rehabilitation Act of 1920; and a token start was made of federal-state cooperation. The act was amended from time to time and thoroughly revised by the Vocational Rehabilitation Amendments of 1954, which provided grants to states upon a matching basis according to formulas prescribed by Congress.[76] The same year amendments to the Hospital Survey and Construction Act provided federal funds to assist in the building of rehabilitation facilities.[77] These two enactments established a basis for effective cooperation between the Federal Government and the states.

While the Vocational Rehabilitation Act provides for industrially disabled persons as well as others, the federal-state program has not achieved maximum effectiveness for the victims of industrial accidents and diseases because states have lagged in establishing adequate rehabilitation programs under their workmen's compensation acts. To achieve maximum results, steps toward rehabilitation should be begun soon after injury occurs. This requires administrative procedures to identify rehabilitable cases early and refer them to appropriate rehabilitation agencies. Continuance of some physical handicap after rehabilitation should be recognized, or an injured worker may resist rehabilitation. Compensation acts should include adequate provisions for medical care, including artificial appliances, and benefits for the maintenance of the worker and his family during rehabilitation, and travel and other expenses. There should also be an adequate second-injury fund established to overcome reluctance of employers to hire handicapped workers. Lump sum settlements of claims for permanent disability should be carefully scrutinized and controlled. When a claim has been settled by a lump sum payment and the case closed and with it supervision of rehabilitation, the worker's interest in rehabilitation may lapse.[78]

Progress toward effective rehabilitation programs for industrially injured workers has not been rapid. A few states only, and Puerto Rico, operate rehabilitation centers under their compensation laws. Only about half the states include in their compensation acts provisions relating to rehabilitation of industrially disabled workers.[79] And although all but four states have established second- or subsequent-injury funds, less than a third of the states cover all prior disabilities by second-injury provisions. A third or more of the states with second-injury funds cover only cases of loss of an eye or a bodily member. A number of states still permit waivers of compensation for subsequent injuries by employees suffering from an existing physical handicap.[80] To be fully effective in encouraging employment of handicapped workers second-injury funds should cover all prior disability. Waivers should not be sanctioned.

The factors discussed all bear on the adequacy of workmen's compensation. Most of all, however, whether or not a workmen's compensation system is adequate depends on the level of benefits it provides. Critics of workmen's compensation maintain that the level of benefits is the most conspicuously inadequate feature.

The basic purpose of workmen's compensation is to compensate for economic loss, not for physical injury as such. Compensation for economic loss includes cash benefits to workers for impairment of earning capacity and to dependents in cases of death; provision and payment for medical and related services and care; and funeral expenses in death cases. Reparation for pain and suffering has never been included; but other forms of damage, not economic, have been gradually allowed. Thus there are compromises of the compensation principle in the form of benefits awarded in some states for disfigurement, schedule benefits for certain disabilities without proof of wage loss, extra payments for workers injured through their employers' violations of safety regulations and for minors injured while unlawfully employed, and special benefits for rehabilitation.

Benefits to replace wages are usually expressed as a percentage of wages, payable for a prescribed number of weeks. But what a worker will receive is not necessarily the product of these two, for there are maximum weekly rates, and often maximum total amounts, which will limit total payments. Rates of benefits, the periods for which they are payable, and the maximum amounts, vary greatly from state to state, with no evident justification for wide disparities. Clearly they do not accurately reflect regional differences in living costs.

Benefits for losses of bodily members or of their use, and other specific partial disabilities, are prescribed in schedules and are payable regardless of loss of earning capacity. The wide variations among the states in these schedules reveal more than anything else the capriciousness of benefit levels. Thus in Wisconsin an arm lost at the shoulder is worth 500 weeks of the weekly benefit. Next door, in Illinois, its value is at most 300 weeks, while on the other side of Wisconsin, in Iowa, it is only 230 weeks. In Alabama and several other states loss of a hand brings 150 weeks of benefits, in Wisconsin 400, with values elsewhere between these two extremes. There are variations of 300 percent or more between the highest and lowest schedules for injuries.[81]

Translated into dollar values, differences in payments for schedule injuries may be even greater, for often states with high benefit rates provide a longer period of payments than states with low rates. The arm worth almost $22,000 in Wisconsin is worth only $6,300 in Maryland. In Iowa the maximum for an arm is $8,500, in Arizona $33,000, but in Texas only $7,000. A hand which Hawaii values at more than $27,000 is worth less than $5,000 in Alabama. The total loss of hearing on which Alabama puts a maximum value of $4,950 and Texas $300 more, Arizona values at $33,000 and Hawaii at $22,500. In nine states compensation for temporary disability is part of the allowance for permanent partial disability, hence if paid it may be deducted from the latter; in the other states compensation for temporary disability is in addition.[82]

Benefits for temporary total disabilities are similarly arbitrary. It is generally considered that benefits should equal about two-thirds of wages, to prevent drastic reduction of living standards while at the same time providing little incentive to malinger. Thus, the nominal rate of benefits is about 65 percent of wages in all but a few states. But limits on the amount of wages which may be considered or the benefits which may be awarded in almost all states reduce maximum weekly benefits far below two-thirds of average weekly wages. Indeed, maximum weekly benefits reach 65 percent of average weekly wages in only five states, the District of Columbia, and Puerto Rico. In 23 states such benefits are less than 50 percent of average weekly wages.[83] Income and social security taxes are not withheld from workmen's compensation. Even considering this, however, one finds that in a majority of the states benefits are still under recommended ratios.

In about half the states maximum weekly benefits for total disability are $40 or less; and in about three-quarters of the states not more than $50 weekly.[84] For 1960, gross average weekly earnings of production workers in manufacturing were about $90. Deducting social security and income taxes for which such workers are liable leaves about $73 as the net spendable average weekly earnings for such a worker with no dependents, and about $81 for one with three dependents.[85] In mining, contract construction, and transportation and public utilities average wages are much higher. Only in retail trade, service industries, and banking are average wages significantly lower than for production workers in manufacturing.[86] Maximum weekly benefits in a majority of the states today represent a smaller proportion of average weekly wages than they did in 1911. Then maximum weekly benefits were $10 to $15,[87] and average annual earnings in all industries, excluding farming, were $629.[88]

Although permanent disability presupposes disablement for life, in fewer than half the states are benefits for permanent partial disability paid for life. In the other states "permanent" may mean no longer than about six years (300 weeks) in about eight states, close to twenty years (1,000 weeks) in Wisconsin. While the record for permanent total disability is a little better, more than one-fourth of the states do not provide benefits for life.[89]

Criticisms of benefits in disability cases also apply to provisions for dependents in cases of fatal injuries. In only about nine or ten states, and under the federal laws, are benefits provided for the duration of dependency. About two-thirds of the states limit the duration of death benefits to periods which range from 300 weeks in three or four states to 600 weeks in Rhode Island. A number of other states, while expressing no time limit, achieve it by limiting total benefits payable.[90]

Benefits are also affected by waiting periods. All states but Oregon provide for an uncompensated waiting period before an injured worker becomes eligible for compensation. The longest waiting period is seven days, but this is prescribed in well over half the states. All but three states provide retroactive compensation for the waiting period for disabilities which last longer than periods prescribed. These range from five days in three states to 49 days in California. In more than twenty states disability must continue for four weeks or longer to entitle an injured worker to retroactive compensation for the waiting period.[91] While administrative convenience may justify a waiting period of a few days, neither administrative convenience nor control of malingering justifies the long period so many states require as a condition to retroactive payment of benefits for the waiting period.

Medical benefits have come a long way from the meager allowances of the early acts, which were scarcely more than tokens. About three-quarters of the states, the federal laws, and Puerto Rico today provide unlimited medical care in industrial accident cases, either by express terms of their statutes or through administrative discretion. Several of these states, however, limit medical benefits in occupational disease cases. In the other 25 percent of the states there are limits, some quite narrow, on the amount of medical benefits which may be awarded, or on the period for which they may be paid, or on both.[92]

There is probably little serious disagreement with these evaluations of workmen's compensation. Employers and insurers, in the main, show no disposition to deny that many workmen's compensation statutes are inadequate in some respects mentioned, and that some are inadequate in many respects.

But the situation is different with regard to administrative and judicial decisions relating to liability. Unlike organized labor, which on the whole probably finds liberal trends in administrative and judicial decisions satisfactory, employers and insurers look upon them, in S. Bruce Black's words, as "inconsistent with the basic concepts of the legal system under which they were made, so that the system itself must be strained to accommodate them." [93] This reflects a view that the workmen's compensation system was designed as "a special ad hoc arrangement, under which one group of rights has been substituted for a preexisting group without offering a precedent for the creation of wholly new rights." The course of decision criticized, however, is described as proceeding upon the unspoken premise "that the system is part of an organic pattern of social legislation, which must . . . grow with the other elements of the pattern . . . ," and revealing a "tendency of administrators and courts to convert workmen's compensation in practice into what might be called social compensation." These regrettable tendencies, it is suggested, are often motivated by a desire to redress legislative failures to correct inadequate benefits; surely a dubious practice. They are abetted by claimants' lawyers, whose arguments stretch workmen's compensation beyond its uttermost limits.[94]

The common law, it is agreed, is sufficiently malleable to accommodate such modifications, but a system of statutory liability is said not to be. Stresses in the latter show up in the failure of the level of costs to coincide with declining injury rates, and in lax administration which approves marginal claims and tends to encourage fraudulent ones.[95] Workmen's compensation varies from state to state. Hence enterprises in states in which overliberal tendencies are especially marked must carry a burden of costs which may affect their competitive position.

The logic of these views suggests to Black "tightening the compensation laws so as to define compensable injuries more exactly and narrowly, excluding injuries suffered through acts of God and aggravation of pre-existing ailments, and also, probably, reversing the trend toward compensation for nontraumatic injuries." [96]

Whether or not one believes the workmen's compensation system can survive liberal trends in interpretation, one can scarcely credit that it could survive such drastic regression. But a test is hardly likely. Political currents are moving too swiftly toward greater social responsibility, not less, to admit of legislation so narrowing workmen's compensation, even if sweetened by higher benefits.

A reversal of the course of administrative and judicial decision is even less likely. Granted that "Statute law is . . . less plastic" than the common law,[97] statutory interpretation, especially of social legislation, is a dynamic process. It does not proceed in an impenetrable isolation, untouched and unaffected by changing public policy.[98]

The factor of costs is a relevant consideration. Workmen's compensation benefits and expenditures to provide them have steadily increased. Since the end of World War II benefits rose from $434 million in 1946 to $1,003 million in 1956,[99] and up to $1,290 million in 1960 (including figures for Alaska and Hawaii, not included in earlier totals).[100] During the same period employers' costs, which include overhead or "expense loading" in addition to benefits, went from $726 million in 1946 to $1,630 million in 1956,[101] and $2,019 million in 1960.[102]

But absolute figures as to costs do not tell the whole story. When workmen's compensation statistics, as Skolnik states, "are related to other indexes of economic change, it is evident that the real position of the program has changed very little.... Aggregate benefit payments since 1946 [and to 1956] have risen by 130 percent, but as a percentage of payroll have remained at slightly less than 0.6 percent. The annual cost to employers has stayed at slightly less than 1 percent of payroll ...." [103] In 1960 employers' costs exceeding $2 billion represented about .97 percent of covered payroll. In 1959 the ratio was .93 percent, and in 1958 .95 percent.[104] Workmen's compensation costs in this respect have proved to be fairly stable.

Ratios drawn from these aggregates, however, do not reveal the variations from year to year in each state and the differences from state to state in benefit payments and expenditures. The latter will reflect judicial and administrative policies on issues of legal liability as well as statutory benefit levels, safety programs, rehabilitation experience, administration, and other factors. Benefit levels and administrative and judicial policies do bear directly on employers' costs, even though costs are not solely a function of them.[105] Hence they may affect competition among enterprises in different states. Some state development agencies consider lower workmen's compensation costs significant enough to advertise to attract new industries.[106]

It is hardly novel that competition among the states for industry depresses labor standards and inhibits improvements in them. Congress has often acted on that assumption in enacting national labor laws.[107] So long as workmen's compensation continues as a system solely controlled by the states, its crazy quilt quality will be preserved and reinforced by interstate competition for industry, and improvements in benefits and other conditions reflected in costs are likely not to keep up with the need for them.

Failure by the states to do better with workmen's compensation has shaken confidence in it generally as a system of social insurance; and the position of the railroad workers may be a case in point. For many years the railroad workers' unions unsuccessfully sought workmen's compensation to replace the Federal Employers' Liability Act.[108] The latter authorizes employees injured by their employers' negligence to sue at law for damages, and denies defenses of contributory negligence and assumption of risk, the former merely reducing damages. Carriers opposed workmen's compensation. But positions are now reversed, and the railroad unions are content with FELA,[109] a remedy members of the Supreme Court call "obsolete and uncivilized," "crude, archaic," "unjust," "cruel and wasteful." [110]

In part, the union position is the result of the Supreme Court's liberal rule under FELA that "the test of a jury case is simply whether the proofs justify with reason the conclusion that employer negligence played any part, even the slightest, in producing the injury or death for which damages are sought," which is "significantly different from the ordinary common-law negligence action," and makes it possible to reach the jury with a case which in an "ordinary common-law negligence action" might not survive defendant's motion for a directed verdict.[111] And large jury verdicts are not uncommon in FELA cases.

As Jerome Pollack points out, however, spectacularly large verdicts go to only a few, after years of litigation which drains off a substantial share of the damages.[112] But what has happened in the states to workmen's compensation doubtless gives railroad workers a jaundiced view of that remedy.[113]

Over the past half century workmen's compensation took redress of work injuries out of the jungle and brought to industrial and commercial workers and employers the benefits of legal order. But today a system of fifty separate state laws, with no mandatory external standards of adequacy, is no more sensible than would be withdrawal of the Federal Government from regulation of wages and hours and collective bargaining. At the very least, states which have made their workmen's compensation adequate, or which are disposed to do so, need help from the national government. Such cooperative federalism strengthens state initiative.[114] Federal leadership through exhortation or example is not enough. During the latter half of the 1950's the U. S. Department of Labor sponsored what, in effect, was a model workmen's compensation law for the states. The tangible results of this seem to have been minimal. The case is strong for federal workmen's compensation, or at least federal standards. Federal workmen's compensation for workers subject to radiation injuries was the subject of bills introduced in the 87th Congress following hearings by a subcommittee of the Joint Committee on Atomic Energy.[115]

There are no longer constitutional obstacles to federal workmen's compensation or federal standards. The narrow 1911 reading of the

Constitution which made impossible a general federal workmen's compensation law under the commerce clause covering virtually all industry, and not merely transportation, was changed a quarter of a century ago.[116] Despite the broad reach of the interstate commerce power, however, federal workmen's compensation resting on it would perforce leave some workers uncovered.

Moreover, one must question whether supplanting the state agencies is a politically feasible alternative, even were it to be sound in principle.[117] If not, a more practicable means to this end borrows from the unemployment compensation experience. Mandatory minimum federal workmen's compensation standards for state laws could achieve the end desired and preserve the present system of state operations. Unemployment compensation achieves minimum standards of administration through the taxing power of Congress and a credit against the federal unemployment tax for state taxes.[118] In a similar approach to workmen's compensation which, unlike unemployment insurance, is privately financed, Congress might condition an employer's federal income tax deductions for workmen's compensation expenditures upon the state law's complying with minimum federal standards.[119] Or, if this be considered constitutionally doubtful, compliance with the federal standards could at least be made a condition for receipt of federal grants which Congress could provide to assist administration of the state laws.

But federal standards will not solve the problem, suggested by some students of the subject, of whether workmen's compensation has outlived its usefulness and should be replaced.[120] Workmen's compensation, no longer the sole social insurance program, may now more or less overlap total and permanent disability benefits under the Social Security Act,[121] or temporary disability insurance programs established by law [122] or by collective bargaining, or even unemployment compensation. It may impinge on still other programs. In such a context different considerations from those formerly relevant may apply in evaluating workmen's compensation.

Great Britain, in 1946, decided to abolish workmen's compensation. Effective 1948, the National Insurance (Industrial Injuries) Act replaced it with a system of compulsory contributory government insurance within the comprehensive National Insurance program, and providing higher benefits than for unemployment and sickness.[123]

Britain also provides a right of action for damages to an employee injured by his employer's tort. Fellow servant's negligence is not a defense,[124] nor is contributory negligence which may be proved only to reduce damages.[125] The right to damages is in addition to the government insurance, but in certain cases damages may be reduced by half the value of the insurance because the employer pays part of the cost of it.[126] Unlike American laws, Britain's workmen's compensation act did not bar damage suits by an injured worker against his employer, but before the 1948 changes the employee was permitted only to elect between compensation and an action for damages.[127]

Proposals have been made for employer's liability acts to supplement American workmen's compensation, but no such legislation has been enacted.[128] And for many years the Social Security Administration recommended "a comprehensive basic national system of contributory social insurance ... [which] would include insurance against wage loss in periods of disability and against costs of medical care ... as well as old-age and survivors insurance and unemployment insurance." [129] Only insurance against total and permanent disability has been adopted.

Workmen's compensation and its place and future in our economy present problems which deserve careful study and consideration. The problems are national in scope and significance, and should be studied on that basis under the leadership of the Federal Government. Random local investigations cannot accomplish what the situation requires. Employer and employee organizations, insurers, and state governments should all cooperate with an agency of the Federal Government in this examination. The Committee on Economic Security of the 1930's, from whose work emerged plans for the Social Security program, provides a model which might be adapted to a study of workmen's compensation and its alternatives.

Notes

1 Freund, *Standards of American Legislation* 22 (Univ. of Chicago Press, 1917).
2 Douglas, Vicarious Liability and Administration of Risk, 38 Yale L. J. 584 (1929); Steffen, Independent Contractor and the Good Life, 2 U. Chi. L. Rev. 501 (1935).
3 Priestley v. Fowler, 3 M. & W. 1, 150 Eng. Rep. 1030 (1837); Farwell v. Boston & W. Ry., 45 Mass. (4 Met.) 49 (1842).
4 Wambaugh, Workmen's Compensation Acts: Their Theory and Their Constitutionality, 25 Harv. L. Rev. 129, 130 (1911).
5 Cf. Freund, *Standards of American Legislation* 21 (1917): "The imperative necessity of developing economic resources retarded adequate

protection against mechanical dangers until it was possible to combine safety with the effective carrying on of industry; the former had to yield to the latter. . . ."

6 Haferbecker, *Wisconsin Labor Laws* 39 (1958), refers to the results of a study reported in the 1907–08 biennial report of the Wisconsin Bureau of Labor and Industrial Statistics revealing that 52% of the accidents studied were due to the hazards of the industry, more than the total of those due to the fault of the employer (11%) and to the employees' lack of care (24%).

7 E.g. First Report to the Legislature of the State of New York by the Commission Appointed under Chapter 518 of the Laws of 1909 to Inquire into the Question of Employers' Liability and Other Matters 68–69 (March 19, 1910), Documents of the Senate of the State of New York, 133d Sess., 1910, Vol. 25, No. 38.

8 *New York Laws* 1910, chaps. 352, 674.

9 201 N.Y. 271, 94 N.E. 431 (1911).

10 California, Illinois, Kansas, Massachusetts, New Hampshire, New Jersey, Nevada, Ohio, and Wisconsin. Commons, who "participated in the agitation, enactment, and, for the first two years, in the administration of the accident compensation and safety laws," writes that "when a committee of the Wisconsin legislature, after 1909, took up the matter of drafting a bill for accident insurance, they determined to avoid unconstitutionality by proposing a 'voluntary' bill, wherein only those employers who registered with the [Industrial] Commission their acceptance of the new law were deemed to be 'under the law.'" *Institutional Economics* 854–55 Macmillan, 1934; Univ. of Wisconsin Press, 1959).

11 State ex rel. Davis-Smith Co. v. Clausen, 65 Wash. 156, 117 Pac. 1101 (1911).

12 The Court upheld a mandatory law, New York Central R.R. v. White, 243 U.S. 188 (1917); an elective act, Hawkins v. Bleakly, 243 U.S. 210 (1917); and Washington's exclusive state fund system, Mountain Timber Co. v. Washington, 243 U.S. 219 (1917).

13 Commons, *Institutional Economics* 855.

14 198 U.S. 45 (1905).

15 In 1911 the total of gainful workers was about 38,000,000 and non-farm gainful workers about 26,000,000. Union membership included about 2,300,000, of which 1,800,000 were in AFL unions. U. S. Bureau of the Census, Historical Statistics of the United States, Colonial Times to 1957, Series D 36–45, p. 72, D 735–40, p. 97 (1960).

16 The National Labor Relations Act (popularly known as the Wagner Act), 49 Stat. 449 (1935), 29 U.S.C. § 151 (1959), was approved July 5, 1935.

17 The Employers' Liability Cases, 207 U.S. 463 (1908).

18 Commons, *Institutional Economics* 856, 857.

19 Boyd, *Workmen's Compensation* (1913) contains the text and an analysis of the early workmen's compensation laws.

20 Aaron, *The Employment Relation and the Law* 110 (1957).

21 Commons, *Institutional Economics* 2, 856–58.

22 Ibid. 856.

23 Southern Pacific Co. v. Jensen, 244 U.S. 205 (1917).
24 New York Central R.R. v. Winfield, 244 U.S. 147 (1917).
25 Wolfe, Determination of Employer-Employee Relationships in Social Legislation, 41 Colum. L. Rev. 1015 (1941).
26 Balinski v. Press Publishing Co., 118 Pa. Super. 89, 179 Atl. 897 (1935).
27 254 N.Y. 60, 62–63, 171 N.E. 906–07 (1930).
28 NLRB v. Hearst Publications, Inc., 322 U.S. 111 (1944); accord, United States v. Silk, Harrison v. Greyvan Lines, Inc., 331 U.S. 704 (1947); Rutherford Food Corp. v. McComb, 331 U.S. 722 (1947).
29 Wis. Stat. § 102.07(8) (1961).
30 E.g., Wieda v. American Box Board Co., 343 Mich. 182, 72 N.W. 2d 13 (1955) and cases cited.
31 Wieda v. American Box Board Co., 343 Mich. 182, 72 N.W.2d 13 (1955) and cases cited (heart attack); Jeffreyes v. Sager Co., 233 N.Y. 536, 135 N.E. 907 (1922) (infection); Bailey v. Henry Knapp & Co., 284 Mich. 395, 279 N.W. 875 (1938) (heat stroke); Horn v. Pals & Solow, 299 N.Y. 575, 86 N.E.2d 103 (1949); Stevens v. Village of Driggs, 65 Idaho 733, 152 P.2d 891 (1944) (exposure to cold). Liondale Bleach, Dye & Paint Works v. Riker, 85 N.J.L. 426, 89 Atl. 929 (Sup. Ct. 1914); Di Maria v. Curtiss-Wright Corp., 134 N.J.L. 524, 49 A.2d 243 (1946), affirmed 135 N.J.L. 490, 52 A.2d 698 (1947); Young v. Melrose Granite Co., 152 Minn. 512, 189 N.W. 426 (1922); Schmitt v. Industrial Comm'n, 224 Wis. 531, 272 N.W. 486 (1937) degenerative disabilities.
32 E.g. Atlas Coal Corp. v. Scales, 198 Okla. 658, 185 P.2d 177 (1947) (miner's infected knee from bruises caused by kneeling on rough surfaces over period of time); Webb v. New Mexico Publishing Co., 47 N.M. 279, 141 P.2d 333 (1943) (dermatitis from frequent washing with soap supplied by employer to which employee was unknowingly allergic).
33 Connelly v. Hunt Furniture Co., 240 N.Y. 83, 147 N.E. 366 (1925) (embalmer's helper died from infection caused by scratching pimple on neck with finger infected through handling a gangrenous corpse); McRae v. U.C.C. 217 N.C. 769, 9 S.E.2d 595 (1940) (tubercular fellow employee coughed and some sputum flew into claimant's mouth and he contracted tuberculosis). See also 1 Larson, *Workmen's Compensation Law* § 40.20 (1952).
34 Yellow Cab Co. v. Industrial Comm'n, 210 Wis. 460, 246 N.W. 689 (1933) (taxi starter exposed to extreme cold after becoming heated while changing a tire).
35 Brown v. Industrial Comm'n, 9 Wis. 2d 555, 101 N.W.2d 788 (1960); Wisconsin Appleton Co. v. Industrial Comm'n, 269 Wis. 312, 69 N.W.2d 433 (1955); Mottonen v. Calumet & Hecla, Inc., 360 Mich. 659, 105 N.W.2d 33 (1960); Dwyer v. Ford Motor Co., 36 N.J. 487, 178 A.2d 161 (1962). In Dwyer's case compensation was awarded for the death of a factory laborer who had suffered from angina pectoris and coronary insufficiency for about two years. He suffered a severe attack while at home on a Sunday and did not return to work

until the following Tuesday. He did the usual work of his job that day, and died shortly after returning home from work.

36 1 Larson, *Workmen's Compensation Law* § 40.60 (1952).

37 Carter v. General Motors Corp., 361 Mich. 577, 106 N.W.2d 105 (1960); Johnson v. Industrial Comm'n, 5 Wis.2d 584, 93 N.W.2d 439 (1958); Roberts v. Dredge Fund, 71 Idaho 380, 232 P.2d 975 (1951); Charnon's Case, 321 Mass. 694, 75 N.E.2d 511 (1947); Burlington Mills Corp. v. Hagood, 177 Va. 204, 13 S.E.2d 291 (1941).

38 Bohlen, A Problem in the Drafting of Workmen's Compensation Acts, 25 Harvard L. Rev. 517, 537 (1912).

39 Ibid. 537, 538, 546.

40 Horovitz, The Litigious Phrase: "Arising out of" Employment, 3 NACCA L. J. 15 (1949).

41 1 Larson, *Workmen's Compensation Law* §§ 6.10, 23.61, 29.10 (1952).

42 Cf. Brown, "Arising out of and in the Course of the Employment" in Workmen's Compensation Acts, 7 Wis. L. Rev. 15, 17–18 (1931); Dodd, *Administration of Workmen's Compensation* 682–83 (1936); 1 Larson, *Workmen's Compensation Law* §§ 6.10, 23.61 (1952).

43 Cudahy Packing Co. v. Parramore, 263 U.S. 418 (1923); Bountiful Brick Co. v. Giles, 276 U.S. 154 (1928); Simonson v. Knight, 174 Minn. 491, 219 N.W. 869 (1928); Pacific Indemnity Co. v. Industrial Accident Comm'n, 28 Cal.2d 329 170 P.2d 18 (1946); State v. Industrial Comm'n, 4 Wis.2d 472, 90 N.W.2d 397 (1958).

44 Bitker Cloak & Suit Co. v. Miller, 241 Wis. 653, 6 N.W.2d 664 (1942). But cf. Bennett v. Marine Works, Inc., 273 N.Y. 429, 7 N.E.2d 847 (1937).

45 Bradford's Case, 319 Mass. 621, 67 N.E.2d 149 (1946); Charon's Case, 321 Mass. 694, 75 N.E.2d 511 (1947); Vendome Hotel, Inc. v. Gibson, 122 Ind. App. 604, 105 N.E.2d 906 (1952); American Motors Corp. v. Industrial Comm'n, 1 Wis.2d 261, 83 N.W.2d 714 (1957); Krause v. Western Casualty & Surety Co., 3 Wis.2d 61, 87 N.W.2d 875 (1958); Van Roy v. Industrial Comm'n, 5 Wis.2d 416, 92 N.W.2d 818 (1958). Clemons, Workmen's Compensation: The Personal Comfort Doctrine, 1960 Wis. L. Rev. 91.

46 Linderman v. Cownie Furs, 234 Iowa 708, 13 N.W.2d 677 (1944); Dodge v. Wm. J. Keller, Inc., 304 N.Y. 792, 109 N.E.2d 85 (1952); Tedesco v. General Electric Co., 305 N.Y. 544, 114 N.E.2d 33 (1953).

47 Leonbruno v. Champlain Silk Mills, 229 N.Y. 470, 128 N.E. 711 (1920); Hartford Accident & Indemnity Co. v. Cardillo, 112 F.2d 11 (D.C. Cir. 1940); Newell v. Moreau, 94 N.H. 439, 55 A.2d 476 (1947); Nash-Kelvinator Corp. v. Industrial Comm'n, 266 Wis. 81, 62 N.W.2d 567 (1954); cf. Ognibene v. Rochester Mfg. Co., 298 N.Y. 85, 80 N.E.2d 749 (1948).

48 Plumb v. Cobden Flour Mills Co., Ltd. [1914], A.C. 62; Hurley's Case, 240 Mass. 357, 134 N.E. 252 (1922); cf. McNicol's Case, 215 Mass. 497, 102 N.E. 697 (1913).

49 Kroon v. Kalamazoo County Road Comm'n, 339 Mich. 1, 62 N.W.2d 641 (1954); Stokely Foods, Inc. v. Industrial Comm'n, 264 Wis. 102, 58 N.W.2d 285 (1953); Carey v. Industrial Comm'n, 181 Wis. 253,

194 N.W. 339 (1923); Hoenig v. Industrial Comm'n, 159 Wis. 646, 150 N.W. 996 (1915); cf. Mixon v. Kalman, 133 N.J.L. 113, 42 A.2d 309 (Ct. Err. & App. 1945).

50 Walborn v. General Fireproofing Co., 147 Ohio St. 507, 72 N.E.2d 95 (1947); cf. Chicago v. Industrial Comm'n, 389 Ill. 592, 60 N.E.2d 212 (1945).

51 Lewis v. Industrial Comm'n, 178 Wis. 449, 190 N.W. 101 (1922); Ceisel v. Industrial Comm'n, 400 Ill. 574, 81 N.E.2d 506 (1948); Ellingson Lumber Co. v. Industrial Comm'n, 168 Wis. 227, 169 N.W. 568 (1918).

52 Sheboygan Airway, Inc. v. Industrial Comm'n, 209 Wis. 352, 245 N.W. 178 (1932); 1 Larson, *Workmen's Compensation Law* § 30.22 (1952).

53 Associated Indemnity Corp. v. Industrial Accident Comm'n, 18 Cal.2d 40, 112 P.2d 615 (1941).

54 Cf. Nash-Kelvinator Corp. v. Industrial Comm'n, 266 Wis. 81, 62 N.W.2d 567 (1954); O'Leary v. Brown-Pacific-Maxon, Inc., 340 U.S. 504 (1951); Christiansen v. Hill Reproduction Co., 262 App. Div. 379, 29 N.Y.S.2d 24 (1941), affirmed 287 N.Y. 690, 39 N.E.2d 300 (1942); London Guarantee & Accident Co. v. McCoy, 97 Colo. 13, 45 P.2d 900 (1935).

55 Hartford Accident & Indemnity Co. v. Cardillo, 112 F.2d 11, 15–16 (D.C. Cir. 1940).

56 Harman v. Republic Aviation Corp., 298 N.Y. 285, 288, 82 N.E.2d 785 (1948).

57 Ibid.; Champion v. W. & L. E. Gurley, 299 N.Y. 406, 87 N.E.2d 430 (1949); Buckley v. Gallagher Bros. Sand & Gravel Corp., 300 N.Y. 447, 92 N.E.2d 38 (1950); Detenbeck v. General Motors Corp., 309 N.Y. 558, 132 N.E.2d 840 (1956); cf. Gilbert Pacific, Inc. v. Donovan, 198 F. Supp. 297 (E.D. La. 1961).

58 Bohlen, A Problem in the Drafting of Workmen's Compensation Acts, 25 Harv. L. Rev. 328 (1912).

59 Friendly, The Federal Administrative Agencies: The Need for Better Definition of Standards, 75 Harv. L. Rev. 863, 867 (1962).

60 7 Wis. L. Rev. 15, 20–23 (1931).

61 Larson, *Workmen's Compensation Law* (1952).

62 Cf. Beveridge, *Social Insurance and Allied Services* ("The Beveridge Report") 35–36 (Macmillan, 1942); Lenhoff, Social Insurance Replacing Workmen's Compensation in England, 5 NACCA L. J. 49 (1950); Somers and Somers, *Workmen's Compensation* 178–84 (1954).

63 U. S. Dep't of Labor, Bureau of Labor Standards, Bull. 161, State Workmen's Compensation Laws as of May 1960, 13, Table 2; Chamber of Commerce of the U.S., Analysis of Workmen's Compensation Laws as of January 1962, 25, Chart IV (a).

64 U. S. Bureau of the Census, Statistical Abstract of the United States: 1960, 68, Table No. 75.

65 U. S. Dep't of Labor, Bureau of Labor Standards, Bull. 206, Agricultural Workers and Workmen's Compensation, 3 (June 1959).

66 Chamber of Commerce of the U.S., op. cit. 25, Chart IV (a);

U. S. Dep't of Labor, Bureau of Labor Standards, Bull. 161, State Workmen's Compensation Laws as of May 1960, 16.

67 Chamber of Commerce of the U.S., op. cit. 25, Chart IV (a).

68 U. S. Dep't of Health, Education, and Welfare, Social Security Bull., Annual Statistical Supplement, 1960, 3, Table 4.

69 Chamber of Commerce of the U.S., op. cit. 29, Chart V; U. S. Dep't of Labor, Bureau of Labor Standards, Bull. 161, State Workmen's Compensation Laws as of May 1960, 17–20, Table 4.

70 Chamber of Commerce of the U.S., op. cit. 33, Chart VI; U. S. Dep't of Labor, Bureau of Labor Standards, Bull. 161, State Workmen's Compensation Laws as of May 1960, 19–20.

71 Employers Mutual Liab. Ins. Co. v. McCormick, 195 Wis. 410, 217 N.W. 738 (1928).

72 Moffett v. Harbison-Walker Refractories Co., 339 Pa. 112, 14 A.2d 111 (1940); Masich v. U. S. Smelting, Refining & Mining Co., 113 Utah 101, 191 P.2d 612 (1948), appeal dismissed, 335 U.S. 866 (1948).

73 E.g. Wis. Stat. § 102.565 (1961).

74 U. S. Dep't of Labor, Bureau of Labor Standards, Bull. 161, State Workmen's Compensation Laws as of May 1960, 19; Supplement to State Workmen's Compensation Laws, 5–7 (Dec. 1961).

75 2 Larson, *Workmen's Compensation Law* §§ 78.42, 78.52 (1952). The question can arise in respect of injuries with latent consequences as well as disease. A minor injury, causing no interruption of work, years later may become seriously disabling, after the claim period has expired. In Zabkowicz v. Industrial Comm'n, 264 Wis. 317, 58 N.W.2d 677 (1953), in such a case, the court held that Wis. Stat. § 102.12 (1951), providing for filing within two years from date of injury "or from the date the employe ... knew or ought to have known the nature of the disability and its relation to the employment," applied to industrial disease and not to accident, and barred the claim for consequences arising about three years after the apparently minor injury, even though the employee had consulted a physician immediately after he was hurt and was assured that he had suffered only superficial bruises. But cf. Acme Body Works v. Industrial Comm'n, 204 Wis. 493, 234 N.W. 756 (1931).

A related problem concerns continuing jurisdiction to reopen a case to increase or reduce an award on the basis of later evidence. For example, Wis. Stat. § 102.18 (1961) provides that the Industrial Commission may make interlocutory awards pending final determination of any controversy before it. This has been interpreted to require evidence that the injured employee's disability might increase in the future, otherwise an award, even though stated to be interlocutory, would be considered final and the attempted reservation of jurisdiction to make a further award of no effect. California Packing Co. v. Industrial Comm'n, 270 Wis. 72, 70 N.W.2d 200 (1955). But where there is evidence that the disability is likely to increase in the future, the Commission may reserve jurisdiction to make a further award. Thomas v. Industrial Comm'n, 4 Wis.2d 477, 90 N.W.2d 393 (1958). Power to reserve continuing jurisdiction is desirable, although there are abuses which must be guarded against. See Somers and Somers, *Workmen's Compensation* 163–64 (1954), for discussion of arguments for and against it.

76 68 Stat. 652 (1954), 29 U.S.C. §§ 31–42 (1958).

77 68 Stat. 461 (1954), 42 U.S.C. §§ 291o–v (1958).

78 Somers and Somers, *Workmen's Compensation* chap. 7 (1954); Pollack, Medical Care and Rehabilitation under Workmen's Compensation, 45 Am. J. Public Health 644 (1955).

79 U. S. Dep't of Labor, Bureau of Labor Standards, Bull. 161, State Workmen's Compensation Laws as of May 1960, 54–62, Table 14; U. S. Chamber of Commerce, Analysis of Workmen's Compensation Laws as of January 1962, 45, Chart IX.

80 U. S. Dep't of Labor, Bureau of Labor Standards, Bull. 161, State Workmen's Compensation Laws as of May 1960, 62–64; U. S. Chamber of Commerce, op. cit. 41, Chart VIII.

81 U. S. Dep't of Labor, Bureau of Labor Standards, Bull. 161, State Workmen's Compensation Laws as of May 1960, 35, Table 9.

82 U. S. Chamber of Commerce, op. cit. 18, Chart III.

83 U. S. Dep't of Labor, Bureau of Labor Standards, Bull. 212, Revised December 1961, State Workmen's Compensation Laws 34–37.

84 U. S. Chamber of Commerce, op. cit. 16, Chart II.

85 U. S. Bureau of the Census, Statistical Abstract of the United States: 1960, 222, Table No. 285.

86 Ibid. 224, Table No. 287.

87 2 Boyd, *Workmen's Compensation* §§ 415–16 (1913).

88 U. S. Bureau of the Census, Historical Statistics of the United States, Colonial Times to 1957, 91, Series D 603–17 (1960).

89 U. S. Dep't of Labor, Bureau of Labor Standards, Bull. 161, Dec. 1961, Supplement to State Workmen's Compensation Laws 16, Table 8; 24, Table 10.

90 Ibid. 32, Table 11.

91 U. S. Chamber of Commerce, op. cit. 39, Chart VII.

92 Ibid.

93 Black, The Anomalies of Workmen's Compensation, 7 Ind. & Labor Rel. Rev. 43, 48, (1953).

94 Ibid. 46–50 passim.

95 Ibid. 48.

96 Ibid. 49.

97 Ibid. 48.

98 See United States v. Hutcheson, 312 U.S. 219 (1940).

99 Skolnik, Trends in Workmen's Compensation: Coverage, Benefits, and Costs, Social Security Bull., Aug. 1958, 4, 8, Table 3.

100 Skolnik, Workmen's Compensation Payments and Costs, 1960. Social Security Bull., Jan. 1962, 18, 19.

101 Skolnik, Trends 4, 13, Table 7.

102 Skolnik, Workmen's Compensation Payments and Costs 1960, 18, 24.

103 Skolnik, Trends 4, 30.

104 Skolnik, Workmen's Compensation Payments and Costs 1960, 18, 24.

105 Ibid. 19; Trends 4, 13.

106   E.g. advertisement, Mississippi Agricultural & Industrial Board, Jackson, Miss., in Wall Street Journal, Dec. 20, 1961.

107   E.g. Fair Labor Standards Act of 1938, 52 Stat. 1060 (1938), as amended, 29 U.S.C. §§ 201–19 (1958), as amended, 29 U.S.C. § 203 (Supp. III, 1959–61).

108   35 Stat. 65 (1908), as amended, 45 U.S.C. §§ 51–60 (1958).

109   See Pollack, Workmen's Compensation for Railroad Work Injuries and Diseases, 36 Cornell L. Q. 236 (1951); Pollack, The Crisis in Work Injury Compensation on and off the Railroads, 18 Law & Contemp. Problems 296 (1953); Somers and Somers, *Workmen's Compensation* 318 (1954).

110   Mr. Justice Frankfurter in McAllister v. United States, 348 U.S. 19, 23 (1954); Tiller v. Atlantic Coast Line R.R. Co., 318 U.S. 54, 71 (1943); Wilkerson v. McCarthy, 336 U.S. 53, 65 (1949); and Mr. Justice Douglas in Bailey v. Central Vermont Ry., 319 U.S. 350, 354 (1943).

111   Rogers v. Missouri Pacific R.R. Co., 352 U.S. 500, 506, 509 (1957).

112   Pollack, The Crisis in Work Injury Compensation on and off the Railroads, 18 Law & Contemp. Problems 296, 309 (1953).

113   Another factor which doubtless influences the railroad workers is the sickness insurance provided under the Railroad Unemployment Insurance Act, 52 Stat. 1094 (1938), as amended, 45 U.S.C. §§ 351–67 (1958), as amended (Supp. II, 1959–60), and the disability and survivor's benefits under the Railroad Retirement Act, 49 Stat. 967 (1935), 50 Stat. 307 (1937), as amended, 45 U.S.C. §§ 228a–z–1 (1958), as amended (Supp. II, 1959–60).

114   See Helvering v. Davis, 310 U.S. 619, 672 (1937); Steward Machine Co. v. Davis, 310 U.S. 548 (1937).

115   H.R. 1267, H.R. 2731, 87th Cong., 1st Sess. (1961).

116   See e.g. NLRB v. Jones & Laughlin Steel Corp., 301 U.S. 1 (1937); United States v. Darby, 312 U.S. 100 (1941); Wickard v. Filburn, 317 U.S. 111 (1942).

117   An example of Congressional reaction to a possible upsetting of long-established patterns and agencies of state regulation was the enactment of the McCarran Act, 59 Stat. 34 (1945), 15 U.S.C. §§ 1011–15 (1958), confirming state regulation and taxation of the insurance business after United States v. South-Eastern Underwriters Ass'n, 322 U.S. 533 (1944) had held the insurance business subject to regulation under the commerce power the first time the question was squarely presented. But since Paul v. Virginia, 8 Wall. 168 (1868), "negative implication from the commerce clause was held not to place any limitation upon state power over the business. . . . [And] the states took over exclusively the function of regulating the insurance business in its specific legislative manifestations." Prudential Insurance Co. v. Benjamin, 328 U.S. 408, 414, 415 (1946).

118   Federal Unemployment Tax Act, Int. Rev. Code of 1954, §§ 3301–09.

119   Somewhat analogous are provisions of the Internal Revenue Code regulating deductibility of contributions to pension, profit sharing, and stock bonus plans. Int. Rev. Code of 1954, § 404(a).

120 See Somers and Somers, *Workmen's Compensation* 248–90 (1954). See general discussion in Larson, The Welfare State and Workmen's Compensation, 5 NACCA L. J. 18 (1950); Larson, The Future of Workmen's Compensation, 6 NACCA L. J. 18 (1950).

121 In 1956 Congress amended the Social Security Act to provide disability benefits to totally and permanently disabled insured persons 50 years of age or over, but under 65. 70 Stat. 815 (1956), 42 U.S.C. § 423 (1958). Such benefits were to be reduced by the amount of workmen's compensation payable monthly. 70 Stat. 816 (1956). Provisions for reduction of benefits were repealed in 1958. 72 Stat. 1025 (1958). In 1961 the requirement that an individual have attained the age of 50 was eliminated. 75 Stat. 134 (1961), 42 U.S.C.A. § 423 (1961). Criticism of these amendments and the trend it is believed they represent is expressed in Symons, Expansion of Our Federal Social Security Laws Is Threatening the Destruction of Our State Workmen's Compensation System, 29 Ins. Counsel J. 379 (1962). Symons points out that an injured employee may be "able, in *combined* Social Security and Workmen's Compensation disability benefits, to draw" more than the amount of his wages for working. Ibid. 389.

122 California, New Jersey, New York, and Rhode Island have state laws relating to temporary disability.

123 National Insurance (Industrial Injuries) Act, 1946, 9 & 10 Geo. VI, ch. 62. Recommendations leading to the abolition of workmen's compensation were included in the Beveridge Report, *Social Insurance and Allied Services,* 35 ff. (Macmillan, 1942).

124 Law Reform (Personal Injuries) Act, 1948, 11 & 12 Geo. VI, chap. 41.

125 Law Reform (Contributory Negligence) Act, 1945, 8 & 9 Geo. VI, chap. 28, § 1(1) (2).

126 Munkman, *Employer's Liability* 22–23 (4th ed. 1959).

127 Ibid.

128 Somers and Somers, *Workmen's Compensation* 191–93 (1954), referring to proposals by Samuel B. Horovitz and Arthur J. Altmeyer.

129 Federal Security Agency, 1947 Ann. Rep. 9. See also 3–9; 1948 Ann. Rep. 115; 1949 Ann. Rep. 43; 1950 Ann. Rep. 30; 1951 Ann. Rep. 30; 1952 Ann. Rep. 36. Recommendations by the Social Security Board for a comprehensive social insurance system go back at least to 1943. Social Security Board, 8 Ann. Rep. 32–40 (1943).

8   ELIZABETH BRANDEIS

Migrant Labor in Wisconsin

Introduction

A mid-twentieth-century John R. Commons, in search of a labor problem to engage his talents, might well choose the plight of the migrant farm worker. In Wisconsin he is typically a Spanish-speaking American citizen—a Texas Mexican—who comes to the state with his family to work in our fields and orchards. Here is a labor problem to intrigue the scholar, to arouse the humanitarian, and to challenge the skill of the social inventor.

Today in Wisconsin as elsewhere the migrant farm worker is low man on the labor totem pole. And between him and wage earners in all other employments the gap seems to be growing wider year by year. In other occupations real wages have been rising, working hours have been falling, and security has been broadened and enhanced, by laws, by collective bargaining, and by employer practices. But migrant agricultural workers have had little or no share in these gains. In addition migratory life creates special problems, calling for special government services and regulations; and these are still grossly inadequate. Why is this so? Despite a plethora of national investigations and publications, precise knowledge about these migrants is still strangely lacking. Despite all sorts of groups concerned about their plight, little has been accomplished to ameliorate their condition. To extend to migrants in agriculture existing legislation which protects other workers encounters unexpected opposition. And when the migrants are brought under such laws, the remedies do not seem to fit the situation or work out as they should. What is wrong?

The migratory labor problem is nationwide. A majority of states use migrants, and most migrants work in several states in the course of a year. Some government action at the federal level is clearly appropriate, but state action will remain indispensable whatever the Federal Government does. This essay sketches the over-all picture, but it gives details only for Wisconsin. The state affords a good case study; the problems here and the attempts at their solution are typical. And Wisconsin happens to be the state in which the author is trying in a small way to learn more of what is actually happening and why, in order to formulate and promote action on behalf of the migrants our farmers need and use.

Migrants in Wisconsin

A LOOK BACKWARD

Wisconsin's substantial use of migratory labor began with the acute farm labor shortage of World War II. Probably long before that, when Wisconsin was a major wheat state, it used "harvest hands" who moved from state to state—single men "riding the rails." But when Wisconsin farmers turned to dairying, they needed relatively little seasonal labor and probably managed their harvesting largely by "swapping." Beginning in the early 1900's some specialized crops, such as cherries in Door County, and perhaps peas and other canning vegetables, needed harvesters. Sugar beets, especially, required a lot of hand labor, both in cultivating and harvesting. Probably most of this seasonal work was done by Wisconsin people until World War II, except in sugar beets; the sugar refining companies had long recruited out-of-state workers to work on the farms where sugar beets were grown. They did the tedious "stoop labor" of thinning and blocking, and later the harvesting of the beets. Early in the century these out-of-state workers were mostly recent immigrants, first Belgians and later German-Russians. Probably in the 'twenties, as these immigrants got farms of their own, the refining companies began to recruit Mexicans living in Texas. Whether born in Mexico or Texas, these workers were Spanish-speaking. They came in family groups, usually brought by labor contractors known as "crew leaders." The wives and children worked in the fields along with the men. How many came, how many worked in crops other than sugar beets are among many unknowns in the migrant story.

We do know that around 1920 the employment of young children (probably Wisconsin children as well as migrants) in specialized kinds of agriculture led those concerned with child welfare to push for an amendment to bring agriculture—hitherto entirely exempt—under the state child labor law. Investigations by the Wisconsin Industrial Commission in the early 'twenties found children working long hours in beet fields and cranberry marshes when they should have been in school. The cherry growers defeated the proposed amendment in 1921 and 1923. But it was passed in 1925, after the cherry growers were persuaded to withdraw their opposition. The amendment was very moderate. It did not bring agriculture under the general provisions of the child labor law, but gave the State Industrial Commission power to regulate the employment of children under 16 in "cherry orchards, market gardening, gardening conducted or controlled by canning companies, and the culture of sugar beets and cranberries." [1] In the commission's report for 1924–26 the director of the Woman and Child Labor Division, Maud Swett, gives this bit of history:

> From 1867–1925 provisions of the child labor law have not applied to children engaged in agricultural pursuits. During the last few years, however, certain types of agriculture, such as the harvesting of sugar beets, cherries and cranberries, and market gardening, have become specialized in form, taking on many of the characteristics of factory work. In these industrialized forms of agriculture certain evils relative to the employment of minors have crept in. Chief among these complaints are those with reference to the interference with attendance at school, the lack of careful supervision, long hours and in some instances unsuitable or harmful work and lack of proper sanitation and housing. [2]

Although Miss Swett mentions several crops, the order issued by the Industrial Commission under its new power was limited to sugar beets. Issued in 1926, this set no general minimum age for employment, merely limited child labor up to 14 to eight hours a day and 48 a week. [3] To get the children into school, it provided that those under 14 who had not completed the eighth grade "are prohibited from working while the school in the district in which they are employed is in session." [4] That the children involved included migrants—whether Texas Mexicans or others—can be inferred from the further provision that records must be kept of "the last residential address of each migratory family." [5] In subsequent reports Miss Swett refers to the order regulating "the employment of migratory children in sugar beet fields." This order was finally dropped in the late 'thirties because of the new federal regulation of child labor in sugar beets, to be described below.

In all the years up to 1960, no other order was issued by the Wisconsin Industrial Commission regulating child labor in the other crops to which its power extended. Children—whether migrant or Wisconsin children it is hard to determine—certainly worked at cherry picking in the 'twenties and 'thirties. Miss Swett inspected the orchards at the harvest season and urged on the growers the working and living conditions for children which she thought should be provided. Apparently the orchard owners preferred to make the changes she urged rather than have the commission issue an order. But all this throws little light on the amount of migrant labor in Wisconsin during these years.

Then came the acute farm labor shortage of World War II. A nationwide farm labor program operated under Agricultural Extension brought to Wisconsin German prisoners of war and foreign workers from Mexico and the British West Indies to harvest a variety of fruits and vegetables. Texas Mexicans continued to be brought to the state by the sugar companies, and attempts were made to put them to work in other crops between the two seasons of sugar beet work. It seems probable that 1947 was the first year that Texas Mexicans were used in substantial numbers in cultivating and harvesting crops other than sugar beets. About 5,000 of them were in the state that year. In addition, foreign migrants numbered about 2,800. [6] It was probably assumed that the use of migrants in Wisconsin agriculture would diminish from then on. Instead it increased. Wisconsin State Employment Service (WSES) reported nearly 9,000 domestic migrant workers in 1953 and nearly 12,000 in 1954. The ten-year average for 1950–60 was around 11,000 workers (not counting children under 16, though many of them work). Mechanization of one harvesting operation after another in the past decade did not seem to reduce the over-all demand for migrant labor. At least through 1961 mechanization was offset by other factors which increased demand.

SOME RECENT FACTS AND FIGURES

How many migrants came to Wisconsin?—In 1961, a year of exceptional crops, WSES counted 12,686 domestic migrants working in Wisconsin plus 5,039 children under 16, many of whom worked, too. Most of these were Texas Mexicans—10,770 out of the 12,686.[7] How many additional migrants worked in the state without using the Employment Service is not known. The sugar-refining company recruited directly in Texas without using the service, but the staff of WSES believe that most of these Texas Mexicans registered with them after beet cultivation was over and thus got into their count. Figures for 1960 indicate that migrants worked in 28 of the 71 counties of the state.[8] The largest concentrations were in Waushara and Oconto, mainly to harvest cucumbers for pickling, and in Door, to pick cherries. Smaller numbers were used to harvest peas and sweet corn for canning, to thin and block sugar beets, and to work in miscellaneous vegetables, including mint—much of this in mucklands. The migrants stayed in one location for lengths of time varying from over five months in vegetables, where they plant, weed, and harvest, to four weeks in cherries, where they merely pick. In sugar beets, migrants in recent years were used only in the early season—late May to early July—to thin and block. The harvesting was done by machine without the use of migrant labor.

In addition to these domestic migrants the WSES brought to Wisconsin in 1961 approximately 1,300 foreign workers. Most of this group were Mexican nationals. (The conditions under which these foreign workers could be brought in will be discussed later.)

Evils inherent in migrant life.—Obviously there are evils inherent in migratory work apart from the wages, hours, and working conditions, the criteria by which other kinds of jobs are judged. First, for the migrants there are days of travel from "home base" and then from one job to the next, days lost so far as earnings go. If the migrants are brought from Texas by crew leaders, they usually travel in overcrowded buses or trucks, often ill-protected in case of bad weather, and with few stops en route to eat or sleep. No wonder a car of his own to make the trip is often the first thing a migrant worker buys. It is far better than riding in a truck, even if it too is overcrowded when the whole family is aboard.

Then consider the living conditions for migrants in the places where they stop to work. For them living conditions are part of working conditions. It is natural, if not inevitable, for the employer to furnish living quarters for temporary workers who come from far away. For single men (such as foreign workers) the employer usually furnishes meals too. But for "family type" labor it is customary to provide some kind of stove for cooking. The need for some kind of laundry facilities is obvious. Water supply and sewage disposal problems are sure to arise in a migrant camp. Yet where workers are needed and used often for as little as five or six weeks in the year, it is understandable that employers are reluctant to invest the sums needed to provide housing which would be even minimal for year-round living.

So all over the country the housing typically available for migrant workers and their families has been the most visible evidence of their substandard conditions. Migrant families are too often crowded into shacks with rudimentary sanitary arrangements, inadequate cooking and laundry facilities. Though Wisconsin's State Board of Health has worked on this problem for more than a decade, there remain many migrant camps in the state which can only be called rural slums. It is really immaterial whether, as is often alleged, the homes in which the migrants live in Texas are no better than the housing in these Wisconsin camps. Actually many migrants, perhaps the majority, spend more time "on the road" than they do in Texas, so camp conditions are the more important. It is touching to see the enthusiasm of migrant women for fixing up their "homes" in a Wisconsin camp, if they are given any encouragement. They sometimes even plant flowers beside the door to enjoy "when we come back next year."

For the children, migrant work means broken and shortened schooling. Every study has shown retardation in school. Retardation increases with age; tests show that the children are on the average one or more school years behind their age group at age 6 and 7, but three or more years behind at age 11 and above.[9]

Finally, Texas Mexicans in Wisconsin are usually regarded as foreigners because they speak Spanish; and their dark skins often make them subject to discriminatory treatment in stores and movies and sometimes even in taverns and churches.

Why then do Texas Mexicans travel so far to work in Wisconsin? Earnings and employment must look a lot better than in Texas. How good are they?

Earnings and working conditions.—Earning figures in Wisconsin are hard to come by. Most migrants are paid on a piece-rate basis. How many hours they work and how much they earn per hour, day, or week seems to be largely unknown. The U. S. Department of Agriculture by the use of its statistical samples and techniques gives 85½¢ as the average cash hourly earnings for agricultural wage workers of all types in 1961 in the East North Central Region of which Wisconsin is a part. For Wisconsin alone the figure was 86½¢. Incidentally 85½¢ was the lowest regional average outside of the South. The average for the Pacific Region was $1.25.[10] The national average of 83½¢ in 1961 should be compared with $2.32 an hour for production workers in manufacturing and with the figure for the lowest nonagricultural classification, laundries, of $1.26.[11] Wisconsin's 86½¢ for farm workers should be compared with $2.41 an hour for production workers in manufacturing and $1.37 in laundries.[12] The gap between farm workers and laundry workers looks even wider when we reflect that about three-fourths of laundry workers are women.

Hourly wage figures for migrants only are not available. However, for 1959 the U. S. Department of Agriculture did provide a figure for daily average earnings specifically of migrant farm workers, by regions. For the North Central Region the figure was $6.00 a day.[13] In that year average daily earnings in Wisconsin in laundries were $9.74; in manufacturing $18.61 a day.[14]

Since most migrants work in several states, what they earned in Wisconsin in a particular year would give little indication of their annual earnings. Average annual earnings for migrants must be reckoned on a national basis. Estimates by the U.S. Department of Agriculture for 1961 (excluding migrants with less than 25 days of work in agriculture during the year) show that migrant workers earned on the average $6.25 a day and $677 for the year, working an average of 109 days in agriculture. Their earnings from work outside agriculture add another $225 for the year.[15] These figures indicate a drop in daily and yearly earnings from 1960 when the comparable figures were $6.65 a day and $819 for the year, for an average of 123 days of farm work. However their earnings from nonagricultural work was slightly less in 1960 than in 1961, an average of $197.[16]

While wages of other workers have been rising in recent years, the annual and daily earnings of migrant farm workers seem to be going down. In 1954 the national annual average was $794, the daily average

$6.40. In 1956 these figures went up to $935 per year and $8.05 per day.[17] But, as noted in the preceding paragraph, both the annual and daily averages were lower in 1960 and 1961, dropping from the high of $935 per year in 1956 to $677 in 1961. For Wisconsin it is possible to compare at least one piece rate paid in 1961 with that prevailing in 1946. It is somewhat startling, in view of changes in price levels, to find that 20¢ a pail for cherry picking, the rate set by the Industrial Commission to meet the minimum wage in 1961, was reported as the "most common prevailing wage" for cherry picking in 1946.[18] If 20¢ a pail for cherry picking is representative of other rates paid to migrants in the early postwar period, it would suggest that their "real" earnings in Wisconsin have fallen substantially in the past decade or more. It would take 30¢ in 1961 to equal the purchasing power that 20¢ had in 1946.

For migrant farm workers in Wisconsin, as elsewhere, there is no legal restriction on hours of work and no time and a half for overtime.[19] In general, actual hours are probably very long per day and frequently too short per week as well as per year. That is, on good days when the crop is ready, these workers, women and children as well as men, are urged, if not required, to work "from sun up to sun down"—as textile mill workers did in New England more than a century ago. But in many weeks, bad weather or a crop unready to harvest means days without work or pay. For Wisconsin we have no figures on this. In New York (where weather and crops are similar) an attempt was made in 1959 in a study of migrants to find out how many days of work were completely lost. The figures show that no work was available on one-fifth of the regular workdays. This lost time of course reduces earnings substantially.[20]

What working conditions are part of migrant jobs? The accident rate is very high in mechanized agriculture, but this does not apply to most of the work migrants do. As for other physical conditions, they are usually assumed to be highly desirable—outdoor work in the fresh air. However, it should be noted that, except for cherry picking, almost all the work migrants do involves "stoop labor," which even those accustomed to other kinds of hard physical work find extremely distasteful in large doses. In fact, the use of children is often defended on the ground that they do not have so far to stoop, or find continued squatting as difficult as adults do.

Wide and Deep Concern for Migrants

In view of the condition of migrant farm workers, it is perhaps not surprising that humanitarian concern for their welfare began years ago. As stated at a Senate committee hearing in 1959. "There have been nearly 60 occasions in the last 50 years when the American conscience, disturbed temporarily by the paradox of poverty amid plenty, has prompted investigations and recommendations in the hope of eventually alleviating this malignant social problem. Four of these reports were issued between 1909 and 1930, the remainder have come forth ... at the rate of nearly 2 each year." [21] The most important of these reports was made in 1951 by the President's Commission on Migratory Labor in American Agriculture. In 1954 President Eisenhower established a permanent President's Committee on Migratory Labor made up of the secretaries of Agriculture, Labor, Interior; Health, Education, and Welfare; and the Administrator of the Housing and Home Finance Agency. This committee, through a small staff and working representatives of these federal agencies, promotes joint federal-state action on behalf of migrants.

Meanwhile many private organizations have for years been working in various ways to help migrants, both with direct services and in promoting government action at all levels. The U. S. Department of Labor counts 28 such organizations.[22] The Migrant Ministry of the National Council of Churches is probably the oldest. It dates its work with migrants from 1920, when it started a day care center for migrant children in Hurlock, Maryland. The National Council of Catholic Women has also been working for migrants for years. More recently the Catholics have set up a special Bishop's Migrant Committee, and in many areas the National Council of Catholic Men is also active. The National Council of Agricultural Life and Labor, the National Sharecroppers Fund, and the National Advisory Committee on Farm Labor are concerned with migrants' problems, as are the American Friends Service Committee, the National Child Labor Committee, and the National Consumers League.*

* The National Consumers League and its state affiliates were probably the first to study the migrants' plight. In 1905 the Philadelphia and New Jersey leagues arranged for a survey of "the seasonal migration of Italian pickers to New Jersey" from Philadelphia. The findings were published in *Charities and the Commons* for November 4, 1905, and reprints were circulated by the National Consumers League.

Activity at the state level is also widespread. In recent years many states have set up official committees to study the problems of migrants and promote a variety of activities on their behalf. Five such committees were established before 1954. Since then, partly because of promotion by the President's Committee, 24 other states have followed suit. Rather surprisingly, this list of 29 states does not include California,* which ranked first in its use of domestic migrants in 1961, employing 66,900 in the peak period.[23] Three other states that use substantial numbers of migrants—Kansas, Missouri, and Montana—also lack an official state committee. But private groups, especially church groups, are functioning in all these states.

The state committees vary in size from 10 to 40 members. In six states (Maryland, Oregon, New Jersey, Texas, Rhode Island, and Oklahoma) they were established by legislative action; in the others by executive action of the governor. Members represent those departments of the state government that are concerned with migrants, as well as a variety of private organizations and individuals concerned with migrant problems. The amount of activity has varied widely from state to state. Some committees have considerable achievement to their credit. All indicate wide recognition of the migrant situation.[24]

In Wisconsin in 1950 the governor, at the request of the Governor's Commission on Human Rights, appointed an Interagency Committee on Migrant Problems. In 1953 this was converted into a State Migrant Committee under the auspices of the Wisconsin Welfare Council, with representatives of departments of the state government, of church groups, and of many other concerned groups, as well as representatives of growers who use migrant labor. This committee promoted various activities, including legislation such as the migrant camp law described in the next section. In 1960 this nonofficial state committee was disbanded, to be succeeded by a somewhat smaller official committee, the Governor's Committee on Migratory Labor, again made up of representatives of the state departments concerned with the migrant problem, representatives of growers using migrant labor, of church and other groups, and a few interested individuals.

---

* Though California has no official state committee on migrants, it has taken much legislative and administrative action which benefits migrants: agriculture is covered by workmen's compensation; there is a camp housing law; and in 1961 minimum wage rates were set for women and minors over 16 in agriculture, and agricultural workers were brought under the state disability insurance law.

In addition to this statewide committee, county or local committees have been organized in some areas in Wisconsin. In others a local Protestant or Catholic group has provided a school or some other direct service for the migrants who came there. Most of these local committees have rallied strongly in support of various proposed bills and administrative orders dealing with migrant problems; their representatives have appeared at hearings, talked and written to legislators, etc. Other groups not serving migrants directly also have supported some of these proposals: the Wisconsin sections of the League of Women Voters, the American Association of University Women, the AFL-CIO, etc. In short, the plight of migrant workers, especially migrant children, has a wide and strong appeal. All kinds of people want to help them.

Government Protection of Migrant Workers

It is clear that migrants are a disadvantaged group and as such have aroused widespread humanitarian concern. Further it appears that groups which want to help migrants believe that government action, state and federal, is needed. What has been accomplished? What laws and regulations exist to protect or serve migrant workers and their families in one way or another?

FEDERAL

The principal federal laws which might be expected to protect migrant farm workers are (1) the Fair Labor Standards Act (FLSA) and (2) Social Security's old-age, survivors, and disability insurance (OASDI).

Actually, FLSA exempts agriculture completely so far as its wage-and-hour provisions are concerned. If there were a federal minimum wage for agriculture even approximating the present $1.15 per hour for other workers, it would obviously force a considerable increase in migrant wages in most parts of the United States.

The child labor provisions of FLSA also exempt agriculture, with one very important exception. During the hours and days that the school in the district is in session, no child under 16 may be employed in agriculture. To the extent that this requirement is enforced or observed, it keeps migrant children out of the fields during school hours when their parents are doing spring work and takes them out in the fall after school has started. The Wage and Hour Division of the U. S. Department of Labor makes a gallant attempt to enforce this 16-year limit. It has devoted much of its inspection manpower to the task in spring and in fall ever since the provision was enacted in 1949. But there are great areas to be covered in short periods; violations have continued at a high rate.[25]

The difficulty of enforcing this federal provision is enhanced by the absence of state regulations to back it up. The failure of most states to require a state child labor permit in agriculture puts a great burden on the federal inspectors. In Wisconsin, for example, though no child may be legally employed in "commercialized" agriculture under the age of 12, those from 12 to 18 do not have to have the permits required in almost all other occupations.[26] In other employments federal inspectors can ask to see the state permits for children they suspect are under age. In agriculture it is obviously far more difficult to detect or prove a violation of the federal 16-year minimum age if the child asserts he is 16 or over.

Even though not fully complied with, this federal child labor provision is immensely important. However, it should be noted that when the Wage and Hour Division orders the children out of the fields, this does not automatically put them into school. Do state laws require school attendance by migrant children, or even require the local schools to accept them? The answers to these questions for Wisconsin are discussed below.

During the summer months then, the present federal provision offers no protection against agricultural work at any age, however young. Amendments to FLSA now pending in Congress would set a minimum age for summer work in agriculture.

The second federal statute which should give some protection to migrant agricultural workers is OASDI. Originally agriculture was completely exempt. A beginning of coverage for agricultural workers came in 1950. The present provision dates from 1956. But no one really knows how many migrant workers are actually building up accounts through payment of tax by themselves and their employers. The tax is collected from employers by the Internal Revenue Service. In its reports no attempt is made to distinguish between migrant and nonmigrant agricultural workers. But a comparison between the number of hired agricultural workers for whom tax was paid in 1960 (as reported by Internal Revenue) [27] and the U. S. Department of Agriculture's estimate of hired workers employed in agriculture 25 or more days in the same year [28] indicates about 250,000 such workers for whom no OASDI tax was paid. It is safe to guess that most of these hired farm workers lost to OASDI were domestic migrants. In 1960 the total number of such migrants was about 409,000.[29] Thus it is possible that for over half of them the presumed protection of OASDI will prove nonexistent when the time comes for them to claim benefits.[30]

Many of these migrant workers are lost to OASDI because of the special provisions in the act which define what wages are required and who is the employer for agricultural coverage. A farmer must pay the tax for a worker if he pays him $150 in a year, or if the worker works for him on 20 or more days in a year if wages are figured on a time basis. However, the statute makes the crew leader the employer if he arranges with the farm operator to furnish workers and if he pays the workers on his own behalf or on behalf of the farmer.[31] How many crew leaders understand their obligation in this respect, pay the tax for themselves and deduct and pay for the worker? It is said that in Wisconsin most wages are paid directly by the grower or processor. If this is true, few crew leaders here are "employers" by the OASDI definition. Perhaps a larger proportion of migrants have their tax deducted and paid here than in many other states. But how many Wisconsin farmers who pay migrants directly pay them enough or employ them long enough to meet the earnings requirement? And when they do, do these farmers all actually pay the tax for themselves and their migrants? Since Internal Revenue does not distinguish migrants from other farm workers, there is no figure for migrants paying tax in Wisconsin to compare with the Employment Service figure of migrants working in Wisconsin.

It is not easy for Internal Revenue to collect the OASDI tax for migrants because of the difficulty of determining who are the employers responsible for its payment, and of educating them to compute and pay it. Amendment of the definition of employer of agricultural labor in the OASDI Act would help.[32] But a basic difficulty would remain arising from the nature of the employment of migrant workers.

One group of migrants is protected by a special federal law, the Sugar Act of 1937, which provides a special subsidy to the growers of sugar cane and sugar beets. The act contains a child labor provision and requires the Secretary of Agriculture to set minimum wage rates.

So while working in sugar beets, migrant workers are covered by these provisions. No child under 14 can be legally employed, and those 14 and 15 years old must not work more than eight hours a day or 48 a week. Agents of the U. S. Department of Agriculture are directed to reduce the subsidy payments where violations of these child labor provisions are found.[33] In an endeavor to make these provisions enforceable, Texas Mexicans are urged by the U. S. Department of Agriculture to bring with them birth certificates or other evidence of age for their children 14 and over. But neither the law nor the Secretary of Agriculture requires child labor permits, the essential for enforcing a child labor law. As for wages, the Secretary of Agriculture sets "fair and reasonable" minimum wage rates for sugar beet workers— an hourly rate plus, for specified operations, piece rates which he "finds" will yield the hourly minimum. These rates can vary among geographical areas.[34] In 1961 the hourly rate was 85¢ in Wisconsin.[35] Here (and probably elsewhere) most of the sugar beet work is paid on a piece-rate basis.

Another special federal regulation for migrant workers that should be noted is the Interstate Commerce Commission's rules for their transportation. Long before domestic migrants got this protection, it was included in the standards set up for the use of foreign migrants. For foreign migrants there must be insurance against injury en route; the vehicle must have fixed seats and covering against inclement weather; hours of travel must be limited to 12 per day; drivers must be licensed, etc.[36] Finally in 1956 Congress directed the Interstate Commerce Commission to regulate the interstate transportation of domestic migrants in similar fashion. The Commission has issued regulations listing qualifications for drivers, standards for vehicles, requiring meal stops, etc.[37] But the ICC lacks funds for adequate enforcement, and states have been urged to enact and enforce parallel regulations. Migrants standing in crowded open trucks, carried long distances without stopping, have probably diminished in numbers but have not entirely disappeared.

One other attempt to protect migrant agricultural workers by federal action deserves mention. In 1959, in the face of strong protests from growers using migrant labor, the then Secretary of Labor James P. Mitchell issued regulations to be met by growers who wished to use the Employment Service. These regulations were designed "to make certain, before interstate recruitment of domestic agricultural workers by the U. S. Employment Service, that the wages, housing and facilities, provisions for transportation, and other terms and conditions of employment accord to prevailing standards of employment." [38] The regulations are too detailed to be even summarized here. Obviously this puts a great new burden on Employment Service personnel. They were instructed to determine in each state those "prevailing wages" with which proposed migrant wage rates should be compared. But much stoop labor is done only by migrants. What prevailing wage is there except what they are paid? On housing, the Secretary of Labor's regulations accepted state housing standards, if any. Since Wisconsin has a state housing code, the Employment Service was to help to enforce it—including enforcement for small units below six workers, not covered under the state law.

Growers have continued to oppose this new use of the Employment Service to protect migrant workers. In 1961 they tried to have it outlawed by Congress.

In 1962 the U. S. Department of Labor tried to do more for domestic migrants through the leverage of the Mexican Migrant Labor Program. After holding regional hearings, the Department announced minimum wage rates per hour which must be paid to Mexican "braceros." Piece rate earnings were to be translated into hourly earnings for each pay period to be sure that they equaled this hourly minimum. The rate for most of the country outside of the South was set at $1.00 an hour. This was designated as an "adverse effect minimum wage." In other words, the Secretary of Labor found that to pay foreign workers less than $1.00 per hour would have an adverse effect on the wages of domestic workers. Apparently an employer who used both Mexican braceros and domestic workers in 1962 would have to pay the $1.00 an hour to the domestic workers, too. What effect this "adverse effect" rate would have on growers not using any braceros was not clear. The requirement that they must pay "prevailing wages" in order to use the facilities of the Employment Service still stood. Was the "adverse effect wage" the prevailing wage? Apparently not.

To this writer it seems doubtful whether denying use of the Employment Service can or should be used as a way to enforce a minimum wage or other minimal conditions for domestic migrants, especially where the wages and other conditions are specified only in terms of "prevailing standards of employment." Even after these standards are translated into more specific terms (such as the $1.00 an hour wage) can Employment Service personnel effectively inspect and check on wages actually earned per hour, and a wide variety of working and living conditions besides? This is certainly a backhanded way to protect domestic migrants from substandard conditions. It is scarcely an effective substitute for a definite minimum wage, for better enforcement of existing transportation regulations, or a well-enforced housing code.

STATE

Wisconsin's laws and orders for the protection of migrant agricultural workers and their families rank high in comparison with those of most other states.

Minimum wage.—The state minimum wage law applies only to women and to minors up to age 21, but for these workers it is all-inclusive; agriculture has never been excluded. Minimum hourly rates are set by the Industrial Commission and are low in comparison with rates set in many other states. As set in 1960 they provide for agriculture 75¢ an hour for women and minors 16 and over, and 65¢ an hour for minors under 16.[39] How enforceable are these minimum wage rates?

In the first place, most migrant farm workers are paid on a piece-rate basis. Of course piece rates are common in industry too and do not make an hourly minimum wage unworkable. The simplest way to handle the problem—the method used in enforcing the Fair Labor Standards Act—is to put the responsibility on the employer to divide the earnings of each worker for the payroll period by the hours he worked, to determine whether his earnings per hour equaled the minimum hourly rate. Wisconsin, however, has long had a formula which makes it possible to employ some workers at a given piece rate who do not earn the hourly minimum. Under its 1960 orders an employer is deemed to have complied with the order if 65% of the workers in the plant covered by a given hourly rate have earned 5¢ above it for all hours worked in a given payroll period. The hourly earnings of the remaining 35% of the workers involved may fall any distance below the hourly minimum wage.[40] This appears to solve the problem of workers whose output is low for any reason. But obviously it assumes that the employer keeps a record of hours worked so that he can convert individual piece-rate earnings into hourly earnings, to make sure that 65% of the workers involved have met the test explained above. In industry, records of hours worked are normally kept. But migrant-using agricultural employers throw up their hands at the suggestion that such records should or can be kept. Even large-scale operators declare it is impossible. The workers, they say, generally go into the fields or orchards when they choose. Are they working? How much time is actually working time?

After the issuance of the 1960 minimum wage rates, various grower groups and the Wisconsin Farm Bureau as their spokesman asked the Industrial Commission to set specific piece rates for various agricultural occupations, such as cherry picking, which would be accepted as meeting the minimum wage. In June 1961 the Industrial Commission modified its minimum wage order by adding the following: "The Commission may, also, upon the application of an employer or group of employers covered by this section, approve specific piece rates for any particular kind of employment on the basis of such tests or studies as it deems adequate." [41] This proviso puts the burden on the commission to decide, when an application is made, what piece rate or rates for a specific agricultural operation will yield earnings in accordance with the formula (5¢ above the minimum to 65% of the women and minors involved). To the extent that such rates are set by the commission, growers are relieved of the obligation to keep records of hours worked.

To keep track of hours worked by domestic migrants apparently seems to growers everywhere an unreasonable requirement. In New York such a requirement (not part of a minimum wage law) was repealed as to piece-rate workers in 1961 though restored in 1962.[42] In California the first minimum wage order for agricultural employment, issued in 1961, reflects the same attitude. It provides a minimum hourly rate of $1.00 for women and for minors over 16 employed on an hourly basis, but for piece-rate workers it provides merely a $4.00-a-day "call in" minimum wage to meet the complaint of workers called to work only to find little or none available.[43] It is assumed that, if there is picking to do, earnings at piece rates will run far above this minimum. The California Industrial Welfare Commission refused the suggestion that they should set minimum piece rates; something like 500 piece rates would have been involved.

Another problem in applying a minimum wage to agriculture using migrants was partially sidestepped in the California orders by excluding minors under 16. Growers in both California and Wisconsin declare that much harvesting by migrants is done on a family basis; the children pick into the parents' pails or baskets. Where a piece rate is set under the Wisconsin order, as was done for cherry picking in 1961, the employer is presumably complying with the order so long as he credits the head of the family at the established piece rate for every pail of cherries brought to the weighing station. Yet a man's output is probably greater than a woman's or a child's. How can we tell whether the piece rate yields the hourly minimum for the women and children?

The Wisconsin Industrial Commission has undertaken to determine on request by employers what piece rate will yield the hourly minimum. In asking for a piece rate in 1961 the cherry growers offered to make "test runs" which commission personnel could observe. But test runs cannot be made until the crop is ready to harvest. In fact conditions change from one part of the season to another. A piece rate adequate at the height of the harvest might well be inadequate in terms of hourly earnings in both the early and late parts of the season. And one year differs from another; a poor crop means that it takes much longer to fill a pail. Piece rates set on the basis of test runs in 1961 were not necessarily appropriate in 1962.

Regardless of these difficulties, the Wisconsin Industrial Commission set a piece rate for cherry picking for 1961 before the picking season started. The rate set was 20¢ per nine-pound pail. During the picking season the commission staff conducted three test runs of women and minor pickers. That the cherry crop was exceptionally good may account for their conclusion that 20¢ a pail was more than adequate throughout the season to yield the minimum hourly rates for women and for minors subject to the "65% formula" described above. It remains to be seen whether it will be as adequate another year. At any rate it was continued in 1962.

Hours of work.—As for any limit on the hours of work of women or minors, such as Wisconsin provides for most other occupations, there is none in agriculture. The women's hour law does not cover agriculture at all, and the child labor order described below does not limit hours of work.

Child labor.—Wisconsin's child labor law covers agriculture to only a very limited extent. To be sure, the state compulsory education law requires school attendance up to age 16 and in effect bars employment during school time. But outside school hours and during vacations, there is no limitation on child labor in agriculture at any age or for any hours—with one rather narrow exception. As mentioned on p. 199, the Industrial Commission has had, since 1925, power to regulate the employment of children under 16 in certain kinds of agriculture loosely called "commercialized agriculture." To make clear the extent of the commission's power, the provision had best be quoted again and more fully: "The Commission shall have power ... to fix ... reasonable regulations relative to the employment of children under 16 years of age in cherry orchards, market gardening, gardening conducted or controlled by canning companies, and the culture of sugar beets and cranberries." [44] Up to 1960 the Commission had never used this power except for the one order, limited to sugar beets, which was dropped after the federal Sugar Act was passed in 1937. In 1960 the commission, following a formal request from the Governor's Commission on Human Rights, set 12 years as the minimum age in all the kinds of agriculture to which its power extends. The 1960 order is weak in two respects. First, there is no requirement for child labor permits for children 12 and over. The long history of child labor laws shows conclusively that a minimum age for employment cannot be adequately enforced without some provision to determine the age of the child. Perhaps in due course this order will be strengthened by the addition of some kind of permit requirement. Another difficulty in enforcement was created by the inclusion of two subsections to meet the growers' contention that Texas Mexicans want their young children in the fields with them, not to work but to keep the family together and because there is no one to leave them with. So the order provides that

(1) The presence of a child under 12 at the place where his parent or guardian is employed, if merely for the purpose of supervision, is not prohibited by this order, and

(2) An employer is not deemed to have permitted a child to work at employment prohibited by this order if he has notified his employees of its provisions and has made reasonable effort to enforce such provisions and has not acquiesced in children under 12 performing such work.[45]

It is obvious that the commission's inspector cannot tell whether or not the children in the field or orchard just stopped working when warned of his coming. And who can say whether the employer "acquiesced"? Yet unless and until we provide summer schools and child care centers, or wages for men high enough to persuade mothers of young children to stay out of the fields, we shall find it difficult to answer the argument for this weakening of the agricultural child labor order.

Another weakness is the wording of the child labor law itself, which gives the Industrial Commission power to regulate child labor only in specified kinds of agriculture. It happens that the crop which today uses the most migrants in Wisconsin is cucumbers grown for pickling. The cucumber growers allege that the provision in the child labor statute does not cover pickles—though the distinction between pickling and canning is a narrow one.[46]

Thus in 1962 regulation of child labor in commercialized agriculture in Wisconsin consisted of a 12-year minimum age, no limitation on hours of work, no permit requirement to make it possible to determine the actual age of a child, and subsections which make presence at the workplace no proof that the child is "working." In short, Wisconsin's regulation of child labor in agriculture adopted in 1960 looks decidedly embryonic. It is much more like the original child labor law of 1877 than like the mature body of child labor regulations which apply to other occupations today. We can only hope that it will not take as long for this embryo to grow to maturity.

In Wisconsin, migrant children are covered by the state compulsory education law and should be in school if they are in the state in spring or fall while the schools are in session. Some growers have done excellently in seeing that the local school accepts the children of their migrant workers. In some other places it is generally (though erroneously) believed that the compulsory school law does not apply to migrant children, and local school officials turn them away. A law passed in 1961 provides that school districts operating summer schools will get the same state aid that is available in winter.[47] It is hoped that this financial aid will stimulate the setting up of summer programs in school districts to which migrant families come in summer. An experimental public summer school in Manitowoc County in 1960 and 1961 was highly successful.

On the whole, when we compare Wisconsin's protection of migrant workers from low pay, long hours, and work at too early an age with protection afforded workers in other occupations, we can see how short a distance the state has come in applying its protective standards to migrants.

Social insurance and public assistance in Wisconsin.—When we turn to social insurance we find that in Wisconsin agriculture is completely excluded from unemployment compensation. It was also completely excluded from workmen's compensation until 1961. In that year the state's workmen's compensation law was amended to cover the farmer who employs six or more agricultural workers for 20 days or more in a year.[48] This should cover most migrants. It puts Wisconsin into the small group of states which effectively include migrant agricultural workers in their workmen's compensation laws—only nine in number at the end of 1961.[49] The traditional exclusion of agriculture is of course entirely unjustified. As a whole, agriculture is a highly hazardous occupation; probably only mining and construction rank above it in accident rate. The new Wisconsin provision will still leave the typical Wisconsin dairy farm outside workmen's compensation, but it represents a big forward step, especially for migrant farm workers.

Migrants in Wisconsin are very largely excluded from assistance programs available to other workers in case of sickness or other misfortune. Residence requirements bar help other than emergency help from county welfare departments.

Migrant housing law.—Wisconsin has tried for many years to provide one kind of protection much needed by migrants—namely, regulation of their housing. In 1949 the State Board of Health under its general powers issued a set of minimum standards for migrant labor camps. A special migrant camp law was passed in 1951, strengthened in 1957 and 1961.[50] It applies to camps housing six or more migrant workers. The code sets minimum standards of space per person, ventilation, toilet and washing facilities, water supply, screening, waste disposal, etc. Years of educational work by sanitary inspectors have brought substantial progress, but general compliance is still lacking. Some growers continue to flout the regulations, which are now compulsory. Inspectors must first locate the camps; some are still operated without application for the required certificate or conditional permit. In 1961 the State Board of Health certified 378 camps as meeting its minimum standards and gave conditional permits to 45 more to operate temporarily while making the improvements required. It estimated there were another 50 to 100 camps not registered at all, presumably because the operators knew they could not meet the board's standards. So even in 1961 a visit to some of the camps where migrants were living could startle the visitor, the living conditions were so far below what one expects to find in Wisconsin today. Large families crowded into shacks with broken screens or none on the windows, a few nails on which to hang clothes; barely room for some double beds, often broken down, and a small kerosene stove. Outside, no receptacles for garbage; the garbage scattered about. The service building with the running hot and cold water required by the code often either lacking or out of order. In short, there was a long way still to go in migrant housing.

In summary, much labor and social insurance legislation, both federal and Wisconsin, exempts agriculture in whole or in part. Further, some legislation which seems to protect migrants does not fit them very well and cannot be adequately enforced because of the peculiarities of the employment situation of migrants. Finally, some special legislation needed because of their special situation has been enacted, but this too is difficult to enforce and compliance is probably far below the level achieved for other workers.

REGULATIONS FOR FOREIGN MIGRANTS

Let us compare briefly the body of legislation affecting domestic migrant workers with the regulations governing the employment of foreign migrants brought to this country under agreements with Mexico and the British West Indies and the similar terms applying to migrants who came to the mainland from Puerto Rico under the standard contract accepted by the Commonwealth. Under the agreement between Mexico and the United States, contracts between the Mexican migrants and their employers must be made under the supervision of representatives of both governments, and must normally be for not less than six weeks. Work must be guaranteed for three-fourths of the workdays, i.e. six days a week, beginning with the day after the workers' arrival at the place of employment. If work is not available, the Mexican worker must be paid what he would have earned had he worked the guaranteed number of days. Further, subsistence (three meals a day) must be furnished at no cost to the worker whenever he is not afforded the opportunity to work 64 hours or more in a two-week period; it must be at the rate of one day's subsistence for each eight hours or fraction thereof that employment offered is less than 64 hours. Records of hours worked and earnings must be kept. Thus the average hourly earnings of a Mexican worker are available for use in computing the amount due him when the days of work are short. Wage rates must be not less than those prevailing for domestic workers doing similar work.[51]

The employer of Mexican nationals must furnish workmen's compensation insurance at no cost to the worker, and nonoccupational accident and health insurance must be available at a reasonable cost to be paid by the workers. Housing and transportation are regulated, with detailed minimum standards specified.[52]

Very similar regulations apply to other foreign migrants and to those Puerto Ricans who are under the standard contract accepted by the Commonwealth of Puerto Rico.

While up to 1962 the prevailing wage standard may have done little for the foreign migrant, the other items in these agreements provided real protection which was sadly lacking for domestic migrants. As noted above, few states include agriculture under workmen's compensation. Only one state, California, requires any provision of nonoccupational health insurance for farm employees [53]—even with the worker paying for it. Housing and transportation are probably much better regulated for foreign migrants than for Americans, even in Wisconsin. Most important, perhaps, is the work guarantee given foreign migrants. No one knows how many days of work Texas Mexicans lose in Wisconsin because the weather is bad or because the crop is not ready to pick, etc. This is something which greatly needs investigation. We do know that there is no guarantee of work or pay or subsistence to protect them, as braceros are protected when they lose earnings for these reasons.

Why Have Migrants Shared so Little in Labor's Gains?

With all the active concern for migrants in so many different groups, why do the results look so meager? Why is their standard of living so far below that of other workers in Wisconsin as well as elsewhere? Why do they seem to be losing in terms of annual income and daily or hourly earnings, a loss not offset by gains of other kinds? There is no one answer to these questions; a few reasons may be indicated.

One reason is the traditional American belief, still strong, that agriculture is "different"; that farm workers do not need and farmers cannot and should not be expected to provide the wages, hours, and working conditions now regarded as minimal standards of decency in the rest of the economy. For example, it is generally believed that, because of its highly seasonal nature, hours of labor in agriculture cannot possibly be limited in any way, and farmers cannot be expected to pay time and a half for overtime. It is argued that agriculture is inevitably highly seasonal and farmers cannot possibly stabilize employment. How these seasonal workers live the rest of the year is not the farmers' business. Because farm work is out of doors, it is believed that it cannot hurt children, however young or whatever the length of their working day.

Closely related to these assumptions about agriculture is the view that farmers have not shared in American prosperity. Their own "wages" or over-all earnings are too low to permit them to absorb the additional labor cost which higher wages and better conditions for their migrant workers would entail. In a highly competitive sector of the economy, it is said, the farmers cannot pass on added costs to the consumer. And anyway, if they could and raised the price of food, wouldn't that hurt more people than it would help?

Next consider that migrants are not year-round residents in Wisconsin, or any other state. They stay only a few months in the state, often only a few weeks in a locality. So there is a strong reluctance to accept responsibility for them—to spend money, private or public, on their behalf. Many farmers strongly resent being required to build adequate housing, because it will be used for only a short time each year. Many taxpayers are reluctant to see public money spent to give education to migrant children, whether it goes to enlarge school facilities to make room for migrant children for a few weeks in spring and fall or to set up summer school programs by which they can make up somewhat for their broken and shortened winter schooling. Texas should provide their schooling; why should Wisconsin? Similarly there is resistance to spending money for relief or medical assistance for migrants in need. They are nonresidents, why not just ship them home? In short, many farmers and many taxpayers think that somehow they should be able to bring from Texas just "hands" to harvest or cultivate the crops—not whole people, who bring their children along, too, with all the various needs these family groups involve.

Actually, just because they are migrants they need special services that residents do not need or perhaps even want, things that cost money, private or public, probably both. For example, if the women are to work in the fields, as they naturally want to with wages so low, what about the babies and young children? There should be day care centers for them and summer schools for the slightly older children. And what about health services? Foreign governments require a health insurance program for workers coming to the United States. Local hospitals in Wisconsin, left with the unpaid bills of migrants who became sick here, are beginning to think some such health insurance program should be required for domestic migrants. Who should pay for all this?

And migrants need special government regulations, just because they are migrants. For example they need regulation of the trucks and buses in which crew leaders transport them from Texas. The Interstate Commerce Commission now regulates this, but there is not enough money for enforcement. Wisconsin should provide regulation, as some other states do. Then regulation of the housing provided for migrants is essential. Wisconsin has done relatively well on this, but it is hard to convince some employers of migrants, and some other people too, that government should spend money to enforce regulation of migrant housing, and thus add to the farmer's costs, also. Do all Wisconsin residents have running hot water and showers and laundry facilities, they ask. Aren't these "do-gooders" pampering the Texas Mexicans, who "never had it so good" at home?

So much for attitudes and opinions. Next consider the economics of the situation. At first it seems surprising that market forces do not operate to bring wages and working conditions in seasonal agriculture somewhere near those which prevail in other segments of the Wisconsin economy. The great disparity could not continue without the migrant workers from Texas. Wisconsin residents do not work for these wages or under these conditions. Why do Texas workers come so far to get so little? The short answer is: they are better off than if they stayed at home. The average hourly wage in agriculture in Texas in 1961 was 74½¢, as against Wisconsin's 86½¢.[54] About 100,000 Texas Mexicans left their state in 1960 to do seasonal farm work in the North and West.[55] (The figure for 1961 is not obtainable.) And why have wages stayed so low in Texas? It seems highly probable that farm labor wages in Texas were held down by the annual importation of Mexican nationals. In 1960, 103,700 foreign farm workers worked in Texas; in 1961 the figure was 104,100.[56]

This arrangement for importing Mexican workers, described on p. 218, is embodied in a statute always referred to as Public Law 78. This provides for a treaty between the United States and Mexico which is supposed to protect both Mexican and American workers. Under the treaty, Mexican nationals must be paid the "prevailing wage for comparable agricultural work in the area" and may be brought in only if adequate domestic labor is not available. How is a domestic labor shortage determined? Up to 1961 the description given in the report of the President's Commission on Migratory Labor ten years earlier seemed still valid: "Farm employers meet in advance of the season and decide on the wage they intend to pay.... Whether the wage agreed upon is sufficient to attract the labor supply needed is apparently not usually considered an important factor in making the decision." [57] If the domestic supply was not adequate at the wages growers were offering, the Employment Service certified to a labor shortage and Mexican nationals were brought in to meet the labor demand. Thus farmers, in setting a wage for seasonal work, could ignore the good old economic law of demand and supply, because the statute in effect provided an unlimited supply of seasonal labor at whatever price the farmers set. As Secretary of Labor Goldberg testified in June 1961 at a Senate committee hearing: Domestic migrants "are forced to compete, as are no other workers in the country, with a large body of foreign workers brought into the country yearly with the approval of the National Government and under conditions which could hardly be more effectively designed to add to the depressed economic condition of these domestic workers." [58]

New attempts were made in 1962 to limit the importation of Mexican braceros by a more rigorous interpretation of the wording of Public Law 78 and the treaty with Mexico.[59]

Though Wisconsin in recent years has used relatively few foreign workers, the numbers brought into the United States to increase the farm labor supply elsewhere, especially in Texas, obviously affected the situation here. Texas Mexicans came north to work because the wages and other conditions, though low by Wisconsin standards, were better than they could get in Texas.

Ironically, as described earlier in this essay, the Mexican nationals, in fact all foreign migrants, are protected by certain "fringe benefits," including a work guarantee, which are not required for American migrants. So working in Texas, at lower wages than prevailed for similar agricultural work in Wisconsin, these foreign migrants perhaps were actually better off than the domestic migrants who came to Wisconsin from Texas to try to improve their condition.

Why has legislation, state or federal, done so little to improve the condition of American migrants working in agriculture? Perhaps the basic difficulty lies in the character of the prevailing employer-employee relation. This relation can be described as casual, short-time, disorganized, unstructured, and preindustrial. However described, it is so out of date in modern industrial America that conventional protective labor and social insurance laws do not fit. And the attempts to devise more appropriate laws or regulations have so far not been very successful.

When Carey McWilliams described the large-scale use of migrants in California agriculture years ago, he gave his book the arresting title *Factories in the Fields*. But actually, except for the size of the work force, the elements of industrial organization implicit in the word "factory" were and are almost entirely lacking. If the fruit and vegetable fields resemble factories, it is the factories of the very early 1800's, not of the twentieth century. In Wisconsin, though farms using migrants have not reached the size found in California, many of them can also be called factories, if only the number of workers employed is considered. But the industrial organization or discipline which prevails today in manufacturing or other kinds of nonagricultural economic activity is almost completely lacking. This creates baffling problems in applying government protection to these workers.

In the first place, a protective labor law assumes a known employer to be responsible for observing its provisions. In the same way a social insurance law assumes a known employer to pay his required tax or premium and to deduct and pay in the employee's tax, if any. Yet in the use of migrant labor in Wisconsin (as elsewhere) it is not always clear who the employer is. Is it the farmer on whose land the migrants work? Or the crew leader who brought them from Texas and who may be paid a lump sum which he distributes among the crew? [60] Or the canning or other processing company which provides workers to cultivate or harvest the crop it has contracted to buy? Or is there possibly no employer at all, as some of the farmers who grow cucumbers in Wisconsin allege? For years, the cucumber pickers' pay has been 50% of the price which the processor pays for the cucumbers. This, according to some growers, makes the pickers not employees but "independent contractors."

Protective labor laws assume not only known employers but also known employees. It is the employee who must be paid not less than the minimum wage (perhaps with time and a half for overtime). Similarly a child labor law assumes a child who asks to be an employee. It then puts the responsibility on the employer to assure himself that the child is not too young to be legally employed at the given job, or, if old enough, works only the permitted hours. For the most part social insurance laws, too, apply to employees,[61] and make their employers responsible for paying taxes on their behalf.

But where migrants work in agriculture in Wisconsin and elsewhere, the growers frequently allege that they really do not know just who are their employees. Presence at the workplace, they say, cannot be used as evidence of employment. In cherry picking, for example, the grower pays by the pail and makes no attempt to determine who filled it. WSES describes the arrangement in this way: "In the cherry harvest . . . family members work together as a unit and one payment is made each week to the family head for the total pails picked by the entire family." [62]

Wisconsin cherry growers frequently declare that those who are in the orchard are not necessarily employees. Texas Mexicans want their children with them. They often take even the babies into the orchard —whom would they leave them with in the camp, anyway? Further, one can't assume the women are working all the time; they take time out to nurse their babies, and so on. You can't tell about the children; some may not work at all; most don't work as long as their parents. As for the hours worked, even the men, we are told, set their own hours. Many of them start at daybreak and work till dark to earn as much as possible; others choose to knock off at noon. There is no set starting time and no quitting time.

At a Senate hearing in June 1961 the executive secretary of Michigan Field Crops, an association of growers, gave a similar description of how Texas Mexicans work. He said their foreign workers were paid by the hour and supervised in groups of 25. But domestic migrants, he declared, could not be paid on an hourly basis, and he explained why: "It just is not possible," he said, "to pay family type labor unsupervised by the hour. You have no idea how they work. You do not know how many there are—how many in the field, when they start and when they stop. . . . some of them are younger people, some women, some of whom are old people who do not want to work all day or cannot work all day, but can contribute something to the family income." He concluded that if it were necessary to pay domestic migrants on an hourly basis "we could not employ them—that is all." [63]

Any other employer of hundreds or even dozens of workers would think it impossible to run his business that way. Even if he pays wages on a piece-rate basis, he pays to individuals and thinks it necessary to keep track of their hours of work. He knows that children must not be permitted to work if they are below a given age. He objects to the presence of nonworkers or quasi workers in the workplace. He recognizes the necessity of having supervisors who keep track of what is going on. The workers are checked in and out, by time clock or otherwise, and the hours between are assumed to be hours of work.

As already suggested, baffling problems arise when the attempt is made to give agricultural migrant workers the protection afforded industrial workers. The unstructured or disorganized relation between the domestic migrants and the people for whom they work causes real difficulties. It is at least partly responsible for the failure to collect OASDI tax for and from about half these workers. It is largely responsible for the unsatisfactory character of Wisconsin's agricultural child labor order. It makes very difficult the enforcement of the state's minimum wage order; for when wages are paid on a piece-rate basis to the family head, how can we possibly know whether each individual member of the family is paid at least the minimum? Difficulties in providing workmen's compensation for migrants will come to light as the 1961 law operates. In view of the uncertainties as to who is the employer in a given situation, there will undoubtedly be questions as to who should buy the required insurance. If a child is injured in field or orchard, a question may well arise as to whether or not the accident occurred "in the course of employment" and hence whether it is or is not compensable.

It is really immaterial whether the lack of structure or the diverse and confusing forms of the employment relation are due to the desires of the workers or the growers. It may be true, as growers often allege, that Texas Mexicans, or at least some of them, like to be free to start and quit work when they choose and to have their children in the fields with them, whether they work or not. But it is also true that the farmers who need and use migrants have largely failed to assume the responsibilities assumed by employers in other segments of the economy. Further, it seems clear that they have not provided wages or working or living conditions which Wisconsin residents will accept; that is why they have to turn to migrants. Strong public sentiment has developed for government action on behalf of these migrants, because they are not able to secure improvement in their conditions by their own efforts. But effective government action will not be possible without better structuring of the employment relation in the kind of agriculture which uses migrant labor. Some clarification of law and fact is needed as to who employs whom. For protective labor legislation and social insurance laws can function only by putting certain responsibilities on known employers in relation to their known employees.

Conclusion

From the point of view of its organization, or the relation of its workers to its employers, agriculture is perhaps going through a transitional period between what in manufacturing were called the handicraft stage and the factory stage. In England and to some extent in the United States, this transition in manufacturing was a period of confusion and of worsening conditions for the workers.[64] Perhaps something analogous is happening in American agriculture today.

Agriculture in the United States is far advanced in technology. In fact, in recent years it has moved much faster in mechanization and increased productivity than any other segment of the economy. But some crops still need hand labor, especially in harvesting. It is generally believed in Wisconsin that residents of the state will not do that kind of back-breaking stoop labor. Perhaps they would if wages were more nearly comparable to wages in nonagricultural work. But believing as they do, Wisconsin food processors and farmers have contrived in various ways to secure a seasonal labor force willing to do stoop labor at wages and under conditions well below those prevailing in other segments of the economy. The domestic migrants involved do not number more than about 12,000 in Wisconsin; about half a million in the United States as a whole. Perhaps the miracles of technology will shrink these figures rather rapidly in the near future. But as of 1961 the number was large enough to cause concern in those who like to think of the United States as an "affluent society." And if most of these stoop labor jobs do disappear in the next few decades, they will leave behind an ugly residue of children grown into adults with so little education that they will be unable to function in the modern economy.

As the President's Commission on Migratory Labor concluded in 1951: "The issue . . . is job standards . . . Public policy must encourage farm employers to build reliable jobs for reliable people, not to maintain obsolete and intolerable standards. The management of our farms must learn to do what management in industry and commerce have done ... We must build toward an agriculture that will yield a decent American income for those who provide labor." [65]

A decade later, action still needs to be taken in Wisconsin as elsewhere to implement that policy. We need laws and regulations specifically adapted to the special problems involved. If we seek to follow in "John R's" footsteps, we must try to find out more about what is actually happening and why. This should help us devise more effective government action to better the condition of agricultural migrants.

Notes

1 Wisconsin Statutes, 103.77 (2).
2 Wisconsin Industrial Commission, *Biennial Report* (1924–26), p. 38.
3 This attempt to limit the children's hours of work sounds reasonable. But then (and even now) limitation of hours in agriculture was unrealistic and very difficult to enforce.
4 It was in this a forerunner of the present provision on child labor in agriculture in the Fair Labor Standards Act (this provision was enacted in 1949).
5 For the full wording of the order see *Biennial Report*, p. 39.
6 George Hill, *Texas Mexican Migratory Agricultural Workers in Wisconsin*, Agricultural Experiment Station Stencil Bull. 6 (University of Wisconsin, 1948), p. 4; and Salick, Long, and Sorden, *The Wisconsin Farm Labor Program, 1943–1947*, Agricultural Extension Service, College of Agriculture, University of Wisconsin, 1948. Mimeographed.
7 Wisconsin State Employment Service Fact Sheet, "Migratory Workers in Wisconsin, 1961." Mimeographed.
    It should be noted that the WSES count includes migrant workers in "seasonal food processing," i.e. in freezing, canning, and pickling plants. Nobody knows what figure should be subtracted to get the figure for field workers only.
8 U. S. Department of Health, Education, and Welfare, Social Security Administration, Children's Bureau, *Children in Migrant Families*, a report to Committee on Appropriations, U. S. Senate (Dec. 1960), p. 59.
9 See the findings of a study made in Wisconsin in 1960 as part of a research project of the University School of Education, financed by the U. S. Office of Education. It is reproduced in U. S. Senate, Subcommittee on Migratory Labor of the Committee on Labor and Public Welfare, Hearings April 12 and 13, 1961, 87th Cong., 1st Sess., p. 349. Many other studies showing similar retardation could be cited.
10 U. S. Department of Agriculture, Statistical Reporting Service, Agricultural Estimates Division, *Farm Labor* release, Jan. 10, 1962.
11 Figures secured from Wisconsin Industrial Commission, Statistical Department.
12 Ibid.

13 U. S. Department of Agriculture, Economic Research Service, Agriculture Information Bull. 238, *The Hired Farm Working Force of 1959*, p. 43, Table 29.
14 Figures secured from Wisconsin Industrial Commission, Statistical Department.
15 U. S. Department of Agriculture, Economic Research Service, Farm Population Branch, Economic and Statistical Analysis Division, Advance Report, *The Hired Farm Working Force of 1961*, July 1962.
16 U. S. Department of Agriculture, Economic Research Service, Agriculture Information Bull. 266, *The Hired Farm Working Force of 1960*, p. 43, Table 27.
17 Ibid.
18 Salick, Long, and Sorden, *The Wisconsin Farm Labor Program, 1943–1947*, Ap. C, p. 15.
19 For one small exception see p. 209 of this book, on the federal Sugar Act of 1937. This act limits hours for children 14 to 16 years old to eight per day, but it is doubtful whether any attempt is made to enforce this rule.
20 New York Department of Labor, Pub. No. B-116, *Employment and Earnings of Migrant Farm Workers in New York State* (Aug. 1960), p. 9.
21 U. S. Senate, Subcommittee on Migratory Labor of Committee on Labor and Public Welfare, Hearings Aug. to Dec. 1959, 86th Cong., 1st Sess., p. 320.
22 U. S. Department of Labor, Bureau of Labor Standards, Bull. 236, *Programs of National Organizations for Migrant Farm Workers and Their Families*, Dec. 1961.
23 U. S. Department of Labor, Bureau of Employment Security, *Farm Labor Market Developments* (Jan. 1962), p. 18.
24 For data on these committees see U. S. Department of Labor, Bureau of Labor Standards, Bull. 215, *State Migratory Committees. Their Organization and Programs*, 1960.
25 In 1959 the Wage and Hour Division of the U. S. Department of Labor found 4,389 children working in agriculture in violation of the act, the great majority of them under 14. The division reported that "illegal employment of children under 16 years in agriculture constitutes the most numerous type of violation covered by the child labor provisions of FLSA." *Child Labor Today* (1959), p. 3.
26 See discussion of the Wisconsin provision on p. 215.
27 The number was 1,910,000. Figure obtained through OASDI Field Office in Madison.
28 The number was 2,162,000. U. S. Department of Agriculture, Economic Research Service, Agriculture Information Bull. 266, *The Hired Farm Working Force of 1960*, p. 7.
29 Ibid., p. 8.
30 Figures are not available to make this comparison for 1961, but it is unlikely that the gap has been narrowed substantially.
31 U. S. Department of Health, Education, and Welfare, Social Security Administration, Bureau of Old-Age and Survivors Insurance, *Social Security Handbook*, Jan. 1, 1960, sec. 731, p. 101 and pp. 103–6. Or

see U. S. Code, Title 42, subchap. 2, sec. 409 (2) and sec. 410 (0).

32 Ibid.

33 Sugar Act, Public Law 414, 75th Cong. Or see U. S. Code, Title 7, sec. 1131 (a).

34 Ibid. (c).

35 Information obtained orally from Leo Ley, administrator of this program in Wisconsin for U. S. Department of Agriculture.

36 Public Law 78, 82d Cong., as amended, Standard Work Contract, Art. 7 and Joint Operating Instructions No. 1 as published by U. S. Department of Labor, Bureau of Employment Security, Oct. 1959, under title *Information concerning Entry of Mexican Agricultural Workers into the United States.*

37 U. S. Senate, Subcommittee on Migratory Labor of the Committee on Labor and Public Welfare, *The Migratory Farm Labor Problem in the United States.* A report together with individual views (Sept. 1961), p. 19.

38 U. S. Department of Labor, Bureau of Employment Security, *Annual Report, Fiscal Year 1960,* p. 82.

39 Wisconsin Administrative Code, Ind. 72.04.

40 Ibid., Ind. 72.02 (4). "Where payment of wages is made upon a basis or system other than time rate, the actual wage shall not be less than provided for in this order, but if the piece rates paid for any particular kind of work yield to 65% of the women and minors employed thereon 5¢ per hour more than the minimum hourly rates prescribed in paragraph (1) then such piece rates are deemed adequate for such employees and differences between earnings at these rates and the prescribed hourly rates do not have to be made up by the employer."

41 Ibid., Ind. 72.04 (3). Effective July 1, 1961.

42 New York Session Laws of 1961, chap. 300; of 1962, chap. 87.

43 California Industrial Welfare Commission, Order No. 14–61. See also discussion of this subject on p. 224 of this essay.

44 Wisconsin Statutes, 103.77 (2).

45 Wisconsin Administrative Code, Ind. 70.16.

46 They also claim that the adult migrants who harvest cucumbers are "independent contractors," not employees, because their pay is set as one half of the price paid for the cucumbers (see on p. 223 of this essay). If the adult migrants are not employees, it might be claimed that the migrant children work for their parents and hence are not subject to any order issued under the child labor law. At first glance this claim seems possible because that law contains a provision that children working on a farm for their parents are not subject to it. Wisconsin Statutes, 103.67 (4). However this provision would not seem to apply to migrants. It reads: "Nothing in 103.64–103.82 shall be construed to apply to the employment of a minor engaged in domestic or farm work performed outside school hours in connection with the minor's own home and directly for his parent or guardian."

47 Wisconsin Session Laws of 1961, chap. 572.

48 Ibid., chap. 387.

49 Alaska, California, Connecticut, Hawaii, Massachusetts, Ohio, Puerto Rico, Vermont, and Wisconsin.

50 Wisconsin Session Laws of 1961, chap. 470; Wisconsin Statutes, 146.19.
51 Public Law 78, 82d Cong., as amended, Migrant Labor Agreement of 1951, as amended, Standard Work Contract as amended, published by U. S. Department of Labor, Bureau of Employment Security, Oct. 1959, under title *Information concerning Entry of Mexican Agricultural Workers into the United States.* Or see U. S. Code, Title 49, sec. 303 (b) and 304 (3a) and Title 7, sec. 1461. For amendments in 1961 see Public Law 345, 87th Cong. See especially Art. 16 of the Agreement and Art. 10 of the Standard Work Contract. Special contracts for four-week periods are permitted, but then 160 hours of work must be guaranteed, which would amount to eight hours a day on five-sixths of the workdays.
52 Ibid. See Art. 19 of the Agreement and Arts. 2, 3, and 7 of the Standard Work Contract.
53 California Legislature, Assembly Bill 1663, 1961.
54 U. S. Department of Agriculture, Statistical Reporting Service, Agricultural Estimates Division, *Farm Labor* release Jan. 10. 1962, p. 15.
55 U. S. Department of Labor, Bureau of Employment Security, *Hired Farm Workers in the United States* (June 1961), p. 30.
56 Ibid. and U. S. Department of Labor, Bureau of Employment Security, *Farm Labor Market Developments* (Jan. 1962), p. 22.
57 Report of the President's Commission on Migratory Labor, *Migratory Labor in American Agriculture* (1951), p. 59.
58 U. S. Senate, Subcommittee on Agricultural Research and General Legislation of the Committee on Agriculture and Forestry, Hearings June 12 and 13, 1961, on *Extension of Mexican Farm Labor Program,* 87th Cong., 1st Sess., p. 105.
59 For the earlier discussion of this see above, p. 211.
60 This is said to be rare in Wisconsin, more common in some other states.
61 OASDI now does make provision for the self-employed—a category singularly inappropriate for migrant farm workers for several reasons.
62 Wisconsin State Employment Service, *Migratory Labor in Wisconsin Agriculture, 1959,* p. 13.
63 Hearings in n. 58 above, p. 98.
64 Cf. John R. Commons, "American Shoemakers, 1648–1895," in *Labor and Administration,* 1913.
65 Report of the President's Commission on Migratory Labor, *Migratory Labor in American Agriculture* (1951), p. 24.

9 DAVID B. JOHNSON

Prevailing Wage Law

A perennial problem of administration is how to eliminate functions after the need for them has disappeared. This is not a matter peculiar to government, but perhaps it has received greater attention there than in other spheres of administrative activity. For instance, the first Hoover Commission listed several examples of redundant governmental activities which either were duplicated by other agencies or had not been discarded after the original need had changed.[1]

Is it not possible that protections created by social legislation may also become obsolete? Recently it has been alleged that this is the case with prevailing wage laws applicable to work performed on government contracts—that the laws were enacted at a time when competitive bidding by employers for government contracts resulted in exploitation of workers. Since then, according to this view, the National Labor Relations Act, other minimum wage legislation, and a strong labor movement have made prevailing wage laws unnecessary.

In light of the changed circumstances of the 1960's some questions are appropriately raised concerning prevailing wage legislation. These include: (1) Is it necessary for government to continue to support wage standards which are far above anything that could be considered exploitative? (2) If the first question is answered in the affirmative (as it will be if one believes that the consequences of competitive pressures are as great as ever), questions still remain as to whether established wage standards are (a) appropriate and (b) properly administered. It is the purpose of this essay to try to answer these questions. We shall begin by examining the origin and operation of prevailing wage policy in this and other countries; then analyze in somewhat greater detail this country's principal prevailing wage statute and current problems of its administration; and conclude with some recommendations for modifications in present policy. Because their records and reports became available after this essay was written, little consideration is given here to recent hearings held by a subcommittee of the House Committee on Education and Labor.

Prevailing wage legislation differs from minimum wage law. Minimum wage law in the United States has had the threefold purpose of preventing the most flagrant kind of exploitation, guaranteeing a minimum rate standard, and removing wages at the lowest level from the ill effects of competitive forces. Prevailing wage regulation has the more limited purpose of taking wages out of competition in bidding for government contracts. But it has a much broader effect upon the workers covered by it since it specifies the rate to be paid each individual. In the United States prevailing wage law applies broadly to "public works" (typically described as "construction, alteration, and/or repair ... of public buildings or public works") done under contract. In some other countries it is applied uniformly both to public works of this sort and to contracts for supplies and equipment. United States wage regulation on Federal Government contracts of the latter type is handled by a prevailing *minimum* wage law, the Walsh-Healey Act,[2] enacted in 1936. The two kinds of laws are quite different. The intent of prevailing wage law is that wage rates on government contracts should mirror conditions existing in the immediate area of the work. Consequently each person employed under the contract is required to be paid the rate he would receive doing the same kind of work on a similar project in the locality. But prevailing minimum wage law requires only that all covered workers be paid not less than a minimum figure which is established beforehand. This kind of regulation does not control the rates paid to covered employees who receive more than the minimum. Because the Walsh-Healey Act presents somewhat different problems, this essay is limited to an analysis of prevailing wage law.

Prevailing Wage Law in the United States

State legislation on the prevailing wage antedates federal law by many years, the first state law having been passed in Kansas in 1891. The Davis-Bacon Act,[3] regulating wages on public works performed under contract with the Federal Government, was passed in 1931, and a majority of the existing state laws followed during the next four years.

The first effective federal law regulating wages of nongovernment employees, the Davis-Bacon Act preceded passage of the Wagner Act and the era of large-scale union organization; it preceded passage of minimum wage legislation and most parts of our social security program. The explanation of this precocity is the extent of organization on both employer and employee sides in the construction industry. The building trades unions were among the strongest and (aside from the railroad unions) perhaps politically the most effective force in a weak labor movement in 1931. The employers have long been associated in trade groups in the building industry and therefore could not have been expected to oppose removal of wages from the area of competition on government work. Furthermore, the period was one in which the evils of "destructive competition" were constantly being stressed. Agreements for the mitigation of competition were common. Shortly afterward this feeling was written into law in the National Industrial Recovery Act.

The basic requirements of the Davis-Bacon Act are

That the advertised specifications for every contract in excess of $2000, to which the United States . . . is a party, for construction, alteration, and/or repair, including painting and decorating, of public buildings or public works of the United States . . . and which requires or involves the employment of mechanics and/or laborers shall contain a provision stating the minimum wages to be paid various classes of laborers and mechanics which shall be based upon the wages that will be determined by the Secretary of Labor to be prevailing for the corresponding classes of laborers and mechanics employed on projects of a character similar to the contract work in the city, town, village, or other civil subdivision of the State in which the work is to be performed, . . . and every contract based upon these specifications shall contain a stipulation that the contractor or his subcontractor shall pay all mechanics and laborers employed directly upon the site of the work, unconditionally and not less often than once a week, and without subsequent deduction or rebate on any account, the full amounts accrued at time of payment, computed at wage rates not less than those stated in the advertised specifications, regardless of any contractual relationship which may be alleged to exist between the contractor or subcontractor and such laborers and mechanics . . . .

All contracts subject to the act must also contain stipulations that the government may withhold payments to the contractor for the purpose of reimbursing workers if they have been underpaid, and that the government may terminate the contract in the event of a violation, prosecute the work to completion by other means, and hold the original contractor liable for any excess costs. The rates for each classification of worker to be employed on a project are issued by the Department of Labor to the contracting agency before the commencement of work. Schedules of the rates are included in advertised specifications and in contracts for performance of the work. The rates are determined on the basis of evidence gathered by the Department of Labor. If a contracting agency fails to award its contract within ninety days of issuance of a determination, a new one must be requested. Employers are required to file weekly payroll affidavits, to have payroll records available for inspection, and to maintain them for a period of three years following completion of the contract. Contract rates must be posted at the jobsite. Violations may result in blacklisting for a period of three years.

The standards of the Davis-Bacon Act, and its related statutes, the Copeland Act and the Contract Work-Hour Standards Act of 1962, have been applied also to work performed under authority of various loan guarantee and federal grants-in-aid programs to the states.[4]

STATE LAW

Thirty-three states now have acts calling for payment of prevailing wages on their own public works performed under contract.[5] A great part of the state legislation follows closely the pattern of the Davis-Bacon Act, but some innovation should be noted. Several states have added premiums, allowances, and other fringe benefits to the rates predetermined for payment under the contract. And a number of states have substituted the criterion of the negotiated rate, where one exists, for the Davis-Bacon method of determining prevailing rates.

Trends in application of the laws have been mixed since 1931. The prevailing rate principle has been applied more broadly as government public works have expanded to include housing, airports, hospitals, and highways. Also the absolute quantity of public construction work has increased greatly: from $2.7 billion in 1931 to $17 billion in 1961. But public construction as a percentage of gross national product is about what it was in 1931: 3.5% that year, 3.3% in 1961. As a percentage of all government expenditure, it declined from 22% in 1931 to 11% in 1960. Although it dominated all construction during the early years of these laws (41% in 1931, 59% in 1934, 76% in 1942), it had declined to 29% in 1961.[6] Thus, while prevailing rate legislation has fairly broad applicability, its impact has been felt more widely during depression and wartime, when government expands public works programs. Somewhere between a half million and a million workers are currently covered by the federal and state laws.

Legislation Elsewhere

One of the purposes of this essay is to consider whether any of the experience of foreign countries can be applied to our own problems.

As in other areas of protective labor legislation, the United States lagged behind Europe in enacting wage regulation under government contracts, although the first state law coincided with Britain's first parliamentary action in this field. In 1891 the House of Commons passed the following resolution: "That in the opinion of this house, it is the duty of the Government in all Government contracts to make provision against the evils recently disclosed before the Sweating Committee, to insert such conditions as may prevent the abuse arising from sub-letting, and to make every effort to secure the payment of such wages as are generally accepted as current in each trade for competent workmen." [7]

Sidney and Beatrice Webb have attributed the adoption of prevailing wage regulation to the trade unions.[8] The record of debate on the British Fair Wages Resolution shows early consideration of the criterion of negotiated rates in determining what was "fair." The 1891 resolution did not contain such wording, but a new resolution adopted in 1909 did. The general effect of the 1909 resolution was to make specific the terminology used in 1891. In requiring that contractors "pay rates of wages and observe hours of labour not less favourable than those commonly recognized by employers and trade societies," the resolution adopted the criterion of the trade union rate in cases where the employees were organized. It also added "hours" to the prevailing standard, an amendment designed to prevent employers from paying prevailing weekly wages for longer than prevailing weekly hours of work.

In the absence of trade union organization the standard was to be that which prevailed "amongst good employers." And where the district had no ascertainable prevailing practice, that in the nearest district where similar industrial circumstances existed was to be used. This then still represented a compromise with those who opposed encouragement of collective bargaining through this device, and a recognition that the resolution was not to be used to promote union organization where it did not otherwise exist. The resolution regulated subcontracting in specific terms and made the prime contractor responsible for observance of its terms in case subcontracts were permitted.

There were no further changes in the resolution until after World War II. At that time an entirely new Fair Wages Resolution was adopted, representing a substantial change. Notably it adopted negotiated rates in the district as its sole wage criterion, whether or not the contractor himself dealt with a union representing his employees. It also added "fair" conditions of labor to "fair" wages. It recognized in specific terms the freedom of employees to be members of trade unions, and required employers to maintain "fair" wages, hours, and working conditions for *all* workers employed, whether or not such employment was on the government work. The employer is further required to give an assurance, before he can be placed on the register of firms invited to tender, that he has complied with the general conditions required by the resolution for a period of at least three months. Under the 1909 resolution questions of compliance were left to the contracting departments. Under the new resolution complaints of noncompliance are reported to the Ministry of Labour and, if not disposed of by it, are referred to arbitration. The contractor is required to notify his employees of the existence of the resolution by posting it in the workplace during the period of execution of the contract.

There are several contrasts between British and American prevailing wage regulation. The first difference is that the British resolution is not a law. Rather, it is an expression to the contracting departments of the will of Parliament on the subject of wages and working conditions under government contracts. As such it does not provide legal penalties for noncompliance. It merely states that government contracts should contain an expression of the conditions in the resolution. Thus, the contracting departments embody the terms of the resolution in their contracts. A breach of the requirements of the resolution may be dealt with by a damage action at common law. In practice this eventuality does

not arise, partly because a damage action leaves the issue of performance of the contract unresolved, but more importantly because the resolution and other legislation provide better alternatives.[9]

A second major difference from the American law is the universal
applicability of the British resolution. Unlike the American law it applies to all government contracts. The most important difference, however, is the use by the United Kingdom of the criterion of wages and
other conditions of employment which have been established by negotiation or arbitration. The chief effect of this is to shift most of the re-
sponsibiltiy for administering the provisions of the resolution to the
trade unions and the employers, whereas in the United States system
determination of prevailing conditions is a governmental responsibility.

The British have not stopped at applying the prevailing wage principle to government contracts. It has also been used as a device to assure
that certain employers who receive government subsidies or require
special licenses to operate will not use a favored position to exploit their
employees. Six industries have thus been brought under the provisions
of the Fair Wages Resolution since 1925. These are sugar, road transport, cinema production and exhibition, civil aviation, housing, and
television.

In general these clauses in statutes regulating these industries simply
say that in the absence of negotiated conditions the terms and conditions of employment on the work covered by the legislation will be no
less favorable than such terms would be for employees of a contractor
subject to the requirements of the Fair Wages Resolution. Disputes
about what these wages and conditions of employment ought to be, if
not disposed of by negotiation between the parties or conciliation by
the Ministry of Labour, are referred to the Industrial Court for settlement. Industrial Court awards must be observed in the employment
contract unless changed by negotiation. These clauses are specific requirements of law and may be enforced by withdrawal by the government of the license, subsidy, grant, or other protection for which they
are a quid pro quo.

The British prevailing wage policy functions very well, at least in
periods of full employment. Its virtue is a great economy of government
regulation. The resolution itself is short (as are the clauses included in
the six statutes), and there are no regulations issued by the Ministry of
Labour, which has the principal responsibility for enforcement. There
is no single person in the entire British Government who devotes his

time solely to enforcement of fair wages regulation. The operation of the resolution is of a piece with the general philosophy of British labor law, which is to encourage in all its aspects the determination of wages, hours, and working conditions by the accepted institutions of negotiation between associations of employers and associations of employees, aided by conciliation services provided by the government where necessary and by arbitration where agreement eludes the parties. This system does not operate with the kind of precision as to rates which is a part of the American prevailing rate legislation, but the lack of criticism of its operation by employee and employer groups indicates that it has succeeded in eliminating the exploitation stemming from competition for contracts—which is its principal purpose.

CANADIAN PREVAILING WAGE LAW

Canadian law in this field is almost as old as its British model. Canada first adopted a fair wages policy in 1900. A resolution of the House of Commons, this was modeled after the British Fair Wages Resolution of 1891. It was later implemented by an Order in Council of June 7, 1922, subsequently amended in 1924 and 1934. Beginning with the 1922 regulations Canada made a distinction between the handling of building and construction contracts (designated as "A" conditions) and supply and equipment contracts ("B" conditions). In 1935 the distinction was emphasized further when the Fair Wages and Hours of Labour Act was passed. This act, devoted mainly to wage rates, also contains an 8-hour-day and 44-hour-week restriction. It is applicable to "construction, remodelling, repair, or demolition of any work" under government contract or in cases where the Dominion Government subsidizes, contributes, loans, or advances money for such work. In addition, the method of establishing fair wages and hours for contract employees also applies to a segment of direct government employees paid on an hourly basis. Unlike the British resolution, which applies to all ranks of employees, the Canadian law applies only to laborers and mechanics.[10]

In several significant aspects the operation of the Fair Wages and Hours of Labour Act is similar to that of the Davis-Bacon Act, which was also given its present form in that year. The regulations issued pursuant to the act [11] specify the kinds of projects [12] and the manner in which wages and hours are determined. As under the Davis-Bacon Act, when a department is contemplating performance of work, it must communicate facts of the contract to the Minister of the Labour Department, who then furnishes to it appropriate schedules of the rates of wages and hours in the district in which the work is to be performed.

As in the American case, this involves a predetermination of rates. It may also involve a predetermination of hours at a figure lower than the 8-hour-daily or 44-hour-weekly maximum written into the law. But where the Canadian regulations depart from the United States regulations is in the definition of wage criteria. Here Canada moves in the direction of the wording of the regulations in the British resolution, for here negotiated conditions are recognized. The regulations state: "By the term 'current wages' and the term 'hours of labour fixed by the custom of the trade' . . . are meant respectively the standard rates of wages and hours of labour either recognized by signed agreements between employers and workmen in the district from which the labour required is necessarily drawn, or actually prevailing although not necessarily recognized by signed agreements."

In other respects the Canadian act and regulations are similar to the United States act. Submission of payroll affidavits and posting of wage rates at the worksite are required, and records must be kept available for inspection. The government department may withhold funds in case of default in wage payments. As in the British resolution, and not the Davis-Bacon Act, the prime contractor must get approval before subcontracting any of the work. Subcontractors are bound by conditions in the prime contract. None of the work under the contract may be performed in the homes of workmen.

The chief way in which the Canadian law differs from that of the United States is that the regulations issued under it allow the Minister of Labour to recognize negotiated rates and hours to be prevailing or "fair" within the meaning of the act.

THE LAW OF FRANCE

France's legislation in this field originated in 1899 [13] under the sponsorship of the Socialist Minister of Labor, Alexandre Millerand. The law was revised in 1937 [14] during the Popular Front and again in 1940 [15] and 1955.[16] It covers all contracts of the national government, departments, communes, and public charitable establishments. Wages must not be less favorable than the rates usually paid the same occupations and classifications in the locality where the work is performed. Representative collective bargaining agreements or custom provide the standard for wages, hours, and other conditions of employment.

The specifications and the contract language refer to the legislative provisions and the collective agreements in force rather than to specific rates and conditions. In this respect French law is like British law in extending negotiated conditions to unorganized employees of government contractors. The law has an unusual provision which allows a contractor to pay certain physically handicapped workers as much as 30 percent less than other workers in the same category, although the proportion of physically handicapped workers must not exceed 20 percent. Posting of the wage scales is required. Contractors' records are inspected by the government, which may withhold amounts necessary to pay workers who have not received full compensation as required. The requirements apply to hours and other conditions of employment as well as to wages. The law has special provisions for the protection of home workers, who are perhaps a larger proportion of the work force in France than they are elsewhere.[17]

THE ILO CONVENTION

Prevailing wage law was recognized as a desirable objective of public policy by an International Labor Conference in 1949. At that time a convention and a recommendation on the subject were approved.

The convention [18] is a comprehensive document which applies to three kinds of government contracts: construction of public works; manufacture of materials, supplies, or equipment; performance of services. Working conditions covered include wages, hours, allowances, and other conditions of labor "not less favourable than those established for work of the same character in the trade or industry concerned in the district where the work is carried on—(a) by collective agreement or other recognized machinery of negotiation between organizations of employers and workers representative respectively of substantial proportions of the employers and workers in the trade or industry concerned; or (b) by arbitration award; or (c) by national laws or regulations." [19]

When no such criteria exist for the measurement of prevailing conditions in the district where the work is to be carried on, the clause included in the contract is to ensure conditions not less favorable than those established by collective bargaining, arbitration, or national regulation "for work of the same character in the trade or industry concerned in the nearest appropriate district," [20] or "the general level observed in the trade or industry in which the contractor is engaged by employers whose general circumstances are similar." [21] Such terms are to be advertised along with contract specifications to be sure that prospective contractors will be aware of them. Fair and reasonable conditions of health, safety, and welfare are to be attained as appropriate according to national circumstance.

The convention is to be brought to the notice of all persons concerned, by proper advertising, with the contract specifications, and by posting of notices at the worksite. Enforcement measures are to include adequate record keeping and systems of inspection. Suggested sanctions are the withholding of contracts for failure to observe the requirements of the labor clauses and withholding of payments under the contract for the purpose of making workers whole for underpayments. The convention provides for exemption of areas where it seems impracticable to enforce the provisions because of sparse population or lack of industrial development. This provision was intended for underdeveloped countries and was accompanied by clear restrictions on the designation of such areas.

The recommendation which accompanies the convention suggests application of the principles of the convention to cases where private employers are granted subsidies or licenses. It also suggests more specific conditions to be covered by the labor clauses, including normal overtime rates, specific limitations on daily and weekly hours, shift hours for continuous process operations, and holiday and sick leave provisions.

The convention has been ratified by twenty-one nations [22] and has also been made applicable with or without modifications to forty non-metropolitan territories of four of the ratifying nations: Belgium, France, the Netherlands, and the United Kingdom. Several nations have adopted prevailing wage laws or other forms of regulations applicable to public contracts but have not ratified the convention. These are Canada, Pakistan, Switzerland, the Union of South Africa, the United States,[23] India, and New Zealand. The states which have laws or regulations and have also ratified the convention are France, Guatemala, Israel, Italy, Morocco, the Netherlands, the United Kingdom, and

Uruguay.[24] For the most part these laws use collectively bargained conditions as criteria for what is prevailing. Israel goes beyond this and adopts the trade union rate without reference to negotiations.

Data on prevailing wage legislation are insufficient for generalizing on the circumstances in countries which have adopted it other than to indicate that the problems arising from competitive bidding are universal. Adoption is not explained by the presence of strong labor movements in all cases. In fact some countries, notably Norway and Sweden, have asserted to ILO that the existence of strong union organizations has made prevailing wage regulation unnecessary. Nor is it clear why the convention was not adopted by ILO in 1935, say, rather than 1949, since such legislation is usually associated with depression. There is considerable information however about the circumstances under which the American legislation was enacted.

The Davis-Bacon Act

HISTORY OF THE ACT

One of the most common allegations against the Davis-Bacon Act is that it was depression legislation, passed when unions were weak, and is therefore no longer necessary.[25] While it is true that this law and many state acts originated in depression, the circumstances of passage of the ILO Convention and subsequent encouragement of passage of prevailing wage law by member countries during a period of generally high employment indicate that these laws also have some other basis. In this connection we should not ignore the fact that nine states in this country have adopted new laws or substantially changed their old legislation during the last decade.

Nevertheless the Davis-Bacon Act clearly *was* depression legislation. Its enactment two years before the New Deal reflects more than a desire to protect the welfare of working people. Moreover its sponsor in the House, Representative Robert L. Bacon of New York, indicated that he had introduced such a bill as early as 1927.[26] Earlier proposals had the support of construction employers as well as of labor organizations, as did the Davis-Bacon Act itself.[27] Passage of the law in 1931 apparently came as a result of a ruling by the Comptroller General that an administrative device (notifying bidders they were to pay prevailing rates) to take wages out of competition on government work was illegal in the absence of a statute.[28] Thus the bill as introduced had the backing of all the departments concerned with the government's building program, including Treasury, Labor, War, Navy, and the Veterans Bureau.

The Federal Government had entered upon an eight- to ten-year building program. The bill was said to be necessary as part of the government's program for stimulating the economy by providing employment and maintaining wage levels. The bill's supporters gave heaviest emphasis to the argument that successful bidders on government building projects were importing labor from distant localities and paying them wages below those prevailing in the local community. Not far below the surface in this discussion it is possible to detect dissatisfaction with the general requirement of acceptance of the lowest bid. There was as much sentiment in the construction industry as in Congress or among other groups to favor home industry. At one point in the debate Representative Bacon said: "This bill, my friends, is simply to give local labor and the local contractor a fair opportunity to participate in this building program." [29] Building contractors favored passage of a prevailing wage bill, although the Associated General Contractors of America had indicated in a letter to the President which was introduced into the record [30] that they thought the wording of the bill was "uncertain" and that it should be modified to provide for predetermination of rates by the department doing the contracting and for their inclusion in the specifications or advertisements for bids and in the contract itself.

The Comptroller General of the United States favored similar amendments on the ground that they would reduce doubt and uncertainty. The vote was not recorded. Among those who spoke in support of it were Fiorello LaGuardia of New York, Adolph Sabath of Illinois, William Connery (who later cosponsored the Wagner Act) and John McCormack, both of Massachusetts.

The identical bill had already been passed unanimously by the Senate almost without discussion.[31] Senators Couzens of Michigan and La Follette of Wisconsin spoke for it.

The act was given its present form in 1935. Hearings held by the Senate in 1933 [32] and 1934 [33] had developed evidence of widespread flaunting of the prevailing wage principle. This resulted partly from the absence of predetermined rates. Under the 1931 law the Secretary of Labor made a rate determination only when the parties were in dispute about it. Such decisions did not operate retroactively. In a period of generally declining rates this might provide additional incentive for rate cutting. Also widespread was the practice of employers taking kickbacks from employees on public works. This was really a form of job peddling, which could be expected in a labor market where demand was limited and wage rates sticky. The rates in construction declined less than in other industries for a number of reasons. First, the government under Hoover and Roosevelt had urged that rates not be cut. Second, building trades unions were strong enough to resist cuts. Third, employers and employees alike recognized that in many cases "prevailing" rates were sheer fiction and that actual rates paid were much lower. The existence of the prevailing rate law had therefore necessitated arrangements which would preserve appearances of conformance but would result in payment of the actual rates.

The most significant amendments in 1935 provided for predetermination of rates by the Secretary of Labor and penalties for wage kickbacks.[34] The 1935 law also provided a reduction of the minimum limitation on covered contracts from $5,000 to $2,000; extension of coverage to public works as well as public buildings; addition of "painting and decorating" to "construction, alteration, and repair" (added at the request of the painters' union after the Comptroller General had ruled painting of existing buildings out from coverage, the new wording first raised the issue of whether or not the act applies to maintenance work); clarification of the standard of comparison for rates to specify "corresponding classes of laborers and mechanics employed on projects of a character similar to the contract work"; provision for the contracting agency of the government to withhold from the contractor amounts necessary to reimburse employees who had not been paid the proper wage; authority for the contracting agency to cancel the contract where there were breaches of the wage stipulation; disqualification of violators of the act from bidding on government contracts for three years; and provision for suits by aggrieved employees against the contractor's bond when funds withheld were insufficient for full reimbursement.

JUDICIAL INTERPRETATION OF THE ACT

Considering the length of time the law has existed, there have been remarkably few court cases, partly because of an early decision (1933) that the Secretary of Labor's wage determinations are not subject to attack on judicial review.[35] A few years later the Fifth Circuit Court of Appeals decided that determination of rates by the Secretary under the Davis-Bacon Act is valid without a formal hearing.[36] These views were further reinforced by the Lukens Steel case, decided under the Walsh-Healey Act in 1940; [37] the judgment in this case declared that the act was designed for the benefit of employees, not contractors, and that it did not bestow litigable rights on those desirous of selling to the government if they disagreed with a wage determination by the Secretary of Labor. This decision is generally believed to have validated the Davis-Bacon Act as well as the Walsh-Healey Act. Written by Justice Black, the decision is not unlike that of the New York Court of Appeals in 1927, written by Justice Cardozo,[38] upholding the New York prevailing wage statute.

In 1954 in the Binghamton case [39] the Supreme Court applied the same reasoning to the Davis-Bacon Act and cited the Alliance, Gillioz, and Lukens cases. In this case the court also declared that the government was not obligated to reimburse a contractor for rates higher than he had expected to pay, even though the government had failed to disclose the existence of higher rates at the time the contract was made. The effect of these decisions has been to emphasize the importance of opinions issued by the Department of Labor and the Comptroller General. Until very recently, however, the opinions of the Solicitor of Labor were not publicly released as a routine matter. The division of authority between the two agencies is still not always clear. Often their views on administration of the law appear to be in conflict.[40]

CRITICISM OF THE ACT

In recent years two broad questions have been raised about the Davis-Bacon Act. These are (1) Is the law administered fairly and equitably to all affected parties? (2) In view of changed circumstances since its enactment thirty years ago, is the act still necessary? The issues are discussed here in reverse order.

How valid is the assertion that the law has outlived its usefulness? Let us return to the original reasons for passage. The chief one was that although competitive bidding for government work was desirable in order to reduce costs, economy should not be obtained at the expense of labor standards. Since competition would otherwise result in depressing labor rates and other conditions by importation of labor from low-rate areas, it was necessary to assure that standards existing in the vicinity where the work was to be performed would be maintained.

In what ways have the circumstances changed so as to warrant repeal of the law? There are several. Most important has been the increased strength of the unions representing affected employees. While the building trades were relatively well organized when the law was passed, the general upsurge of union organization and growth of the practice of determining employment conditions through collective bargaining have occurred since then. Most though not all work in the building and construction industry is performed under negotiated conditions. While the unions can be expected to police their agreements on government work, the threat to the maintenance of general standards remains. This is perhaps especially a problem in this industry, where the casual nature of employment prevents normal operation of the representation machinery of the National Labor Relations Act. In building and construction, unlike manufacturing, the choice of operating with organized or unorganized employees is made by the employer, who may select nonunion workers if he is willing to meet the difficulties this involves. Therefore, although the unions are much better able to maintain negotiated standards than they were in 1931, in my opinion prevailing wage protection remains necessary in order to prevent lowering of labor standards through the operation of competitive pressures where there is lump sum bidding.

But the importance of lump sum bidding has declined. Although conventional building and construction projects continue to be performed under fixed price contracts, much government work involves construction of unique facilities and development of new processes while construction goes on. Changes in design occur after building starts. In these circumstances costs cannot be predicted and lump sum bidding is abandoned. The government procurement agency therefore selects contractors to perform particular jobs and negotiates contracts providing for government payment of all appropriate costs. To the extent that cost type contracts are used, the importance of prevailing rate regulation declines, because competitive wage-cutting pressures on the contractor decrease when all his wage costs are reimbursed. (Competitive pressure on wage rates does not disappear completely so long as the contractor has part of his work force engaged in nongovernment commercial activity.)

In any event, as long as some construction is performed by lump sum contracts, the need for legislation remains. In the interests of uniformity of application it is desirable for the legislation to apply, as at present, to all government contracting for public works, whether fixed price or cost type.

A third factor which has changed since 1931 is the existence of minimum wage law. The Fair Labor Standards Act, enacted in 1938, by providing a minimum standard of rates protects the worker against exploitation. It is argued that since the nation has adopted a general philosophy of guaranteeing a specified minimum it is improper for government to maintain a separate set of guarantees at a much higher level—indeed at a level which some employers feel they cannot or should not be required to adopt. This argument is less persuasive than it at first seems, since the minimum wage law is totally inadequate in meeting the objectives of prevailing wage law. The difference between the legal minimum hourly rate and prevailing rates in the building industry may be anywhere from nothing to about $4.00 an hour. In most cases it is at least $1.00. Therefore the amount of rate shaving which could occur legally by using a minimum rather than a prevailing rate standard for government contracts is great enough to warrant rejection of the minimum rate standard of FLSA for government contracts. The objection to maintaining a rate standard above that of the national policy expressed in FLSA has no reasonable basis since the two laws have entirely different functions.

Let us examine the issue from the other side. Have circumstances changed so as to alter the attitudes of beneficiaries of the law? Who benefits from the act? Three principal groups: (1) the covered employees, (2) other employees in the industry, and (3) employing contractors. Covered employees benefit from the guarantee that they will receive the prevailing rate in the area without needing to resist rate-cutting pressure from their employer. Other employees benefit since payment of the prevailing rate on the government work further reinforces its prevalence. Employing contractors benefit by having the element of labor cost removed from competition. In addition union organizations representing workers in the building trades also benefit since the law usually acts so as to support negotiated rates. Circumstances since passage of the act do not appear to have changed so as to diminish any of these benefits. The building trades unions have vigorously supported the legislation and have been active in behalf of broadening amendments. Employing contractors have not generally opposed the law. In 1960 John Dunlop stated that not one employer association in the building industry had called for repeal of the law.[41]

Clearly the greatest opposition has come from outside the building industry. The chief spokesman for employers has been the Chamber of Commerce of the United States. The industrial unions within the labor movement are reluctant to criticize, for various reasons, but it would be safe to assume that there is something less than overwhelming enthusiasm for the law on their part. The nature of the opposition indicates that if the argument for continuation of the law can be sustained, aspects of its administration may bear revision.

There are two broad problems of administration of the act: determination of the rates and coverage. These issues are not altogether independent of one another, but certain facets may be discussed separately.

Until recently opponents have devoted their main criticism of the operation of the act to determination of rates, questioning (1) the accuracy of the wages determined; (2) the scope of the area from which wage evidence is obtained for application to particular projects; (3) whether rates found to be prevailing accurately reflect rates for employees "on projects of a character similar to the contract work"; and (4) whether rates found to be prevailing accurately reflect rates for "corresponding classes of laborers and mechanics" in the area.

Implicit in each of these specific issues is the question whether the rates determined to be prevailing contain an inflationary bias which produces a ratchet effect in the vicinity of the work, with attendant consequences for the community wage structure, area employment, and union organization. Immediate responsibility for administration of the act within the Department of Labor rests with an Assistant Solicitor with a staff of about 20 attorneys who have responsibility for issuing determinations. During 1962 this group processed around 50,000 determinations. Thus, on the average, each lawyer staff member handled about 2,500 determinations during the year, or almost ten each working day. Data upon which the determinations are based is furnished by employers and unions in the area of the proposed project, by contractor associations, and by state agencies. In relatively rare instances an on-the-spot survey of rates is made by the department staff; and in the case of very large projects in areas remote from cities, hearings may be held. But for the most part the determinations are made in Washington on the basis of indirect evidence submitted by parties at interest or by state labor agencies. Department of Labor representatives believe that their staff should be larger to perform this work. The difficulty of attaining accuracy is attested by the fact that several thousand "inadvertencies" each year correct mistakes in determinations already issued.

The problem of the area from which prevailing rates are obtained involves interpretation of the phrase in the statute: "city, town, village, or other civil subdivision of the State in which the work is to be performed . . ." This is not difficult in urbanized areas where negotiated rates are recognized by most employers. But in rural areas there may be no single prevailing rate. In these circumstances the published procedures [42] of the Secretary of Labor provide for finding the rate paid to the majority of those employed in the area in each classification in construction similar to the proposed undertaking. If there is no majority paid at any one rate, then the rate determined is that paid to the greatest number of employees in each classification, provided these constitute more than 30 percent of those employed. That failing, an average rate is calculated from the evidence at hand. It is alleged by critics that this procedure is impracticable in some rural areas because the necessary evidence is not obtainable, for reasons which stem from limited staff and available time, and that the rates determined are those prevailing in an urban area sometimes far removed geographically from the site of the proposed project.

Both of these criticisms, questioning the accuracy of the predeterminations and the area from which evidence is obtained, look valid until scrutinized more closely. If indeed they are sound criticisms, the solution is obviously to devote a larger staff to gathering the necessary information. If critics of the law believe that the problem involves misrepresentation of actual rates, then they ought to bend their efforts to increasing the Department of Labor's appropriation. It is doubtful, however, that accuracy is the real problem. The staff depends largely upon ascertaining the negotiated rate for the area. And this certainly is the only realistic view for them to take. While additional staff would prevent some of the mistakes which result in issuance of "inadvertencies," the main result would be the same. In most cases the negotiated rate in effect is the only rate for which labor can be obtained in quantities necessary to perform the work. As such it has to be the prevailing rate.

The issue of determination of rates for "projects of a character similar" presents like problems. In the case of a large project, such as an atomic energy industrial facility or an Air Force test facility in a rural area, it may not be possible to find projects of a similar character within the same state. According to a strict interpretation of the law this necessitates finding rates which are unrealistic in that they are too low to attract labor. Conversely, it is alleged that rates for a small project may be set with reference to rates being paid on a much larger project in the area, merely as a matter of practicality, even though the larger project is dissimilar in character.

The criticism as to the large project is certainly valid. In order to have rates high enough to attract the necessary labor for a very large project, it is sometimes necessary for the Department of Labor to predetermine rates based on rates paid in another state, yet the law states that the rates "shall be based upon the wages that will be determined by the Secretary of Labor to be prevailing for the corresponding classes of laborers and mechanics employed on projects of a character similar to the contract work in the city, town, village, or other civil subdivision of the State in which the work is to be performed. . . ." This wording is unrealistic and does not recognize the necessity in some cases of looking beyond the borders of a state.

The criticism is also valid in the converse situation, of a very small federal project. Here the effect may be to increase rates more than is necessary, and sometimes to increase the cost of the project. There may also be a lasting effect upon the rate structure in the community.

And finally, in comment on the fourth of the specific issues, the Department of Labor (again as a matter of practicality) in all cases applies its preconceptions about "classes of laborers and mechanics," using the classifications of the building trades unions. This means that, with the exception of perhaps four crafts, no rates for helper classifications are determined, even though in some areas it may be the practice for nonunion contractors to pay differentiated rates within other classifications according to skill.

This issue is but a facet of two sweeping criticisms made concerning administration of the law. One is that the predetermined rates almost always reflect the influence of the building trades unions and in fact are in almost all cases their negotiated rates. The other is that the Department of Labor always finds that "corresponding classes of laborers and mechanics" are building trades classifications even though evidence is presented which purports to show that other work of a similar character in the area is performed by nonbuilding trades workers. The latter problem of administration of the law is a part of the larger dispute among employers, industrial unions, and building trades unions over assignment of work and questions of representation.

This then comes down to the problem of coverage by the terms of the act. It is clear that the act applies only to contracts of more than $2,000. It is not clear what the terms "construction, alteration, and/or repair" mean. Indeed, the question of coverage and who is to have authority to determine coverage is the most important issue in the administration of the law. Let us examine some of the background of the issue.

The act itself does not give administrative authority to any single agency of the government. It provided that the Secretary of Labor shall determine prevailing rates to be included in contracts, that the contracting agency shall handle enforcement through the device of withholding accrued payments necessary to cover shortages in wages, and that the Comptroller General of the United States shall distribute such money to workers to whom it is due and shall maintain a blacklist of contractors who have disregarded their contractual obligations. (The worker may also sue the contractor if the accrued payments withheld are insufficient.) Because this division of authority resulted in some confusion in administration of the act, Reorganization Plan No. 14 of 1950 was made effective. This gives the Secretary of Labor authority to "prescribe appropriate standards, regulations and procedures, which shall be observed by [procurement] agencies," and also directs him to make "such investigations, with respect to compliance with and enforcement of such labor standards, as he deems desirable." [43] Pursuant to this authority the Secretary has issued regulations containing standards applicable under the act.[44] These standards have been helpful in spelling out the obligations and responsibilities of government agencies and contractors where the work is covered by the act. They also provide for investigations by the Secretary of Labor where he thinks it desirable in order to obtain compliance with the act and the regulations, and for hearings. According to the regulations the Secretary is the final arbiter of all questions relating to application or interpretation of the regulations or the act, as well as of other related statutes. The regulations themselves are ambiguous as to the meaning of "construction, alteration, and/or repair"; but the Secretary's regulations provide him with complete discretion in the matter of deciding questions of coverage.[45]

It is this aspect of administration of the law which causes the greatest distress for contractors and procurement agencies and constitutes a legitimate area for outside criticism and suggestions for ameliorative action. The legislation enacted in 1931 is not properly applicable to some of the conditions existing thirty years later. Both technology and the kinds of contracts entered into by the government have changed considerably, and there are now many contracts which call for items to be "built" for the government which are not necessarily "construction, alteration, and/or repair." The missile-testing facilities of the Department of Defense provide the best current example of the problem of application of the act. Much of the work carried on under missile contracts is experimental in nature, and according to the Department of Defense much of the construction under such contracts is inseparable from testing. That is, the structure involved in the test is not completed in the sense that a building project is completed, then used for testing missiles. Rather, the creation of the facilities for testing and the actual testing are parts of one integrated operation. Another example is the installation of equipment at operational missile bases. Here the building trades unions claim the work to be covered by the Davis-Bacon Act, while Department of Defense procurement officials and contractors have argued that it is part of engineering and manufacturing and therefore covered by the Walsh-Healey Act instead. A third and somewhat older coverage controversy has occurred in the atomic energy program, where major maintenance work in government-owned, contractor-operated plants has been in dispute. Building trades unions view the work as "alteration or repair" while contractors have considered it to be outside coverage of the act.

In all three of these situations contractors have argued against any requirement that they pay prevailing wages (construction rates) to their manual employees on disputed work. This is not simply because the predetermined rates are higher;[46] presumably the higher wages could be recovered from the government under the terms of the contract. The problem for the employer is in the effects the higher wages required by the prevailing wage law will have upon the rest of his employees. It is not practicable for an employer to operate with two sets of employment conditions. The real effect of a decision that certain work is covered by the act, then, is to cause the work to be sub-contracted to a construction contractor who employs building trades workers. Thus the decision amounts to making a jurisdictional award in favor of the building trades union. It may be asked why the pre-vailing rates predetermined by the Secretary of Labor need to be building trades rates. Could they not be production or maintenance worker rates? The answer is that this could not happen under the present statute for two reasons: (1) The words "construction, altera-tion, and/or repair" for purposes of coverage have not been considered separable. If the Secretary found particular work covered by the act, he could not very well find it to take the production worker rate. (2) It is probably not practicable to issue predeterminations of prevailing rates outside the building and construction industry.[47] In any area where these workers are organized there tends to be only one rate for each classification, because the building trades unions have a virtual monopoly in representation of craftsmen in the industry, and because of multiemployer bargaining. The same thing is not true of production worker rates because of the multiplicity of unions in one industry and because most employers bargain individually with unions. It would be extremely difficult in most areas to find anything which could ac-curately be designated as a prevailing rate among production and maintenance workers.

In sum then, what does the attack on the act amount to? I believe that the allegations of inflationary tendencies in the process of deter-mining the rate, of inaccuracy in determinations, and of improper use of "area of the work," while they have some superficial attractiveness, are not telling criticisms of prevailing wage legislation. But the attempt to apply standards involving "projects of a character similar" and "cor-responding classes of laborers and mechanics" is not always successful and in fact is part of the problem of making decisions regarding cov-erage of the law. In the case of coverage, events have outdated the statute. It is not so easy as it once was to classify work as construction of public works, production of equipment, or research; and much test-ing and experimentation performed for the government has aspects of all three.

The ill effect of the dispute over coverage is that it puts the contract-ing agency in the position of contesting application of a law designed to protect working people. Although a finding of noncoverage is un-likely to result in deprivation for the affected employees, it is undesirable from the standpoint of good public administration and the humanitarian intention of the law to have agencies of the government occupied with evading coverage of protective legislation. It would be desirable (although difficult to achieve) if the procurement agencies and the Department of Labor were in accord in their efforts to administer the law.

PROPOSALS FOR CHANGES

Several solutions of the problem of prevailing wage law have been suggested. Repeal of the law in my opinion would result in reinstituting the evils the law was passed to correct. Another perennial proposal has been to make actions of the Department of Labor subject to court review. Consequent delays, however, would probably vitiate the effectiveness of the law. Whether the department's own alternative, an administrative review board, would satisfy the critics remains to be seen.

There have been many suggestions of ways to redefine construction work so as to make a clear-cut distinction between it and production and maintenance work. The most common one has been to itemize specific work which is covered or not covered by the act. The Atomic Energy Commission has adopted this device.[48] The Air Force also proposed a guide of this sort in 1960. The draft was revised by the Solicitor's Office of the Department of Labor, but its authoritativeness was disavowed by the Secretary.[49] A discussion of these suggestions for determination of coverage is contained in the *Report of the Missile Site Public Contracts Committee to the Secretary of Labor.*[50] The committee's own suggestion for determining coverage was a basic standard to be applied on a case-by-case basis: work to be considered covered if it involved providing housing for the missile, not covered if performed to provide an operable missile.

Under either the itemization criterion or the broadly stated standard, the work not covered by the Davis-Bacon Act would presumably be covered under the Walsh-Healey Act. If coverage could be determined in equitable fashion this area of controversy would be eliminated from the administration of Davis-Bacon. A similar problem, however, even if more modest in degree, would continue to exist under Walsh-Healey, since different wage standards have been determined for different industries. With the problem would remain all the attendant pressures from contractors and unions on government authorities for favorable interpretation of the regulations or advantageous modifications. A desirable objective would be to diminish the importance of coverage determinations by bringing the two laws into closer conformity with one another.

A third possibility, worth exploring, is to move in the direction of most other countries which have legislation of this kind; that is, to use the standard of negotiated conditions where they exist. When the Davis-Bacon and Walsh-Healey acts were passed, in 1931 and 1936 respectively, relatively few workers were organized and few employment conditions were arrived at by collective bargaining. Since that time the National Labor Relations Act (which was not validated by the Supreme Court until a year after passage of the Walsh-Healey Act) has made collective bargaining a national policy. There is little reason now, when collectively bargained rates exist, for them not to be equated with prevailing rates. This system might work as follows:

The Davis-Bacon Act would require payment of prevailing rates on government contracts for construction, alteration, and/or repair of public buildings and public works, as at present. Predetermined rates would be building trades rates. These would appear in the advertised specifications for each contract and, when applicable, in the contract.[51] But after a contract was awarded, if the successful firm indicated its intention of operating in accordance with conditions negotiated with a bona fide union recognized pursuant to the National Labor Relations Act, as amended, the firm would be excused from any detailed requirements of paying specified rates. The law should also be made applicable to premiums, allowances, and other supplemental items of compensation, which have become a large part of workers' earnings.[52] The Walsh-Healey requirements would operate in similar fashion.

This policy would reduce the importance of decisions on coverage, since such decisions would not, as now, automatically determine whether the work must be subcontracted by a manufacturing firm. And where there was a bona fide union relationship it would make the question of which law governed a matter of indifference to the contractor and the procurement agency. If a contractor chose to do work with his own forces, the rates paid would satisfy the requirements of either law as long as they had been negotiated with a bona fide union which had been lawfully recognized. Any dispute between the employer and the union representing his employees on the issue of contracting out could be handled under the same kind of procedures applicable to this issue in nongovernment work.[53]

This proposal would not eliminate disputes over assignment of work among building trades unions or between them and industrial unions. But the present Davis-Bacon Act was not designed to handle this problem either. The proposal would eliminate the anomalous circumstance of the Department of Labor, in deciding that certain disputed work is covered by the Davis-Bacon Act, actually overturning a National Labor Relations Board representation proceeding. There have been cases where the NLRB has decided that industrial rather than craft units were appropriate, and industrial unions have been certified, but where the Department of Labor has subsequently found the work to be covered by the Davis-Bacon Act. This has allowed the building trades craft unions to attain what they had been denied by the NLRB or by the workers themselves in NLRB elections. Under our national labor policy disputes over assignment of work are intended to be handled by the NLRB. The Supreme Court has declared it the duty of the board under Section 10(k) of the NLRA to make jurisdictional determinations and to award tasks to particular unions.[54] Under this provision the NLRB has encouraged dispute settlement by the National Joint Board for Settlement of Jurisdictional Disputes in the Construction Industry. It is to be hoped that the constitutional amendment adopted by the AFL-CIO in December 1961 on settlement of internal disputes will also operate to reduce the ill effects of disputes between industrial and building trades unions.

It is somewhat sanctimonious to criticize the Department of Labor for making what are in effect jurisdictional awards by its determinations on questions of coverage. In the first place it has no choice under its interpretation of its responsibilities but to make such determinations. The consequences for contractors and unions are not its doing. Second, the department is not alone in making such decisions; determinations on coverage which are made by the procurement agencies themselves have exactly the same effect. The difference is that the Labor Department is predisposed in favor of coverage while the procurement agencies are not. Nevertheless, it would be desirable from the standpoint of consistent public policy to encourage handling disputes over assignment of work by normal methods, i.e. management and Joint Board decisions, federation dispute settlement agreements, or operation of

Taft-Hartley proceedings. This objective could be attained more easily if prevailing wage law recognized a negotiated wage criterion.

What would be the objections to this proposal? The first would be that negotiated conditions are an improper criterion for finding employment conditions to be prevailing. This objection is based partly upon opposition to the use of a standard negotiated by unions when some employers have no intention of dealing with a union. But this should not be a valid objection if each contractor were allowed to opt for predetermined rates when he did not intend to deal with organized labor. It may also be argued that adoption of the negotiated rate as prevailing is a questionable delegation of legislative power. This has not been regarded as a serious problem in the seven states where such legislation exists.[55]

A more valid objection would be that local negotiators might impose discriminatory conditions in the local agreement upon government work. Such conditions might take the form of high rates in an area where a large government contract was being performed, or fringe benefits or allowances which are framed in such a way as to apply only to government work. This would be especially likely to occur where the contract called for reimbursement of all costs. Here the contractor might not be expected to have the incentive for economizing on labor costs that he would under a system of competitive bidding. This would present a real problem in some cases but could be taken care of by proper supervision by the contracting agency.[56] It has also been argued that this problem would be largely illusory since the concern of the local people with the permanent community wage structure is so great as to inhibit discriminatory action.[57]

It might be argued that the proposal would deprive the Department of Labor of the authority to correct misclassifications of employees. Where a contractor operated under nonunion conditions the Department of Labor would continue to police classifications and rates as at present. If he operated under negotiated conditions, preventing misclassification would be the responsibility of the unions and the NLRB. The legalization of prehire agreements in the 1959 amendments to NLRA, and the 1961 Supreme Court decision in the Radio Engineers case (cited in note 54), are what make the proposal feasible.

A further advantage of adopting the negotiated rate as the prevailing one would be its administrative simplicity. There is very good precedent for this kind of arrangement under Section 7(b) of the Fair Labor

Standards Act,[58] in which employers with seasonal demands are excused from certain overtime premium obligations if they guarantee certain annual hours of work pursuant to a contract with representatives of employees certified as bona fide by NLRB. Further precedent is found in the Portal-to-Portal Act [59] and the Overtime-on-Overtime Law; [60] in both of these the calculation of overtime compensation takes account of provisions in collective bargaining agreements.

Another advantage is that the proposal would diminish the need for government to protect labor standards which are protected by unions anyway. In this sense much of the activity now performed in this field is redundant. Moreover, it is a "service" furnished almost exclusively to the building trades unions. Aside from the existence of rates in building and construction which are more identifiable as prevailing, there seems to be no good reason why the government should reinforce rates in this industry, at a level greatly above that of the FLSA, while not doing the same for rates in other industries which are also subject to the same kind of pressure from competitive bidding on government contracts.

The principle embodied in this proposal is important enough to warrant Congressional consideration. Minimum wage regulation assumes that workers at marginal levels need protection. Implicit in this is the assumption that these workers in need of protection are unorganized and thus subject to competitive pressures among themselves. Prevailing wage legislation also assumes that workers need protection from competitive pressures, but the level it protects is much higher. There is no question here of the kind of exploitation that minimum wage regulation protects against; it is simply a matter of assuring that government bidding procedures will not serve to undermine standards. Prevailing wage legislation is needed to protect the standards of workers who are not organized. Under both kinds of wage regulation, where workers are organized close supervision of the terms and conditions of employment is unnecessary. Our national policy, as expressed in the National Labor Relations Act, encourages the practice of collective bargaining. The principle of substituting negotiated rates and employment conditions for detailed government regulation of wages would reinforce the national policy on collective bargaining and reduce the area of government intervention in the employer-union relationship. This is a desirable goal of social policy.

Notes

1   Commission on Organization of the Executive Branch of the Government, Concluding Report, May 1949, pp. 27–33.
2   41 U.S.C. 11.
3   40 U.S.C. 267a–277.
4   These include work performed in connection with the National Housing Act, the Hospital Survey and Construction Act, the Federal Airport Act, the Housing Act of 1949, Community Facilities and Services Act of 1951, the Federal Civil Defense Act of 1950, and the Federal Aid Highway Act of 1956.
5   For a history and summary of state prevailing rate law, see the author's article "Prevailing Wage Legislation in the States," *Monthly Labor Review*, Aug. 1961, pp. 839–45.
6   The figures in this paragraph have been calculated from Department of Commerce data.
7   *Industrial Relations Handbook*, London, H. M. Stationery Office, 1961, p. 214. The "Sweating Committee" was the Select Committee of the House of Lords on the Sweating System. This committee was established in 1887 and held extensive inquiries in industrial cities throughout Britain. See *Fifth Report from the Select Committee of the House of Lords on the Sweating System*, May 5, 1890.
8   Sidney and Beatrice Webb, *History of Trade Unionism* (New York, Longmans, Green, 1920 ed.), pp. 398–99.
9   E.g., the Terms and Conditions of Employment Act, 1959, requires, in effect, that all employers in a particular trade or industry observe the recognized terms and conditions negotiated by representative unions and employers in the trade or industry.
10 Dominion of Canada, Annual Report of the Department of Labour, 1950, pp. 26–29.
11 Fair Wages and Hours of Labour Regulations, P.C. 1954–2029 and 2030.
12 "Contracts for construction or remodelling of public buildings of all kinds, railways, canals, roads, bridges, locks, dry docks, elevators, harbours, piers, wharves, lighthouses and other works for the improvement and safety of transportation and navigation, rifle ranges, fortifications and other works of defence, dams, hydraulic works, slides, piers, booms and other works for facilitating the transmission of timber, and all other works and properties constructed or remodelled for the Government of Canada."
13 Decret du 10 août 1899.
14 Decret du 10 avril 1937.
15 Decret du 8 mars 1940.
16 Decret du 12 février 1955.
17 Thirty-seventh Session of the International Labour Conference, Summary of Reports on Ratified Conventions, Report III, Pt. I, p. 142; Summary of Reports on Unratified Conventions and on Recommendations, Report III, Pt. II, p. 18; and Report of the Committee of Experts on the Application of Conventions and Recommendations, Report III, Pt. IV, p. 42.

18 *The International Labour Code* (Geneva, International Labour Office, 1951), Arts. 189–98, pp. 145–52, "Labour Clauses in Public Contracts."
19 Ibid., Art. 191, p. 148.
20 Ibid., Art. 191.2 (a).
21 Ibid., Art. 191.2 (b).
22 Austria, Belgium, Bulgaria, Congo, Costa Rica, Cuba, Cyprus, Denmark, Finland, France, Guatemala, Israel, Italy, Morocco, Netherlands, Nigeria, Philippines, Somali Republic, United Arab Republic, United Kingdom, Uruguay.
23 Because our federal system of government grants to the states at least partial authority on most issues, the United States has ratified few conventions. Of the few the U. S. Senate has ratified, almost all deal with working conditions of seamen.
24 Eight other states have ratified but appear to have no laws or regulations of substantial nature: Austria, Belgium, Bulgaria, Cuba, Denmark, Finland (although it has some regulation), Philippines, and the United Arab Republic. Five other states have ratified recently and have not reported on their domestic legislation to ILO: Congo, Costa Rica, Cyprus, Nigeria, and Somali Republic.
25 See testimony of industry witnesses in U. S. Senate, *Work Stoppage at Missile Bases,* Hearings before the Permanent Sub-committee on Investigations of the Committee on Government Operations, Pursuant to Senate Res. 69, 87th Cong., 1st Sess., Pt. 2, pp. 451 and 478. Also House of Representatives, Hearings before the Special Subcommittee on Labor of the Committee on Education and Labor, on H.R. 9656 and 9657, 87th Cong., 2d Sess., March 8, 9, and 13, 1962.
26 *Congressional Record,* 74 (Pt. 7): 6510, Feb. 28, 1931.
27 Cf. House of Representatives, *Employment of Labor on Federal Construction Work,* Hearings before the Committee on Labor, on H.R. 7995 and H.R. 9232, 71st Cong., 2d Sess., March 6, 1930.
28 10 Comptroller General 294. The ruling held that such action was in conflict with another statute which required acceptance of the lowest bid: Sec. 3709, Revised Statutes.
29 *Congressional Record,* 74 (Pt. 7): 6510, Feb. 28, 1931.
30 Ibid., p. 6508.
31 Ibid., 74 (Pt. 4): 3918–19, Feb. 4, 1931.
32 U. S. Senate, Hearings before a Subcommittee of the Committee on Commerce, Pursuant to S. Res. 74, 73d Cong., 2d Sess., 1 (Pt. 5): 789–826, 838–40.
33 U. S. Senate, Hearings before a Subcommittee of the Committee on Education and Labor, Pursuant to S. Res. 228, 73d Cong., 2d Sess.
34 Prohibition against kickbacks appears in the Davis-Bacon Act, but its principal formulation is in the Copeland ("Antikickback") Act, 18 U.S.C. 874.
35 Alliance Construction Co. v. United States, 79 Ct. Cl. 730.
36 Gillioz v. Webb, 99 F.2d 585.
37 Perkins v. Lukens Steel Co., 310 U.S. 113.
38 Campbell v. City of New York, 244 N.Y. 317.
39 U.S. v. Binghamton Construction Co., 347 U.S. 171.
40 The following are some examples of differences between the two agen-

cies: (1) On April 3, 1961, in his first public opinion under the new policy (No. D-B 1) the Solicitor of Labor declared that the Secretary of Labor is the only government official who can issue opinions which may be relied upon as to statutory coverage of the Davis-Bacon Act; and that reliance on the opinion of the District Council of the Army Corps of Engineers is no defense to liability. On April 10, 1961, the Comptroller General issued an opinion that the Solicitor of Labor may not reverse the judgment of a contracting officer when a decision on coverage has been made in good faith and in accord with prescribed regulations of the department from which he draws his authority; that such ruling may not be applied retroactively to contracts awarded or completed, and that the Solicitor's position that the contracting agency should take prompt action to arrange for restitution or withhold funds for workers had "advisory force only." (CG Opinion No. B-144901.) (2) On April 3, 1961, the Comptroller General declared that "it is not mandatory upon contracting agency to modify an existing contract by incorporating new minimum wage rates set out in 'letters of inadvertence' from the Department of Labor where the change in rates was not based upon clerical errors in computing the original rate but represented a change in judgment as to what classification of work was applicable to the contract." (CG Opinion No. 145009.) (3) On June 10, 1957, the Comptroller General declared that "local area practice is controlling with respect to wage rates only and not insofar as it restricts method of performance. Thus, where there is a local ban on spray painting, determination of the wage rate for spray painters 'subject to the practice prevailing in the area' (a phrase added by Department of Labor) does not restrict advertising and award of work to brush painters." (CG Opinion No. 132044.)

41 *Proceedings of the 13th Annual Meeting of the Industrial Relations Research Association,* St. Louis, Mo., Dec. 28–29, 1960, p. 13.

42 Title 29, Subtitle A, Code of Federal Regulations, Pt. 1.

43 Reorganization Plan No. 14 of 1950, 5 U.S.C.A. 133z–15.

44 Title 29, Subtitle A, Code of Federal Regulations, Pt. 5.

45 But it is not entirely clear where the final authority on coverage is. See n. 40 supra.

46 The total wage package may be about the same in either case because of the cost of extra benefits and allowances paid to production and maintenance employees. See the testimony of A. H. Bode of the Bendix Corporation in *Work Stoppage at Missile Bases,* (cited in n. 25 supra), pp. 443–44.

47 Shipbuilding and repair and some kinds of drilling are covered by the act and are exceptions to the statement.

48 See AEC Regulations: Title 41, Public Contracts, chap. 9–12, Labor.

49 This document is reproduced in *Work Stoppage at Missile Bases,* pp. 457–61. The "disavowal" letter appears at p. 46. For an extended discussion of the coverage problem and further suggestions for demarcation of coverage by categories of work, see John R. Van de Water, "Applications of Labor Law to Construction and Equipping of United States Missile Bases," *Labor Law Journal,* 12: 1003–24.

50 This committee was established by the Secretary in April 1961, for the

purpose of recommending "fair and impartial standards and criteria" for determining coverage of work at missile sites and missile test sites. Its report is dated August 25, 1961. Committee members were Thomas W. Holland, chairman, Lloyd Bailer, and Peter Seitz. A year after issuance the report had not been adopted by the Secretary of Labor.

51 Consideration ought to be given to the predetermination of rates only once or twice a year in each area, rather than each time a job is contemplated. This would simplify administration and would sacrifice little in accuracy. No doubt local agreements would soon be coordinated with the date(s) selected.

52 Hearings on a bill designed for that purpose were held by the House Committee on Education and Labor in March 1962. House of Representatives, *Amendments to Davis-Bacon Act, and a Bill to Establish a Work-Hours Act*, Hearings before the special Subcommittee on Labor of the Committee on Education and Labor, on H.R. 9656 and 9657, 87th Cong., 2d Sess., March 8, 9, and 13, 1962.

53 Textile Workers v. Lincoln Mills of Alabama, 353 U.S. 448; Steelworkers v. Warrior & Gulf Navigation Co., 363 U.S. 574.

54 NLRB v. Radio Engineers Union, 47 LRRM 2332. The Board is at present performing this function.

55 The Kentucky statute was found invalid by that state's highest court in 1961 in a case where the law failed to provide necessary guiding standards for determining rates. Kerth v. Hopkins County Board of Education, 346 S.W.(2d) 737. The state legislature amended it in 1962, but the law had been upheld earlier on the specific issue of whether legislative power had been improperly delegated. Baughn v. Gorrell & Riley, 311 Ky. 537.

56 It might be handled by a special procedure, as is being done in the missile program. The Missile Sites Labor Commission, created by President Kennedy by Executive Order 10946 on May 26, 1961, is charged with the responsibility of reviewing collective bargaining practices which may be discriminatory or burdensome to the government. Under this policy the commission has recommended to the Defense Department in at least one case that it disallow payment for certain labor rates which were 31 cents an hour higher than the area rates for all government work.

57 Donald E. Cullen, "Union Wage Policy in Heavy Construction: The St. Lawrence Seaway," *American Economic Review*, March 1959, pp. 68–84.

58 29 U.S.C. ¶¶ 201–19.

59 29 U.S.C. ¶¶ 251–63.

60 Section 8(d) of FLSA.

GERALD G. SOMERS

Policy Implications of Labor Market Analysis

The laborer has been encouraged by society to fit himself for a trade, and when this trade is abolished in the interests of society, the employer, first, and society ultimately, should share the loss with him. The methods by which this can be accomplished are matters of social invention and experiment.

JOHN R. COMMONS, 1899 [1]

It has sometimes been noted that an intelligent discussion of any economic problem, even the most current, can be found in some footnote in Alfred Marshall's *Principles*. In the field of labor, much the same can be said of the writings of John R. Commons. There are few topics falling within the subject matter of this volume which Commons did not explore. The problem of unemployment was one to which he turned frequently, especially in his early discussion of the *Distribution of Wealth* and in his later proposals for employment exchanges and a system of unemployment compensation in Wisconsin. His legislative influence in the development of unemployment insurance has been discussed in this book by Arthur Altmeyer.

As the opening quotation indicates, Commons' approach to unemployment has a modern ring. He was especially concerned with those displaced by mechanization or changes in business organization; these workers he felt had a right to work or to equivalent compensation. Like property owners whose property was condemned under eminent domain, workers cast aside for the sake of economic progress were entitled to special consideration. Since the employer and the public benefited most from these progressive changes, in the form of lower costs and prices, they should join hands in aiding the major loser, the work-ingman. As the concluding section of this paper emphasizes, policies reflecting Commons' viewpoint are now prominent in the attack on technological and other types of unemployment. But Commons also recognized that policies designed to mitigate unemployment must be geared to the cause of the particular unemployment; and it is to this question that we must direct our initial regard.

Causes of Unemployment

A study of unemployment is, in many ways, a study of the pathology of the labor market. Just as medical science frequently concentrates on pathological cases in order to throw light on normally functioning organisms, so may economists gain greater understanding of essential mechanisms of the labor market through examining results of its malfunctioning. The increasing seriousness of unemployment in the United States in recent years has prompted research on the perform-ance of many variables in the labor market as a whole; and this broader analytical attack is found to be essential to understanding the forces creating unemployment.

Political realities often lead to fads in economic research. Since un-employment has frequently had a profound impact on election results, Congressional committees become especially active in promoting re-search on this question in periods of serious unemployment; and be-cause the growth of unemployment cannot be understood in isolation from the broader context of the labor market, this research must spill over into many other areas of labor market behavior. Much of recent labor market analysis has originated in this fashion. Thus, the political and economic misfortune presented by high unemployment levels has had at least one salutary by-product in the encouragement of needed research.

In the discussion which follows, a number of trends in a changing labor market are related to the problem of unemployment. Principal attention is given to factors involved in unemployment in depressed areas and to the traditional redevelopment policies adopted in such areas. This is done because many of the crucial structural factors in unemployment in general converge and are accentuated in depressed areas. Localities of persistent unemployment show the many structural factors at work in the larger economy standing out in sharp relief, accessible for more detailed analysis. They have also provided a laboratory for policy experimentation, with significant implications for the formation of broader national policy.

Stress on one aspect of the unemployment problem should not obscure the interrelatedness of the causal forces. Areas of chronic unemployment are widely scattered across the country, and their persistence is closely related to underutilization of new entrants into the labor force, older workers, Negroes, and rural manpower. The problems of these groups stem from employer hiring practices and lack of skills, training, mobility, and vocational guidance. Automation has disturbing employment effects primarily because of these labor market deficiencies, and technological progress causes a growing shortage of technical manpower because of similar failings in vocational guidance and public instruction.

STRUCTURAL FACTORS VERSUS AGGREGATE DEMAND

There is also a close relationship between structural causes of unemployment and insufficient aggregate demand. Much of the controversy that has recently surrounded this question appears to be misplaced.[2] This is not to dispute the fact of higher unemployment rates in recent years. Whereas unemployment averaged 4.2% of the labor force during the period 1947–57, the rate, seasonally adjusted, has, with the exception of one month, equaled or exceeded 5% continuously since November 1957. At the cyclical peak in 1960 unemployment was still 5% and was above that level in the recovery period during the first half of 1962. In only two other periods during this century, 1908–12 and 1930–41, were unemployment rates more unfavorable. Moreover, these high rates have been accompanied by exceptionally high rates of long-term unemployment (over 15 weeks) and very long-term unemployment (over 26 weeks).[3]

A case can be made equally well that these high rates of unemployment result from structural causes or that they reflect inadequate total demand. In one sense, much of the unemployment among experienced workers can be called "structural" in that workers displaced from one job because of automation, changes in business organization, or similar causes are unable to make contact with another job. The lower the level of aggregate demand, the greater the length of time in between jobs, and therefore the higher the level of "structural unemployment."

On the other hand, it may be argued that structural unemployment would evaporate under the warm glow of a sufficiently high total demand, and that therefore there is no such thing as structural unemployment.

Efforts to prove or disprove an increase of structural unemployment in recent years have not been fruitful because of lack of relevant data. Since automation, increased productivity, and change in specific product demand would affect narrow ranges of occupations, proof of their differential impact would require unemployment data broken down by finer occupational categories than presently exist. Unfilled vacancies, which should grow alongside unemployment if structural factors were increasing, cannot now be measured with accuracy in the United States for lack of reporting requirements on this question. Similarly, changes in geographic mobility, related to job termination in one area and job opportunities in another, cannot be accurately gauged. An attempt to arrive at judgments on this relevant type of mobility from analysis of data on residential moves unrelated to employment opportunities cannot be considered a satisfactory alternative.

Fortunately, as we shall see in discussing depressed areas, there is growing agreement that, regardless of recent trends in either causal category, both structural and demand factors have always been relevant in full-employment policies. Future policies must recognize their close relationship.

LABOR FORCE EXPANSION

One of the most important factors in the persistence of high unemployment rates is the increasing rate of labor force expansion. Whereas the labor force increased less than an average of 900,000 a year in the 1950's, it is expected to experience an average net increase of 1.3 million in the 1960's. The estimated net increase in the present decade is about 13.5 million. Even more significant from the standpoint of manpower absorption in a labor market of structural frictions, there will be a *gross* entry of 29 million, as an estimated 15.5 million withdraw, die, or retire. Such an influx in a period which begins with far from satisfactory employment levels will obviously call for far-reaching measures not only to maintain high and increasing levels of aggregate demand but also to reduce structural obstacles to a smoothly functioning labor market.

The changing age composition of the labor force is also significant in appraising employment potentials. Whereas the number of young people under 25 will grow almost 50%, and workers over 45 by about 40%, those in the 35–44 age group will remain relatively steady during the 'sixties. Unemployment among youths and older workers, now well above the national average, is likely to increase further. In December 1961 the unemployment rate for those under 20 was 12.2%, more than twice the national average of 5.8%. High school dropouts have special difficulties in obtaining employment.[4] For older workers the principal problem is long-term unemployment. In 1961, 800,000 workers were unemployed more than half a year, the largest number in two decades. Although men over 45 years of age represented one-fourth of the labor force, they constituted one-third of these hard-core unemployed.[5] These age concentrations among the unemployed point up the need for improvements in education and training. Employers must also be induced to alter hiring restrictions against older workers.

FROM MASS TO CLASS UNEMPLOYMENT

In addition to higher rates of unemployment among youths and workers over 45, heavy concentrations are also found among Negroes, the unskilled, and the less educated. Nonwhite workers have an unemployment rate about twice as high as that of whites. In December 1961 they constituted less than 12% of the labor force but 22% of the total unemployed and 24% of those unemployed more than half a year. Semiskilled and unskilled workers also have above-average rates of unemployment and are heavily concentrated among the very long-term unemployed. In 1961 they constituted 45% of those unemployed over six months, compared with 24% of the labor force.[6]

There has been a consistent, marked inverse relationship between education level and unemployment indicated in the 1940 and 1950 censuses and in a 1959 sample survey. Moreover, a comparison between these surveys indicates that the relative employment position of persons with little schooling has deteriorated during the past decade.[7] Clarence Long has speculated that low-education levels constitute a major source of structural unemployment. As the average productivity of the work force rises, the gap between the average and these unskilled, ill-educated workers widens, and they are increasingly priced out of the labor market. Their productive contribution is below the "social minimum wage" which an employer would have to match if he were to employ them.[8]

The interrelation among the causes of "class" unemployment is seen in the fact that nonwhites are likely to have less skill and education than whites. Each of these factors is an independent source of higher unemployment rates, and when combined in the same person they present a truly formidable obstacle to gainful employment. Here, too, education and training—for workers, employers, and unions—are indicated. Negroes are deprived of equal opportunities for formal education and training in company programs and apprenticeship programs. Discrimination against them in employment results partly from their consequent lack of skill and partly from prejudicial hiring practices based on color.

AUTOMATION AND PRODUCTIVITY INCREASE

Controversy over the existence or nonexistence of technological unemployment has a long tradition in labor economics. The adoption of the term "automation" and greatly increased research on the technology-employment relationship have done little as yet to improve the factual bases of the argument.[9]

Studies demonstrate a sharp decline in employment opportunities under productivity increase in agriculture, mining, railroads, and in some branches of manufacturing. But case studies in a number of individual plants, and especially in offices, have shown no immediate reduction in employment. On the other hand, a number of case studies of plants shut down as a result of technological change draw a picture of severe and lengthy unemployment among most of the displaced workers.

A reasonable conclusion appears to be that automation, too, is significant as a cause of unemployment only in its relationship to other environmental factors. In a declining economy or a declining industry, the effects of technological advance on employment are likely to be highly unfavorable. In periods, industries, or occupations undergoing rapid expansion, the impact of automation is likely to be absorbed and its employment effects to go unnoticed.

IMMOBILITIES

All of these causes of structural unemployment take on greater significance when adjustments are impeded because of frictions in the labor marketplace. Even normal seasonal unemployment gains in importance as workers seasonally displaced in one industry are unable to obtain employment elsewhere.

Immobility, in turn, is likely to be a function of age, skill, and general employment opportunities. Once again, the interaction of the causes of unemployment comes into play; and any policy proposals designed to combat unemployment must take cognizance of the integrated nature of the problem. The convergence is especially noticeable in depressed areas.

Depressed Areas

In the current controversy over causes of recent increases in the rate of unemployment, between those who stress structural factors and those who emphasize aggregate demand, the former are more likely to give central consideration to areas of chronic and persistent labor surplus, the so-called depressed economic areas. Fortunately, there appears to be developing an area of compromise and mutual agreement between these two schools of thought, best summarized perhaps, in Samuelson's recent statement that policies to increase aggregate demand and those to combat structural unemployment are like two blades of a scissors. Nowhere is this duality of attack on the problems of unemployment more necessary than in areas of chronic unemployment.

It is now almost axiomatic that our legislative concern with depressed areas is badly timed. Apparently our representatives in Congress, and politicians generally, are not aroused over chronic and persistent local labor surpluses until the nation as a whole suffers an excessively high rate of recession unemployment. Only when the national attention is focused on the general level of unemployment, and when in consequence the rate of unemployment in chronically depressed areas goes to almost unbearably high levels, do we see a wave of legislative interest in area redevelopment. In spite of valiant efforts in this direction dating from the 1954 recession, it was not until the recession period 1958–61 that we had the culmination in the Area Redevelopment Act. And yet it is equally axiomatic that very little can be done about the problems of chronic unemployment in depressed areas in a period of national recession. In such a period the establishment of plants in depressed areas—the major plank in any area redevelopment platform —is likely to occur only through pirating them away from other areas.

The ARA specifically prohibits such pirating. If we hope to contribute to the solution of unemployment problems in depressed areas through a program of extensive retraining or relocation, we should remember that in a recession period the questions will arise, Training for what? Relocation where?

At the same time, if we attempt to solve the problems of national unemployment through concentration on aggregative monetary-fiscal policy, without regard to such basic structural problems as those reflected in areas of chronic unemployment, we are likely to have an inflationary price rise long before full-employment levels are achieved. The injection of increased demand into the economy through monetary-fiscal policy gives maximum benefit to expanding areas and industries. Shortages of labor and other factor shortages may develop in these areas and industries while excessively high rates of unemployment persist in the nation's chronically depressed areas. As we discovered in World War II, even unemployment in depressed areas will evaporate under the blazing sun of full employment if the level of employment is high enough. Given sufficient differentials in employment opportunities and earnings, even the notoriously immobile workers of depressed areas *will* move to areas of greater economic opportunity. But as we also learned to our sorrow during World War II, full-employment levels of sufficient magnitude to achieve this reallocation of resources are likely to be accompanied by severe inflationary pressures.

Thus the area redevelopment approach and the monetary-fiscal approach are both necessary, but neither taken by itself is sufficient to result in a substantial inflation-free reduction in unemployment in areas of chronic and persistent labor surplus. If this point is now fairly widely accepted, however, there is considerably less agreement (and perhaps even very little research and speculation) on the appropriate methods by which the two types of policies can be meshed for the most fruitful attack on depressed-area unemployment. Wilcock and Franke have described the reduction in the level of unemployment and, in particular, long-run unemployment, under the impact of growth in the gross national product during recovery from the postwar recessions.[10] Although there has been a reduction in the number of chronically labor surplus areas, and in the number of unemployed within these areas, during these recovery periods of expanding gross national product, it is discouraging to note that many of the truly hard-core areas of chronic unemployment have persisted through all phases of the postwar business cycles. At the present time there continues to be a large number of areas classified as "substantial and persistent" areas of labor surplus. Under these circumstances, major questions to be asked are, What is the specific process by which an increase in aggregate demand makes itself felt in areas of chronic unemployment? What types of industries are first and most substantially affected? What occupations? Workers of what characteristics? Who moves to other areas? What firms move into the depressed areas? etc., etc.

Not only are we very much in the dark about the local impact of national expansion but we know little more about the impact of localized industrial expansion upon employment and unemployment in depressed areas. In instances of local industrial expansion, it is of crucial importance to know how training may be related to company hiring policies and the reduction of area unemployment. It is also important to know the mobility patterns of the workers who are hired by the newly established industrial facility. How many of the workers were unemployed prior to industrialization? How many moved from lower-paying occupations to the new facility? How many moved their homes from great distances in order to work at the new plant? How many reduced lengthy commuting journeys in order to benefit from the convenience of localized employment, or, on the contrary, how many were willing to expand their commuting greatly in order to obtain industrial employment? The answers to these questions will be of the utmost significance in determining the effectiveness of the new industrial facility in reducing unemployment in the local depressed area. Expansion of demand, nationally and locally, is a cornerstone of our attack on problems of depressed areas. The rationale of expansion is to reduce unemployment in such areas, and yet there have been very few inquiries into the total employment effects of increased demand.

It is a basic viewpoint of this paper that intelligent area redevelopment policy must rest on a realistic appraisal of the effects of national and local industrial expansion in the areas, especially as they are related to questions of retraining and relocation. We will return to this point after an examination of some other relevant facets of the depressed-area problem.

THE SIGNIFICANCE OF THE DEPRESSED-AREA PROBLEM

First we want to know what the shouting is all about. How important are depressed areas in the national picture? Are they substantially different from other areas, and if so, in what way?

As we attempt to measure the numerical significance of chronically depressed areas, we inevitably meet the usual definitional bugbears. In our effort to arrive at a total of such areas in the country, we are confronted with the problems of how to define a chronically depressed area and what size of areas to include. The U. S. Department of Labor classifies the country's 150 major labor market areas (in which there is usually a central city with at least 50,000 population) into six groups depending on their rate of unemployment. "Areas of substantial labor surplus" are those in groups D (6–8.9% unemployment), E (9–11.9%), and F (12% or more). The number of areas with a substantial labor surplus has varied from an average of 15 in 1951 to 102 in April 1961 and down again to 63 in March 1962.[11] As is seen in Table 1, the num-

Table 1. *Number of major areas of substantial labor surplus*

Date	Areas of substantial labor surplus * (annual average, D, E, and F areas combined)	Date	Areas of substantial labor surplus		
			D	E	F
1951	15	1961 Apr.	70	18	13
1952	20	May	66	21	9
1953	17	June	63	17	8
1954	42	July	69	11	8
1955	33	Aug.	66	12	7
1956	21	Sept.	56	11	5
1957	22	Oct.	55	8	5
1958	77	Nov.	47	8	5
1959	54	Dec.	48	7	5
		1962 Jan.	47	10	4
		Feb.	46	11	5
		Mar.	47	10	6
		Apr.	47	10	5

* Of the six classifications based on unemployment rates, "areas of substantial labor surplus" are those in group D (6–8.9% unemployment); E (9–11.9%); or F (12% or more).

Source: Data provided by U. S. Department of Labor, Bureau of Employment Security.

ber of such areas fluctuates with the level of national prosperity, but there is considerable stickiness in their reduction even in periods of national recovery. Within this group of areas the Department of Labor has designated a smaller number with truly "hard-core" problems of unemployment as areas of "substantial and persistent" unemployment. In May of 1953 eight major labor market areas were in this group; by 1961 there were 20, and this number continued through the early months of 1962.

The Labor Department's criteria for establishing areas of "substantial and persistent" unemployment are as follows:

1. Unemployment is now 6% or more of the labor force, discounting seasonal or temporary factors; and

2. the annual average unemployment rate has been

a. At least 50% above the national average for three of the preceding four years; or

b. At least 75% above the national average for two of the past three years; or

c. At least 100% above the national average for one of the preceding two calendar years.

Although there has been some speculation concerning the possible use of other criteria for designating depressed areas,[12] there is now fairly general acceptance of these standards. These criteria have also been used under the Area Redevelopment Act for designating urban-industrial "redevelopment areas."

The Bureau of Employment Security also distinguishes labor surplus areas in smaller localities, where the labor force is over 15,000 but not large enough for the area to be classed as a major one. These smaller areas are not subclassified by rates of unemployment. The BES designated 104 smaller areas of substantial and persistent unemployment in April 1962.

Greater difficulty is encountered in designating "very small areas" for purposes of determining the chronic nature of unemployment. The number of such areas increased substantially in early 1962, but the increase does not necessarily reflect a recent worsening in unemployment; it may mean that an area has not until now been called to the attention of the bureau for special survey.[13] It should be noted also that a number of the additions to the list of very small areas resulted from redefinition of the areas involved.

As the economic advantage of a "labor surplus" designation grows, under the impact of federal legislation to aid depressed areas, we can expect increased pressure from localities to alter labor market boundaries and change labor supply classifications. Such pressure is already much in evidence.

In addition to the urban depressed areas to which the U. S. Department of Labor devotes much of its attention, a large number of depressed rural areas are also given considerable weight in the policy formulations of the Area Redevelopment Administration. At the present time there are over 700 of these so-called 5 B areas, in whose designation the Department of Agriculture plays a significant role. Some of the alternative criteria used in designating these areas are as follows: 1. areas of low income; 2. areas of low farm income; 3. rural development counties; 4. areas of low-production farming; 5. very small areas of substantial and persistent unemployment. Finally, 50 Indian reservation areas are included in the scope of operations of the Area Redevelopment Administration.

A recent report by the Area Redevelopment Administration concerning the significance of these 148 urban-industrial areas, 735 rural and small labor markets, and 50 Indian reservations indicates that the areas have a population of 34.7 million people and a labor force of 13.2 million, of whom "the equivalent" of more than 1.4 million were unemployed in April 1962. At this time the areas had 19% of the nation's capital and population and 19% of the labor force, but they had 31% of the country's unemployment. Average unemployment rates in the redevelopment areas exceeded 10%, in contrast with 5.4% nationally. In some of these areas, unemployment rates are as high as 20–30%. In rural depressed areas, suffering a problem of underemployment rather than unemployment, the median family income is less than $1,560 a year, and the median farm income is less than $1,170 a year.[14]

It has been estimated that to bring unemployment down to a 4% level in the urban redevelopment areas would require the creation of an estimated 660,000 direct and indirect new jobs in private enterprise. To make up the underemployment deficit in the rest of the redevelopment areas would require the creation of an estimated additional 300,000 new jobs, directly and indirectly.[15]

It is safe to conclude that trends in the number of depressed areas and their significance in the national economy will compel national concern with this problem for many years to come.

CHARACTERISTICS OF DEPRESSED AREAS *

In formulating action on chronically depressed areas, it is also important to know the distinguishing characteristics of the unemployed,

* The comparisons presented in this section are for major areas only and do not include small or rural areas. Inclusion of the latter would undoubtedly alter the industrial and occupational distribution of depressed area unemployed.

the number of years of excessive unemployment, and the industrial and occupational composition of such areas. A study recently conducted by the Department of Labor on the characteristics of the unemployed in substantial labor surplus areas, based on a special tabulation of data compiled from the Monthly Report on the Labor Force and samples of insured unemployed in such areas, notes that during the period July 1956–June 1957 depressed areas had a higher proportion of unemployed who were male, married, and between the ages of 25 and 54 than areas with a more balanced labor market. In the depressed areas 49% of the men were in this age category, as against 42% in the more balanced areas.[16]

In the depressed areas the concentration of unemployment among regular labor force members and among those who work in manufacturing plants is greater than for the nation as a whole. There is also a much greater incidence of long-term unemployment. One-fourth of the unemployed in depressed areas, according to the study by the Department of Labor, had been unemployed for more than six months, compared with one-eighth of the unemployed in tight or balanced labor markets.[17] On the other hand, the incidence of unemployment among younger workers is less. This lends weight to the usually accepted view that younger workers tend to leave depressed areas in search of employment opportunities. However, it should be noted that the median age in depressed areas is not significantly above that of the nation as a whole, probably because more older people are left in depressed areas and a higher proportion of very young people below working age. It is the group in the category 20–45 who are most likely to leave.[18] The percentage of persons in the 18–44 category in depressed areas is lower than that of the nation as a whole, further corroborating the extent of outward migration.

Industrial and occupational characteristics of unemployed workers in depressed areas are considerably influenced by the inclusion of Detroit (dominated by auto production) in the sample. The survey reveals a high proportion of semiskilled and skilled workers and a smaller proportion of white collar and service workers among the unemployed in depressed areas.

These data emphasize further the seriousness of the unemployment problem in depressed areas and the obstacles in the path of absorbing the unemployed into the ranks of the employed. Compared with other areas, unemployed workers in depressed areas are less likely to be secondary workers or at lower age levels and more likely to have been unemployed for a considerable period.

Another Department of Labor study, made in 1959, of seventeen areas with a chronic labor surplus indicates a relatively high proportion of employment in manufacturing in such areas. The report provides a basis for understanding the reasons for decline in these major labor markets:

Employment trends and overall labor market conditions in each of the 17 chronic areas have been strongly influenced by developments in one or two industries—to an extent where most of them could be labeled as "one-industry towns" with some justification. In 12 of the 17 areas—all but Terre Haute, Ind., New Bedford, Mass., Scranton, Pa., Providence, R.I., and Muskegon–Muskegon Heights, Mich.—a single industry, usually coal mining, textiles, machinery or automobiles, accounted for 20 percent or more of local nonfarm employment totals, either currently (May 1959) or in the spring of 1950. In four of the five exceptions, the major local industry—coal mining in the case of Scranton and Terre Haute, and textiles in Providence and New Bedford—already had been declining sharply for some time prior to 1950. Muskegon–Muskegon Heights has a somewhat more diversified industrial base than most of the other areas in the chronic grouping. Even in this area, however, a few declining industries have accounted for a major share of local jobs.[19]

Tabulations based on analysis of the statistical profiles for 94 labor surplus areas in the urban-industrial complex also indicate a very sharp decline in agriculture, transportation, and mining between 1950 and 1960.

The Attack on Unemployment in Depressed Areas [20]

Area unemployment has been traditionally approached through "operation bootstrap"—a local community redevelopment project designed to attract new employment opportunities. These efforts customarily consist of a cooperative citizen–business–local government venture to raise funds for land purchase and new facilities for low-cost lease or grant to new enterprises. Community development plans are generally accompanied by enthusiastic promotional campaigns and receive the widespread support of state agencies.

The Federal Government has developed a number of programs to further these local efforts. These have included technical assistance, urban renewal and planning, assistance with community facilities, aids to small business, federal procurement advantages, rapid tax amortization, surplus food distribution, and a variety of rural development measures. Under the recently passed Area Redevelopment Act stress is still given to the importance of local and state efforts at "self-development" and to the contributory rather than dominant role to be played by the Federal Government.[21]

Some states, for example Pennsylvania and New York, have scored some notable successes in fostering community development, and there have been occasional local triumphs, as in Nashua, New Hampshire. But for every Nashua there are several Hazeltons (Pennsylvania) where long, strenuous, and costly efforts at community self-renewal have resulted in no significant improvement in local economic conditions. Major areas, such as Evansville, Indiana; Lowell, Massachusetts; Scranton, Pennsylvania; Providence, R.I.; and Charleston, West Virginia, continue to appear on the "substantial and persistent" unemployment lists year after year with discouraging regularity. Many other areas, small in size and "notoriety," have been similarly embedded in the hard-core of unemployment in spite of long local efforts to pull out.

This dismal record of local self-help notwithstanding, as late as 1955 the President's Council of Economic Advisers continued to insist that the adjustment processes could best be left with the local communities, and avoided advocacy of a centralized federal attack on the problem. Two bills designed to provide federal aid to depressed areas were passed in both houses of Congress after 1955 but were vetoed by President Eisenhower. Finally, after a long legislative battle, the Area Redevelopment Act, embodying much of the content of earlier bills, was signed into law by President Kennedy on May 1, 1961.

In view of the magnitude of the problems to be solved and the lengthy travail that preceded passage of the act, some might say the mountain had labored and brought forth a mouse. The new legislation can have far-reaching results only to the extent that it encourages local redevelopment activities in a way not accomplished by the piecemeal federal aids of the past.

The act, whose term is four years, provides for one revolving fund of $100 million to support industrial development in urban redevelopment areas, a second fund of $100 million for similar industrial support in rural areas, a third fund of $100 million for loans for qualified public facilities, and an additional 75-million-dollar fund to provide grants for public facilities. The law also provides annual appropriations for occupational training facilities and retraining subsistence allowances, and finally an annual $4.5 million appropriation for technical assistance to local redevelopment efforts.

In the first year of its operations the Area Redevelopment Administration could boast of only modest gains in the accomplishment of its major objectives. By May 1962, 40 projects in 23 states were approved, involving $10.8 million in federal funds. It was estimated that these projects would create an estimated 10,716 direct new jobs in private enterprise, and 7,500 indirect jobs in trades and services and supporting industries.[22] These achievements will be discussed further below. The administration notes that its major contribution has been in mobilizing local planning and resources. As required in the legislation as a condition of federal aid, 535 areas and 22 Indian reservations submitted local over-all development plans in the first years. These represented 60% of all eligible areas.

In addition to the ARA approach to the problem, increased attention is being given to measures which will create jobs in depressed areas through direct federal spending. A bill to channel public works into chronically depressed areas was passed in the 1962 Congress. Measures such as this are similar, in principle, to the allocation of government contracts to depressed areas on a preferential basis. In both cases a link is provided between expansionary aggregative fiscal-spending policies and the sectional approach customarily adopted in the attack on structural unemployment.

EFFECTS OF PLANT EXPANSION

Let us turn now to the central purpose of this discussion: an evaluation of the effectiveness of depressed-area policies.

As has been noted, the attraction of new industrial facilities into depressed areas is a cornerstone of redevelopment policy. State and local development councils seek to achieve this objective through a variety of inducements, and the ARA through low-cost loans helps new firms get started or existing firms to expand. As of June 4, 1962, the ARA had approved 23 commercial and industrial loans, representing an investment of approximately $5.5 million. It was estimated that this federal investment would result in the creation of 3,500 direct jobs, and 2,400 indirect jobs in supporting industries, trades, and services.[23] Such loans range from $19,500 to the Port Royal Industries in Beaufort, S.C., for establishment of a new woolen knitting mill expected to employ 40 persons, to a $455,000 loan to Technical Tape Corporation as an aid in its expansion to Carbondale, Illinois. It was stressed that the latter is an excellent example of the "seed money" character of Area Redevelopment Administration activities in this field, since the federal loan stimulated additional private and public investment of more than $2.6 million. The loan was expected to produce 700 jobs and an annual payroll of $4.3 million.[24]

Although such developments are encouraging, especially in view of the limited time period in which ARA has functioned, it is necessary to note that estimated job creation resulting from plant expansion is only a rough guide to the total impact of a new plant on a depressed area's unemployment. This consideration is especially pertinent in the establishment of new industrial facilities in rural areas. Unfortunately there have been few studies directed toward appraisal of the reduction of unemployment following industrial expansion to depressed areas. Such inquiries should be a highly fruitful line of research in connection with future redevelopment policies.

Almost all the studies seeking to evaluate the effects of industrialization in rural depressed areas have been conducted by rural sociologists, who have been primarily concerned with the impact on farm, family, and community life, and the socioeconomic adjustments required of new industrial employees.[25] They are less concerned about the prior location, employment status, occupational-income history, and mobility patterns of the workers attracted to the new plant. Nor do they say much about applicants for work at the new plant who were found unacceptable for employment. And yet this type of information is essential for a full appraisal of the effects of plant expansion on employment.

Recent studies on unemployment, mobility, commuting, and job skills in rural depressed areas point up some problems in the new-industry solution to chronic unemployment in these areas. They indicate that the creation of new jobs through plant expansion has not always been paralleled by a proportional reduction in local unemployment. The discrepancy arises partly from the personal characteristics and lack of requisite skills among the local unemployed; partly from the numbers of jobholders who have been transferred into the area from other company plants; of those in pursuit of higher wages and greater employment security who move voluntarily from employment in less desirable jobs to the new industrial facility, either moving their homes into the new area or commuting from considerable distances; and finally, of those who had been commuting to a distant job from their residence in the locally depressed area and now take advantage of the newly afforded opportunity to work closer to home. Any of these people, already employed, may be preferred by the new employer over the local unemployed who possess less "desirable" qualifications from the standpoint of age, education, manufacturing skills, and experience.

The earlier discussion of the characteristics of the unemployed in depressed areas supports the view that a new industrial facility in a rural area may "create" local jobs without a proportional reduction in local unemployment. The unemployed in such areas tend to be older and, unlike those in depressed urban areas, they are not likely to possess manufacturing experience. A recent summary of five studies of the effects of new industrial plants in rural areas of low and moderate farm income substantiates these views.

As in urban industrial labor markets, older rural workers with little industrial experience or skill were least likely to seek or find jobs in rural industries.

These studies underscore the need for more adequate vocational training programs for residents of rural communities, particularly those seeking industrial employment. The educational facilities of rural communities need to emphasize vocational counseling and guidance programs for rural youth that will assist them in obtaining non-agricultural employment. Training and retraining of rural workers on a large scale is essential if their earning capacity and productivity is to be raised to an adequate level.[26]

The obstacle to reabsorption of unemployed older workers in rural depressed areas has also been emphasized in studies of plant shutdown in these areas. Even locally expanding firms are likely to look elsewhere for employees.[27] The effects of preferential hiring are also especially noticeable in two recent studies of company hiring policies for new industrial facilities in areas of substantial unemployment. James Blum appraised the movement of a medium-sized motor vehicle plant to a small community in southeastern Michigan.[28] He summarizes his major findings as follows:

While the large number of unemployed workers in the area presented a substantial pool of labor for the plant, this study indicates that they did not constitute the most important source of workers. The larger proportion of unemployed workers among the unaccepted applicants than among those hired implies than many of the unemployed either did not possess the needed skills or may not have met the employer's hiring standards.

A majority of the new employees were workers already employed, who voluntarily left their jobs to accept work in the new plant. While some came from local non-factory jobs in search of higher earnings and job advancement, the most significant number of voluntary transfers were living in the area and had been commuting as much as 50 miles daily to their previous place of work. Thus, the desire to shorten commuting time and distance may be a significant factor in explaining the voluntary transfers, especially of the professional and skilled workers.

These findings are almost identical with those of an earlier study conducted in Ravenswood, West Virginia, to determine the characteristics of workers hired by the Kaiser Aluminum Company.[29] The firm began operations in this depressed rural community in 1956. At the time of the study, in 1957, there were approximately 1,000 employees; employment had reached its full complement of 3,500 by 1960. When the plant was established, Ravenswood was a small rural community of 1,175. It is located in Jackson County on the Ohio River on the Ohio–West Virginia border. The county had a wholly rural population of 13,900 in 1957. Interviews were conducted with the firm's first 900 employees, and 520 rejected application forms were examined in order to compare qualifications for employment. As in Blum's study, it was found that the company was able to choose younger, more highly educated, and more skilled workers among transfers from other jobs and areas than from among the majority of the local unemployed. As additional hiring continued, selection standards were lowered so that more of the unemployed benefited. In time some were also able to find jobs in new service and trade establishments. But the labor market area as a whole remained relatively depressed.

The establishment of a large aluminum plant in a depressed area of West Virginia is close to the ideal of redevelopment policy; and since few studies have sought to determine fully the employment effects of such plant expansion, it is worth spending some time on this case. Ravenswood and Jackson County are located in the Point Pleasant (W. Va.)–Gallipolis (Ohio) Redevelopment Area. In Table 2 selected characteristics of the area, of the two states in which it is located, of Jackson County, and of contiguous counties are compared for 1960 and earlier years. These data permit a view of "before" and "after" the plant's establishment in 1956. Jackson County is seen to fare better than other sections of the labor market area, but its 1960 unemployment rate of 8.6% was still substantially above the Ohio rate and even a little above the generally depressed unemployment rate in West

Table 2. *Selected characteristics of Ohio, West Virginia, and the Point Pleasant–Gallipolis Redevelopment Area* (minus sign [−] denotes decrease)

Subject	Ohio	West Virginia	Point Pleasant–Gallipolis Redevelopment Area					
			Total	Gallia Co., Ohio	Meigs Co., Ohio	Jackson Co., W. Va.	Mason Co., W. Va.	Putnam Co., W. Va.
POPULATION, 1960								
Total population	9,706,397	1,860,421	114,840	26,120	22,159	18,541	24,459	23,561
% increase, 1950–60	22.1	−7.2	6.3	4.9	−4.6	21.2	3.9	12.1
% increase, 1940–50	15.0	5.4	0.5	−0.1	−3.6	−7.8	5.7	7.7
Net civilian migration, 1950–60	452,800	−427,000	−5,500	−1,300	−2,800	1,200	−2,300	−300
PLACE OF RESIDENCE IN 1955								
Persons 5 years old and over, 1960	8,567,666	1,664,130	102,207	23,487	19,933	16,218	21,550	21,019
Same house as in 1960	4,271,412	937,571	55,771	13,196	11,638	7,254	11,837	11,846
Different house, same county	2,922,368	500,791	26,993	5,940	5,499	3,733	6,348	5,473
Different house, different county	1,201,008	204,058	18,566	4,098	2,654	5,117	3,189	3,508
PLACE OF WORK IN 1960								
All workers, 14 years old and over	3,437,799	526,147	30,797	7,006	5,919	5,014	6,637	6,221
Worked in county of residence	2,925,166	435,359	22,044	5,659	4,179	4,295	4,925	2,986
Worked outside county of residence	387,203	69,134	7,422	921	1,474	541	1,465	3,021
EMPLOYMENT, 1960								
% increase of labor force, 1950–60	16.0	−10.9	5.0	7.7	−7.2	16.9	3.3	9.2
Unemployed	202,284	49,018	3,289	648	765	481	870	525
% of labor force	5.5	8.3	9.4	8.3	11.1	8.6	11.3	7.6
FAMILY INCOME								
Median income, 1959, all families	$6,171	$4,572	$4,310	$4,029	$3,619	$4,707	$4,418	$4,779
Median income, 1949, all families	$3,412	$2,597	$1,864	$1,685	$1,994	$1,391	$1,952	$2,300
% families, income under $3,000, 1959	15.7	32.6	35.9	36.2	43.7	35.0	34.1	30.4

Source: U. S. Bureau of Census, *Statistical Profiles, Point Pleasant–Gallipolis Redevelopment Area.* Prepared for the Area Redevelopment Administration. Series SP, 1962.

Virginia as a whole. The population data lead to inferences of a substantial inward migration from contiguous counties; and this is substantiated by the higher rates of residential mobility in Jackson than in contiguous areas between 1955 and 1960. The Kaiser plant apparently made a significant difference in income in Jackson County between 1949 and 1959, but over one-third of the families still had less than $3,000 cash income in 1959.

It is evident that plant expansion must be substantial to have an appreciable effect in reducing poverty in a depressed rural area, and that many more studies of the employment impact of industrialization are required to serve as a factual base for future industrial redevelopment activities.

RETRAINING AND RELOCATION OF THE UNEMPLOYED

In the trio of redevelopment policies—plant expansion, retraining, and relocation—the first has dominated official thinking for many years, the second has just begun to make itself noticed, and the third still lacks formal recognition. Although the retraining provisions of the Area Redevelopment Act are extremely modest, in many ways retraining can be considered the fulcrum of area redevelopment policies. As studies of industrialization in rural depressed areas demonstrate, industrial plant location in such areas could fulfill its functions of reducing unemployment much more successfully if it were accompanied by programs for development of skills among the local unemployed.

Retraining of the unemployed in depressed areas would not only increase the effectiveness of plant location policy, it is also closely associated with relocation of workers. Out-migration is likely to be viewed by unemployed, unskilled workers themselves as pointless in any circumstances other than tight national full employment. They do not need to be tutored in the statistics of unemployment, which indicate heavy concentrations among unskilled throughout the country, to sense instinctively the folly of leaving friends and familiar surroundings for alien parts where employment opportunities are no better. Similar considerations apply to older workers, the less educated, and racial minorities. Retraining and development of skills, by increasing the bargaining power of these workers, may provide at least some offset to their disadvantage in the labor market and make relocation more fruitful.

Retraining is in an anomalous position. On the one hand, the concept of occupational training is an old one and can claim federal support as early as 1917 in the Smith-Hughes Act. On-the-job training has long been widespread throughout privately owned enterprises. But retraining on a wide scale, as a deliberate governmental means to combat structural unemployment among adults, is a very recent development in the United States. The Area Redevelopment Act is the first introduction of this concept on the federal level. In addition to financial aid for instructors and training in eligible redevelopment areas, the act provides a subsistence allowance to qualified trainees for a maximum period of 16 weeks. The allowance is equal to the average weekly unemployment compensation payment in the state. In the last few years, Pennsylvania, West Virginia, Ohio, California, and other states have passed legislation providing for retraining of the unemployed. There are also many local programs in Michigan, Connecticut, and elsewhere. A growing number of states have authorized the payment of unemployment compensation, as a substitute for formal retraining allowances, to unemployed workers who are not available for work because of enrollment in a retraining course.

Many of the state programs, like the ARA retraining programs, are especially geared to the needs of depressed areas and become part of the area redevelopment arsenal. In a number of areas, including Carbondale in Illinois, Clarksburg and Charleston in West Virginia, and Evansville in Indiana, ARA training programs have been specifically designed to meet the needs of an incoming manufacturing facility. It is expected that this type of tie-in between plant location and retraining of the locally unemployed will increase. The government-subsidized retraining serves as an additional inducement for plants to establish in depressed areas, as well as providing greater assurance of employment upon the completion of training.

This inducement to plants to take advantage of retraining programs in depressed areas by moving in may be lost with the passage of the Manpower Development and Training Act, which took effect July 1962. Under provisions of this act, $435 million is to be spent in a three-year period to encourage retraining of the unemployed and underemployed without regard to area. Although subsistence payments to eligible trainees under this act are still geared to state unemployment compensation payments for adult workers, they are more liberal in that they may be paid for a maximum of 52 weeks. Although there seems to be some disposition in some areas to delay ARA training proposals while awaiting the implementation of the new act, it is not likely that the MDTA will displace the ARA or interfere seriously with redevelopment policies. Since the MDTA is directed almost wholly to unemployed and underemployed workers, with state allotments partly determined by the number of unemployed, it is likely that many of the training programs under this act will also end up in depressed areas. Moreover, except for a small fraction reserved for youth, MDTA funds are to be paid only to unemployed heads of households with at least three years of previous work experience. The ARA has no such restriction or selectiveness and may be favored by employees and local authorities for this reason. Women, especially, who play a prominent role in ARA programs, are more likely to be excluded under the eligibility provisions of the MDTA.

How effective is retraining in reducing the burden of unemployment in depressed areas? Unfortunately, one can only speculate at this point. State and local training programs are too new, small scale, and/or sporadic to serve as a basis for evaluation. There have been some notably high ratios of job placement among trainees in some programs (e.g. in sections of Pennsylvania), but the number of trainees initially enrolled has usually been a very small fraction of the unemployed in the area.

Even the ARA experience to date has been too minor to provide valid generalizations. In a report dated June 4, 1962, only 120 programs had been approved, involving 8,869 trainees and a total expenditure of $5.3 million for training and subsistence.[30] Even these data overstate the progress at that time since many of the courses listed in the report were not scheduled to get under way until several weeks later. And so to that date the ARA had used only a little over a third of its small first-year appropriation for retraining in depressed areas.

At this stage, the best one can do is to offer a few major hypotheses about the effectiveness and problems of retraining, based on scattered data and preliminary investigation:

1. Unless the intensity and resources of retraining programs in depressed areas are vastly increased, approaching the level of concentration achieved in vocational rehabilitation of the handicapped, the truly hard core of the unemployed are likely to be by-passed by the current ARA programs, either in selection for training or in placement after training. The first report on the personal characteristics of 2,512 ARA

trainees, as of March 31, 1962, indicates that 9.1% of the males and 12.3% of the females were over 44 years,[31] whereas the study of unemployment in depressed areas, referred to earlier, indicates that 21.4% of the males and 12.8% of the females among the unemployed in depressed areas were over 44 in the 1956–57 period.[32]

Investigation into a number of ARA retraining programs indicates that, under employer urging, selection procedures favor younger, educable workers. An extension of the training period 16 weeks might develop greater skills and induce a more favorable attitude to the hiring of older workers. The 16 weeks' duration of present courses has also restricted the scope of the program to relatively few occupations.

2. In most depressed areas, relocation allowances would considerably enhance the effectiveness of retraining programs in reducing depressed-area unemployment. A provision for these was stricken from the MDTA in its early stages. As the size and number of training programs increase, training geared wholly to local job opportunities is likely to be seriously restricted.

3. With increased scope given to retraining, selection procedures will have to be modified in the interests of motivating unemployed workers to undertake retraining; and to reach workers who cannot hope to pass currently used selection tests. Experience under a number of the early retraining programs indicates that motivation for entry into training can be a major problem. Workers most in need of retraining are likely to be early school dropouts, unsympathetic with the whole educational process, including such trappings as tests. A number of "failures" among friends and neighbors in selection tests for admission to a retraining program will often serve to discourage many other applicants. Furthermore, present selection tests are generally based on the assumption that the applicant can read and write. This assumption will sometimes be ill founded in chronically depressed areas.

It is recognized, of course, that a number of the unemployed, in depressed areas and elsewhere, are not suitable subjects for retraining. As in the case of older workers, those with little schooling pose a dilemma for Employment Service counselors. On the one hand, it is hoped that the training programs will be of maximum benefit to the hard-core unemployed—the old, unskilled, uneducated, minorities—who, as is noted above, suffer the highest rates and longest duration of unemployment. But the training legislation also cautions the Employment Service to select those who have "a reasonable expectation of employment" upon completion of training. Imaginative use of experiments in selection procedures may well salvage many unemployed workers who are deemed hopeless as a result of standard test batteries. At the same time, others will be found to be unsalvageable through this means, and alternative forms of aid will have to be utilized.

4. Motivation and morale of the trainees, as well as the direct efficiency of the retraining and subsequent job placement, are most likely to be favorable if the trainees are assured of a specific job in a specific company upon completion of their course. This can be done under company-sponsored programs among displaced workers who are to be transferred to branch units, and under a number of ARA courses designed to fill the specified needs of an incoming industrial facility. But it must also be recognized that from the viewpoint of the best long-term prospects highly specific training of this type may be less advantageous than training in more generalized skills.

5. Finally, the effectiveness of retraining, as judged by the dual criteria of job placement and reduction of area unemployment, will be a function of the availability of jobs, locally and nationally, and of the special efforts of the Employment Service to find work for trainees. Although this may seem almost axiomatic, it is probably the fundamental truth in the retraining field, and brings us full circle to the interrelatedness of structural policies and measures designed to increase aggregate and local demand for labor.[33]

Conclusion: Matters of Social Experiment

We hold with John R. Commons that the methods by which problems of unemployment are to be met are "matters of social invention and experiment." If the foregoing discussion is correct, the most useful basis for such experiment will be recognition that unemployment is a many-sided demon which will not be exorcised through a one-sided attack. Not only must the interdependence and interaction of the causes and cures of unemployment be accepted, but, equally important, unemployment must be viewed as only one phenomenon in the broader functioning of the labor market. The most effective policies to combat unemployment will be based on analyses of total labor market behavior: labor force changes, mobility patterns, union-management "security" provisions, education, training, retirement policies, and the gamut of government measures.

Unemployment represents a disease in the labor market, a malfunctioning, a waste of human resources. It is the most obvious waste but not the only one. Many forms of underemployment and underutilization exist, including withdrawal from the labor force which may stem from market imperfections and closed opportunities. Other chapters in this volume, such as those dealing with social security, migrant labor, and minimum wages, are also relevant to an inquiry into the policy implications of labor market analysis.

Some major implications to be derived from labor market analyses are as follows:

1. Policies to combat structural unemployment will be successful only when accompanied by monetary-fiscal policies designed to achieve a high and rising level of aggregate demand. The structural policies, in turn, will enhance the achievement of the full-employment goals of aggregative policies. But to attain maximum effectiveness the two sets of policies should be not only simultaneous but combined. An obvious opportunity for integration exists in depressed areas where tax and spending policies can be given special emphasis in certain localities, as part of total monetary-fiscal policy. But similar combinations of aggregative and structural policies can occur in such expenditures as those to support a Youth Conservation Corps; or in allocation of federal contracts designed to discourage discrimination against older workers or minorities. Federal expenditures on training and other transfer payments—as part of a national monetary-fiscal attack—will serve similar purposes.

2. The substantial reduction of unemployment for many of the "class" unemployed will require "education" of employers as well as strenuous efforts by the Employment service. Older workers and racial minorities are likely to be only slightly more acceptable to a prejudiced employer after training. Employers who traditionally discriminate against these groups in hiring are likely to continue to do so in the absence of specific action to deal with this aspect of the problem.

3. As in many other areas of labor market policy, the most likely development in employment security policies is a "mixed economy" of government and private functions. A precedent has been established in such combined moves as the integration of social security and private pension plans or the joining of unemployment compensation with private supplemental unemployment benefits. These developments, along with privately negotiated severance pay, retraining allowances, reloca-

tion allowances, automation funds, as well as numerous other security provisions recently agreed upon in the longshore industry, steel, autos, and rubber, point the way to a public-private approach.[34]

Here too, however, social experiment is necessary to determine the most effective combination of public and private activities in combating or alleviating unemployment. The essential role that private concerns can play in retraining displaced or unemployed workers has already been noted. Nonetheless the exact nature of public subsidy to private establishments for this purpose presents some thorny problems. Since relocation allowances appear to be anathema politically in the United States, expansion of the private role in this sphere may serve a highly useful purpose. Similar allocations specifically to either the public or the private sector can best be decided by the peculiar competencies in each area.

4. Finally, a careful distinction should be made between short-run structural policies and a long-range plan to achieve the most efficient utilization of manpower and functioning of the labor market. Short-run policies are necessary to alleviate immediate distress and reduce intolerable levels of unemployment in particular areas or industries. They can readily be integrated with a long-range plan, but care must be observed lest they be considered an alternative to a broader approach.

A few examples will illustrate the necessary distinction. The Area Redevelopment Act's approach to depressed-area problems is useful as a short-run, emergency measure. But localized policies, geared to localized problems and possibilities, can at best be a limited attack. It is hoped that the ARA can blossom into a broad regional planning agency, designed to develop resources over large areas of states, with expansion measures geared not to just a locality or a state but to an integrated economic region. The experience with TVA may be instructive in this regard.

The present approach to training, through ARA and MDTA, is another case in point. It is fine as far as it goes, but it cannot go very far in bringing about substantial reductions in unemployment or in improving the over-all allocation of human resources. Advanced technology is creating many shortages of manpower at highly skilled and technical levels. The unemployed, concentrated in low-skill, low-education categories, cannot be trained for these positions. Many of the growing opportunities may not be located in localities or even states where large numbers of unemployed reside. The long-range plan should envisage a continual process of retraining, under cooperative government-private auspices, in which all levels of employees are being constantly upgraded in order to leave openings at the bottom of the occupational ladder for retrained unemployed workers. Relocation allowances and an improved Employment Service clearance procedure would also be fundamental in this over-all plan. An expansion of educational and vocational opportunities for young people, accompanied by improvements in vocational guidance, would be a fundamental part of the long-range goals in this area.

Temporary extended unemployment compensation is a necessary provision in time of widespread unemployment, but it must be considered an emergency, stopgap measure. In a long-range plan, it is hoped that extensions of unemployment compensation (paid out of general taxation and kept separate from regular unemployment *insurance*) could be associated with retraining and/or relocation allowances and perhaps with other devices to provide an incentive toward employment as well as to mitigate distress. In a number of European countries, notably in Sweden, in coal mining in Britain, and in the European Coal and Steel Community, such an integrated system of benefits and incentives has worked with considerable success. Although differences in labor market conditions and labor force homogeneity make caution necessary in efforts to parallel European experience, much can be learned from social experiments abroad.

Most essential of all in any broad long-range plan for the labor market is integration and coordination of policies. The problems cannot be fragmented. Neither can a successful set of policies to improve labor market mechanisms. Proposals for a National Council of Manpower Advisers, to serve as a coordinating agency, have considerable merit. And central in any coordinated plan must be an expanded, revitalized Employment Service.

Notes

1   "The Right to Work," *The Arena*, 21, No. 2 (Feb. 1899): 140.
2   See especially U. S. Congress, Subcommittee on Economic Statistics of the Joint Economic Committee, *Higher Unemployment Rates, 1957–60: Structural Transformation or Inadequate Demand*, 1961; and "Problems of Persistent Unemployment," *Proceedings of the Fourteenth Annual Meeting*, Industrial Relations Research Association (Dec. 28–29, 1961), pp. 16–58.

3   U. S. Congress, Report of the Subcommittee on Economic Statistics to the Joint Economic Committee, *Employment and Unemployment* (Feb. 2, 1962), p. 6.

4   See U. S. Department of Labor, Bureau of Labor Statistics, Bull. No. 1277, *School and Early Employment Experience of Youth: A Report on Seven Communities, 1952–57* (Aug. 1960), pp. 35–36.

5   "The Impact of the Changing Economy on Our Manpower Resources," *Employment Security Review*, U. S. Department of Labor, Bureau of Employment Security (April 1962), pp. 8–15.

6   Ibid., p. 11.

7   U. S. Department of Labor, Bureau of Labor Statistics, *Educational Attainment of Workers, 1959*, Special Labor Force Report No. 1, Reprint No. 2333, p. 115.

8   Clarence Long, "A Theory of Creeping Unemployment and Labor Force Displacement" (Department of Economics, Johns Hopkins University), pp. 7–8. Mimeographed.

9   There has been a voluminous literature on automation in recent years. An excellent summary statement and annotated bibliography can be found in U. S. Department of Labor, Bureau of Employment Security, *Impact of Automation and Technological Change on Employment and Unemployment*, Sept. 1961.

10 Richard Wilcock and Walter Franke, "Will Economic Growth Solve the Problem of Long-Term Unemployment?" *Proceedings of the Fourteenth Annual Meeting*, Industrial Relations Research Association (Dec. 28–29, 1961), pp. 30–49.

11 U. S. Department of Labor, Bureau of Employment Security, *Area Labor Market Trends*, April 1962.

12 See for example Committee for Economic Development, *Distressed Areas in a Growing Economy* (June 1961), pp. 19–20.

13 U. S. Department of Labor, Bureau of Employment Security, *Area Labor Market Trends* (April 1962), p. 12. These are areas with a labor force under 15,000. The number listed by BES increased from 58 in July 1961 to 367 in April 1962.

14 U. S. Department of Commerce, *A Report of the Area Redevelopment Administration*, May 1, 1961–May 1, 1962, p. 2.

15 Ibid., p. 6.

16 *The Structure of Unemployment in Areas of Substantial Labor Surplus*, prepared by the U. S. Department of Labor, included in the report by the Joint Economic Committee, 86th Cong., 2d Sess. (Jan. 1960), pp. 24–26.

17 Ibid., p. 11.

18 This information is based upon a tabulation made by the author from information prepared by the U. S. Bureau of the Census for the Area Redevelopment Administration, in *Statistical Profiles*, Series SP, 1962. One hundred and forty-eight such profiles for the major urban-industrial redevelopment areas will be prepared; 94 were available in May 1962 and were utilized in this tabulation.

19 U. S. Department of Labor, Bureau of Labor Statistics, *Chronic Labor Surplus Areas: Experience and Outlook* (July 1959), p. 8.

20 Community area-redevelopment efforts and proposals for state and fed-

eral action have been described in considerable detail in Congressional hearings dating from 1954 and in a growing number of articles and monographs. The more instructive Congressional hearings include U. S. Senate, Subcommittee to Investigate Unemployment of the Committee on Labor and the Public Welfare, *Causes of Unemployment in the Coal and Other Domestic Industries,* 84th Cong., 1st Sess. (March 7–29, April 12–20, 1955); U. S. Congress, Subcommittee on Low-Income Families of the Joint Commitee on the Economic Report, *Low-Income Families,* 84th Cong., 1st Sess. (Nov. 18–23, 1955); U. S. Senate, Subcommittee on Labor of the Committee on Labor and the Public Welfare, *Area Redevelopment,* 84th Cong., 2d Sess., Pt. 1 (Jan. 4–26, Feb. 3–24, 1956) and Pt. 2 (Feb. 24–27, March 22–29, April 26, 1956); U. S. Senate, Subcommittee of the Committee on Banking and Currency, *Area Redevelopment,* 85th Cong., 1st Sess. (March 6–14, April 9–15, May 8–15, 1957); U. S. House of Representatives, Committee on Banking and Currency, *Legislation to Relieve Unemployment,* 85th Cong., 2d Sess. (April 14–30, May 1–22, 1958); U. S. Senate, Subcommittee of the Committee on Banking and Currency, *Area Redevelopment Legislation,* 86th Cong., 2d Sess. (Aug. 18, 1960). One report should be mentioned: U. S. Senate, Special Committee on Unemployment, *Studies in Unemployment,* 1960.

Other general discussions of "remedies" can be found in Sar A. Levitan, *Federal Assistance to Labor Surplus Areas,* a report prepared at the request of the chairman of the Committee on Banking and Currency, U. S. House of Representatives, 85th Cong., 1st Sess. (April 15, 1957), pp. 13–16; William H. Miernyk, *Depressed Industrial Areas—A National Problem,* National Planning Association Pamphlet 98 (Washington, 1957), pp. v–vii, 37–52; Miernyk, "British and American Approaches to Structural Unemployment," *Industrial and Labor Relations Review,* 12 (Oct. 1958): 12–19; "Distressed Areas—A National Problem," *Labor's Economic Review* (Washington, AFL-CIO), April 1957. Donald R. Gilmore, *Developing the "Little" Economies,* Supplementary Paper No. 10, Committee for Economic Development, 1960; Committee for Economic Development, *Distressed Areas in a Growing Economy,* June 1961; Jacob J. Kaufman and Helmut J. Golatz, *Chronic Unemployment in Pennsylvania,* Bureau of Business Research, Pennsylvania State University, 1960; Lowell E. Galloway, "Proposals for Federal Aid to Depressed Industrial Areas: A Critique," *Industrial and Labor Relations Review,* 14 (April 1961): 363–78; Gerald G. Somers, "The Role of Unemployment Compensation in Depressed Areas," *Proceedings of the Eleventh Annual Meeting,* Industrial Relations Research Association, Dec. 1958; William H. Miernyk, "Problems and Remedies for Depressed Area Unemployment," *Proceedings of the Fourteenth Annual Meeting,* Industrial Relations Research Association (1961), pp. 28–36.

21 See U. S. Department of Commerce, Area Redevelopment Administration, *Your Community and the Area Redevelopment Act,* May 1961.

22 U. S. Department of Commerce, *A Report of the Area Redevelopment Administration* (May 1, 1961–May 1, 1962), p. 3.

23 U. S. Department of Commerce, Area Redevelopment Administration,

Activity Summary Report, June 4, 1962; and Daniel L. Goldy, Deputy Administrator, ARA, Remarks Prepared for Delivery at Meeting of State Planning and Development Agencies, Washington, D.C., May 24, 1962.

24 Goldy, p. 4.

25 See the excellent summary of five recent studies of this type contained in U. S. Department of Agriculture, Economic Research Service, Agriculture Information Bull. No. 252, *Rural Industrialization,* Nov. 1961.

26 Ibid., pp. 1, 31.

27 See Richard C. Wilcock, *Impact on Workers and Community of a Plant Shutdown in a Depressed Area,* U. S. Department of Labor, Bureau of Labor Statistics, Bull. No. 1264 (June 1960), pp. 6–7; H. L. Sheppard, A. Ferman, and S. Faber, *Too Old to Work—Too Young to Retire: A Case Study of a Permanent Plant Shutdown,* U. S. Senate, Special Committee on Unemployment Problems (1960), p. 33.

28 "Sources of Workers for a New Establishment," *The Labor Market and Employment Security,* U.S. Department of Labor, Bureau of Employment Security (May 1961), espec. pp. 1–2.

29 Gerald G. Somers, *Labor Supply and Mobility in a Newly Industrialized Area,* U. S. Department of Labor, Bureau of Labor Statistics, Bull. No. 1261, Feb. 1960.

30 U. S. Department of Commerce, Area Redevelopment Administration, *Activity Summary Report* (June 4, 1962), pp. 8–11.

31 U. S. Department of Labor, Bureau of Employment Security, *Characteristics of A.R.A. Trainees,* March 31, 1962. Mimeographed report.

32 Ibid., p. 7.

33 These "working hypotheses" concerning retraining were arrived at during the initial stages of a study, supported by the Ford Foundation, to evaluate retraining and relocation of unemployed workers in distressed areas.

34 An excellent recent summary of such union-management provisions can be found in Charles Killingsworth, *Collective Bargaining Approaches to Employee Displacement Problems,* a study prepared for the Presidential Railroad Commission, Aug. 1961. Mimeographed.

INDEX